STUDIES IN WELSH HISTORY

Editors

RALPH A. GRIFFITHS   CHRIS WILLIAMS
ERYN M. WHITE

34

THE SOUTH WALES MINERS
1964–1985

C000161693

THE SOUTH WALES MINERS
1964–1985

by

BEN CURTIS

Published on behalf of the
University of Wales

CARDIFF
UNIVERSITY OF WALES PRESS
2013

www.uwp.co.uk

British Library CIP Data
A catalogue record for this book is available from the British Library

ISBN   978-0-7083-2610-7 (hardback)
          978-0-7083-2611-4 (paperback)
e-ISBN 978-0-7083-2612-1

Printed on demand by CPI Group (UK) Ltd, Croydon, CR0 4YY

For Natalie and Elinor
and
In memory of my mother Krystyna (1946–2012),
three generations of Curtis women

SERIES EDITORS' FOREWORD

Since the foundation of the series in 1977, the study of Wales's history has attracted growing attention among historians internationally and continues to enjoy a vigorous popularity. Not only are approaches, both traditional and new, to the study of history in general being successfully applied in a Welsh context, but Wales's historical experience is increasingly appreciated by writers on British, European and world history. These advances have been especially marked in the university institutions in Wales itself.

In order to make more widely available the conclusions of original research, much of it of limited accessibility in postgraduate dissertations and theses, in 1977 the History and Law Committee of the Board of Celtic Studies inaugurated this series of monographs, Studies in Welsh History. It was anticipated that many of the volumes would originate in research conducted in the University of Wales or under the auspices of the Board of Celtic Studies, and so it proved. Although the Board of Celtic Studies no longer exists, the University of Wales continues to sponsor this series. It seeks to publish significant contributions made by researchers in Wales and elsewhere. Its primary aim is to serve historical scholarship and to encourage the study of Welsh history.

CONTENTS

ACKNOWLEDGEMENTS

Writing a book is both a solitary and a communal activity. Writing is solitary in that no-one else in the world understands exactly what you are really doing, no-one else must put in the long hours and years of research, writing, revision, frustration and small triumphs. It is communal in that it would be impossible to make it through the solitary struggle without the help of a great many people. I should like to acknowledge the many debts of gratitude that I have accumulated over the course of my work, the principal ones of which are listed here.

This book has been a long time in the making. It is mainly based on my PhD thesis, research for which began over a decade ago now. First, I would like to thank my doctoral supervisors, Professor Chris Williams and Dr Andy Croll, for their guidance and assistance, both during the years of my PhD research and subsequently. I am also extremely grateful for the generous advice and support which I received from the late Professor Nina Fishman, whose untimely passing is a great loss to the history of the labour movement. The transition from thesis to monograph has also been quite a lengthy process. In this respect, I should like to thank Professor Ralph Griffiths for his extensive and meticulous advice and assistance in revising the monograph manuscript, as well as to thank Sarah Lewis of the University of Wales Press for her prompt and helpful responses to my many and various queries.

Given that my research is a study of the history of the south Wales miners which relies primarily on the publications and internal records of the NUM as its source material, I am especially grateful for the assistance shown to me by the National Union of Mineworkers (South Wales Area). Without the many months I spent working through the archive at the NUM Area Office in Pontypridd, it would not have been possible for me to have completed this book in the form that I intended. Consequently, I should particularly like to thank Wayne Thomas, Dorothy Lewis, Carole Jones and Ron Stoate for being unstintingly helpful towards me during my time there. Much of the rest of my research was conducted at the South Wales

Miners' Library and I should also very much like to thank Siân Williams and the staff there. In addition to this, I should like to note my appreciation of the assistance I received from Darren Treadwell and the other archivists at the People's History Museum in Manchester during my visit there, as well as the staff of the National Library of Wales and the National Archives.

I should like to thank all the people whom I interviewed during the course of my work, whose names are listed in the bibliography. These interviews gave an invaluable 'feel' for the viewpoints of miners during the turbulent period covered by this study. For me, these meetings constituted one of the main highlights of my research programme.

With regards to the photographic illustrations which form part of this book, I should like to thank the following copyright holders for permission to reproduce them: the National Union of Mineworkers (South Wales Area), Martin Shakeshaft, Media Wales Ltd, the South Wales Coalfield Collection at Swansea University, and the National Museum Wales.

I am very grateful to all my friends for their companionship and encouragement throughout the course of writing this book. Particular thanks go to Chris Beck, whose IT skills were largely responsible for the creation of the maps that form part of this book. In addition to him, I should also like to thank Darren and Siân Williams (a different Siân from the one mentioned above!), Shahid Mian, Stephen Marsland, and Ben and Veronica Cottam. It would be remiss, too, not to acknowledge the contribution made by my cats, Hector and Aristotle, who did their inadvertent utmost to hinder the completion of this monograph.

Last but by no means least, I should like to thank my family: Jack Smith, my brother Sam and his wife Lisa, my sister Lucy Strand and her husband Matt, my aunt Mary Harman, my parents-in-law Irene and Paul Charlton, and my sister-in-law Alison Charlton. Finally, three people deserve particular mention: my wife Natalie, for her love and support; my daughter Elinor, who arrived in March 2012; and my mother Krystyna, for her unwavering belief in me throughout my academic career, who sadly passed away earlier this month, just as the final version of the monograph manuscript was being prepared for publication. This book is dedicated to them.

BEN CURTIS
Newbridge, July 2012

ABBREVIATIONS

ACAS	Advisory, Conciliation and Arbitration Service
ANL	Anti-Nazi League
APEX	Association of Professional, Executive, Clerical and Computer Staff
Area	NUM South Wales Area (unless otherwise stated)
ASLEF	Associated Society of Locomotive Engineers and Firemen
AUEW	Amalgamated Union of Engineering Workers
BLOC	Broad Left Organising Committee
BSC	British Steel Corporation
CAWU	Clerical and Administrative Workers' Union (later APEX)
CBI	Confederation of British Industry
CEGB	Central Electricity Generating Board
CLC	Central Labour College
COHSE	Confederation of Health Service Employees
COSA	Colliery Officials and Staffs Area
CP(GB)	Communist Party (of Great Britain)
DHSS	Department of Health and Social Security
EC	Executive Council (of the South Wales NUM unless otherwise stated)
EETPU	Electrical, Electronic, Telecommunications and Plumbing Union
EPEA	Electrical Power Engineers' Association
FBU	Fire Brigade Union
GMBATU	General, Municipal, Boilermakers' and Allied Trades Unions
IMF	International Monetary Fund
ISTC	Iron and Steel Trades Confederation
JNNC	Joint National Negotiating Committee
MFGB	Mineworkers' Federation of Great Britain
MINOS	Mine Operating System
MI5	British Security Service
NACODS	National Association of Colliery Overmen, Deputies and Shotfirers
NCB	National Coal Board
NCC	National Co-ordinating Committee
NEC	National Executive Committee (of the NUM unless otherwise stated)

NF	National Front
NPLA	National Power Loading Agreement
NUGMW	National Union of General and Municipal Workers (later GMBATU)
NUM	National Union of Mineworkers
NUPE	National Union of Public Employees
NUR	National Union of Railwaymen
NUS	National Union of Seamen
OPEC	Organisation of Petroleum Exporting Countries
PLP	Parliamentary Labour Party
ROLF	Remotely Operated Longwall Face
SOGAT	Society of Graphical and Allied Trades
SWMF	South Wales Miners' Federation
SWP	Socialist Workers Party
TGWU	Transport and General Workers' Union
TUC	Trades Union Congress
UCATT	Union of Construction, Allied Trades and Technicians
UCS	Upper Clyde Shipyard
UDC	Urban District Council
UDM	Union of Democratic Mineworkers
Union	National Union of Mineworkers (unless otherwise specified)
VERS	Voluntary Early Retirement Scheme
WCSMC	Wales Congress in Support of Mining Communities
WTUC	Wales Trade Union Council
AAC	NUM (South Wales Area) Annual Conference minutes
ASC	NUM (South Wales Area) Special Conference minutes
EC	NUM (South Wales Area) Executive Council minutes
HSIR	*Historical Studies in Industrial Relations*
IRSH	*International Review of Social History*
LHR	*Labour History Review*
MS	*Morning Star*
NLW	National Library of Wales
PHM	People's History Museum
SW	*Socialist Worker*
SWE	*South Wales Echo*
SWM	*South Wales Miner*
SWML	South Wales Miners' Library
TCBH	*Twentieth Century British History*
TNA	The National Archives
WHR	*Welsh History Review*
WM	*Western Mail*

LIST OF ILLUSTRATIONS

Images 1, 4, 6, 7 and 8 courtesy of National Museum Wales

Images 2 and 11 courtesy of Media Wales Ltd (Source: South Wales Coalfield Collection, Swansea University)

Image 3 courtesy of Media Wales Ltd

Image 5 courtesy of National Union of Mineworkers (South Wales Area) (Source: South Wales Coalfield Collection, Swansea University)

Images 9, 10, 12, 13, 14, 15 and 16 courtesy of Martin Shakeshaft (*www.strike84.co.uk*)

LIST OF MAPS

A NOTE ON CAPITALISATION

South Wales and south Wales

Throughout the text of this book, recurrent references are made to both 'south Wales' and 'South Wales'. The aim of this is not to confuse the reader but to provide a greater degree of clarity about the subject under discussion. Where I have used these terms, 'south Wales' refers to the southern part of Wales, whereas 'South Wales' is used exclusively as an abbreviation of the NUM South Wales Area. The same distinction is also drawn when discussing north Wales and the North Wales NUM. When quoting from a literary source, however, I have retained the original capitalisation format in each case.

INTRODUCTION:
'AN HISTORICAL MISSION TO LEAD IN
CLASS STRUGGLES'

In May 1981, at the South Wales Area NUM annual conference, Area president Emlyn Williams addressed the delegates and told them that the south Wales miners 'are associated in people's minds with resistance and struggles . . . There is no doubt in my mind that miners have an historical mission to lead in class struggles.' This statement expressed the self-image of the South Wales Area and highlighted an important historical trend. During the twentieth century the miners were generally considered to be amongst the most militant sections of the British labour movement, with South Wales in the forefront. This book examines how and why the south Wales miners held this prominent vanguard role.

By the eve of the Great War in 1914, the south Wales miners had acquired a formidable reputation for radicalism. The year 1898 – which saw the bitter six-month lock-out of the miners, together with the subsequent formation of the South Wales Miners' Federation – was a watershed in the history of the south Wales coal industry. The completeness of the miners' defeat spurred them to form a single coalfield-wide union, to match the employers' strength. The SWMF ('the Fed') was founded in October 1898 and when it affiliated to the Mineworkers' Federation of Great Britain (MFGB) in 1899, it was the largest constituent union. Following this, the Taff Vale Judgment in 1901 meant that a series of 'stop days' resulted in the SWMF being fined over £57,000 in damages.[1] Equally aggravating for the miners was the judicial decision in 1908 that compensatory payments for colliers working in difficult, less productive seams ('abnormal places') were not legally binding and could be revoked by employers. Appalling tragedies in this period – the most serious being in Senghenydd in 1913, the worst disaster in British mining history – further embittered mining communities, since they blamed the coalowners' cavalier attitude towards safety for the accidents.

---

[1]   Robin Page Arnot, *South Wales Miners, Vol. 1: 1898–1914* (London: 1967), p. 373.

Consequently, south Wales had a high level of industrial unrest even before the 'Great Unrest' of 1910–14. Between 1901 and 1913, Welsh workers employed in mining and quarrying were 70 per cent more strike-prone than the British average and also five-and-a-half times more strike-prone than the British average for all workers.[2]

This rise in industrial relations tensions prompted a rapid transformation of the miners' political attitudes. The growth of the Independent Labour Party (ILP) in south Wales, particularly Keir Hardie's victory at Merthyr Boroughs in 1900, was undoubtedly a reflection of this process.[3] A further landmark was the affiliation of the MFGB to the Labour Party in 1909. These broad developments ran parallel to the emergence of a more thoroughgoing critique of capitalism within the south Wales coalfield, via the Central Labour College (CLC) and the Plebs' League (which advocated independent working-class education).[4] The CLC's impact on the political culture of the coalfield was immense. A key figure was Noah Ablett, who won a scholarship to Ruskin College and was part of the college strike in 1908 that led to the establishment of the CLC, subsequently becoming the Cambrian Combine Committee vice-chairman and co-author of *The Miners' Next Step*. In January 1909, Ablett and other militants founded the Unofficial Reform Committee (URC). Centred on the Rhondda, this became the nerve-centre of revolutionary syndicalism in the valleys. Its newspaper, *The Rhondda Socialist*, subtitled 'The BOMB of the Rhondda Workers', appeared in August 1911, subsequently claiming a circulation of over 6,000 and a readership higher than that of all other local newspapers.[5]

The Cambrian Combine strike of 1910–11 heralded the emergence of south Wales as a 'storm centre' of industrial unrest. Approximately 11,000 men in four Cambrian-owned collieries took on the mighty Combine and its autocratic owner, D. A. Thomas. The dispute ran from September 1910 to August 1911, longer than any major coal-mining strike in living memory and it involved large-scale and persistent violence not only during the Tonypandy riots of November 1910 but for months thereafter. The miners' struggle became a class

[2] Chris Williams, *Capitalism, Community and Conflict: The South Wales Coalfield, 1898–1947* (Cardiff: 1998), p. 15.

[3] Kenneth O. Morgan, *Rebirth of a Nation: Wales, 1880–1980* (Oxford: 1981), p. 79.

[4] Gwyn A. Williams, *When Was Wales?* (London: 1985), p. 242.

[5] Morgan, *Rebirth of a Nation*, p. 150.

war, replete with battles with the police and a confrontation with the military.[6]

The Cambrian Combine strike was a defining moment in the history of the south Wales coalfield. Furthermore, the dispute played a key role in radicalising British miners, pressuring the government to introduce a colliers' Minimum Wage Act in March 1912. The strike also laid bare the absence of any common ground between capital and labour, dealing a severe blow to the Liberal-leaning ethos of the 'old guard' of the Fed leadership. It inspired SWMF radicals to produce the famous pamphlet *The Miners' Next Step*, a thorough critique of the existing personnel and traditions of their union.

Published by the URC in 1912, *The Miners' Next Step* is the pre-eminent document of British syndicalism. Its spurning of parliamentary politics and its advocacy of syndicalist industrial action and the centralisation of the union under rank-and-file control all connect it directly to the upheavals of 1910–11. It is a full-blooded savaging of trade union officialdom:

> [T]he Executive have the supreme power. The workmen for a time look up to these men and when things are going well they idolise them. The employers respect them. Why? Because they have the men – the real power – in the hollow of their hands. They, the leaders, become 'gentlemen'; they become MPs and have considerable social prestige because of this power . . . Now, every inroad the rank and file make on this privilege lessens the power and prestige of the leader. Can we wonder then that the leaders are averse to change? Can we wonder that they try and prevent progress? . . . The leader then has an interest – a vested interest – in stopping progress. They have therefore in some things an antagonism of interests with the rank and file. The conditions of things in South Wales has reached the point where this difference of interest . . . has become manifest.[7]

This was the situation in the south Wales coalfield when the Great War began in June 1914. The war greatly increased demand for coal, thereby boosting colliery company profits. The miners demanded wage increases commensurate with these profits and the rising cost of living, to which the coalowners proved resistant. Consequently, in July 1915 the entire south Wales coalfield struck, in defiance of the Munitions Act and the newly-imposed Treasury Agreement. After

---

[6] Morgan, *Rebirth of a Nation*, pp. 146–7.
[7] Unofficial Reform Committee, *The Miners' Next Step* (Tonypandy: 1912; new edn, 1991), p. 12.

ten days' stoppage, the miners won all their main points.[8] The government was forced to assume control over the industry for the duration of the conflict. Wartime pressures allowed the miners to make significant advances: in April 1916, it was conceded that all colliery workmen should be members of a recognised union, reinforcing the Fed's central role within the south Wales coalfield. Pay increased, with average earnings more than doubling between 1914 and 1918. Support also grew for the MFGB's call for the nationalisation of the mines. In this way, the war helped to reinforce the combativeness of the years 1910–12 amongst the south Wales miners.

As the war continued, popular resentment of wartime conditions began to appear. Open opposition emerged in response to conscription and news of the Russian Revolution. Conscription was seen as a threat to trade union rights and an infringement of civil liberties: in February 1916, the SWMF only narrowly failed to persuade the MFGB to use strike action against it. The revolutionary upheavals in Russia in 1917 were greeted with widespread and enthusiastic support: Petrograd-style workers' councils appeared in the Rhondda and red flags flew at the pitheads.[9] In August 1917, the Fed called for a peace settlement from the government.[10] At this time, SWMF activist Arthur Horner crossed to Ireland to fight for Irish independence in the Irish Citizen Army. Imprisoned on his return, he was promptly elected checkweigher by Maerdy lodge.[11] In the summer of 1917, the government appointed a Commission on Industrial Unrest. Its report on south Wales painted a picture of deteriorating conditions and rising militancy.

By 1918, it was clear that the popular culture of the south Wales miners had come to adopt radical socialist tones. An enthusiastic contemporary observer claimed that Marx's writings had become household words.[12] Similarly, in 1921 a prominent Swansea Liberal

---

[8] Anthony Mòr O'Brien, 'Patriotism on trial: the strike of the South Wales miners, July 1915', *WHR*, 12/1 (1984), 76–104.

[9] Morgan, *Rebirth of a Nation*, p. 175.

[10] Hywel Francis and David Smith, *The Fed: A History of the South Wales Miners in the Twentieth Century* (London: 1980), pp. 22–3.

[11] Williams, *When Was Wales?*, p. 250.

[12] John Thomas, 'The Economic Doctrines of Karl Marx and their influence on the industrial areas of South Wales, particularly among the Miners' (unpublished essay submitted to the National Eisteddfod at Ammanford, 1922), cited in Francis and Smith, *The Fed*, p. 54.

lamented that 'Marx's *Capital* has displaced the Bible from the minds of thousands of young Welshmen'.[13] In a rules conference in July 1917, the Fed's constitution was rewritten to include the abolition of capitalism amongst the union's objectives.[14] The miners' leaders were also increasingly militant. S. O. Davies, for example, elected Dowlais miners' agent in 1918, was a committed Marxist. A. J. Cook was a member of the Communist Party of Great Britain, describing himself as 'a humble follower of Lenin'.[15] Arthur Horner, the future SWMF president, was a long-term Communist Party member. These were the type of men coming to the forefront in the Fed at this time.

The formation of the Third Communist International and its subsidiary, the Red International of Labour Unions, by the Bolshevik government in Russia in 1919 was the spur for a remarkable episode in south Wales. At a conference in July 1921, the SWMF voted overwhelmingly in favour of affiliation to the RILU – a very rare instance of a British union espousing revolutionary trade unionism. At the 1922 MFGB Conference, the SWMF attempted to persuade the other coalfields to affiliate but was defeated comprehensively. Nevertheless, a conference was held in Cardiff in October 1922 aimed at building SWMF support for the RILU. The Fed even considered affiliating unilaterally, before eventually rejecting this because it feared expulsion from the MFGB.[16]

More generally, the post-war years saw the establishment of the Labour Party's political dominance in the valleys. By 1922, Labour had won every parliamentary seat in the south Wales coalfield. This hegemony was 'of a highly distinctive kind, wreathed in passionate left-wing talk, shot through with Marxism and great blood-red dreams of brotherhood, with at its side a small but highly influential Communist Party and all around it a tradition of pro-Soviet feeling and bitter class battles'.[17]

The immediate post-war period also saw mining trade unionism at the pinnacle of its influence. Employment in the south Wales coalfield reached an all-time high of 271,516 in 1920, while average

[13] Quoted in Morgan, *Rebirth of a Nation*, p. 193.
[14] Francis and Smith, *The Fed*, p. 24.
[15] Quoted in Morgan, *Rebirth of a Nation*, p. 194.
[16] Francis and Smith, *The Fed*, pp. 28, 30–1.
[17] Williams, *When Was Wales?*, p. 265.

earnings were more than treble those of 1914.[18] The MFGB was determined to press for further wage increases and the nationalisation of the coal industry. In order to avert strike action, Lloyd George appointed the Sankey Commission to examine the issue of ownership of the mines. Although the commission's majority report advocated nationalisation, in August 1919 the government rejected this recommendation. The Welsh miners reacted with amazement and bitterness; even the moderate Vernon Hartshorn said that the miners felt 'deceived, betrayed, duped'.[19]

The decline in labour productivity by a quarter between 1914 and 1920 and the collapse in coal export prices in late 1920 meant the industry's return to private control in April 1921 made a clash over wages inevitable.[20] On 31 March, the miners were locked out for refusing to accept a wage cut and the introduction of district-level wage bargaining. The MFGB appealed to its Triple Alliance partners (the NUR and the TGWU) for support, but on 'Black Friday', 15 April 1921, they called off secondary action, thereby ending the Triple Alliance. The miners stayed out until July 1921 before conceding defeat. Following this, average earnings halved in south Wales that year. A coal trade recession further reduced the SWMF's ability to defend its members. Membership fell to fewer than 100,000 and only a vigorous campaign in 1923 restored the membership to about 148,000.[21]

The anthracite strike of 1925 indicated a new intensity of conflict within the south Wales coalfield, provoked when the coalowners dismantled Ammanford No. 1 colliery rather than allow the operation of established practices there. In the bitter six-week dispute, the miners showed unusually aggressive willingness to escalate the strike, to mobilise mass pickets, to use riots and to infiltrate the police with spies. At the height of the strike, SWMF vice-president S. O. Davies called for a workers' army. A miners' Defence Corps was formed in the Amman valley and this held Ammanford for nearly a week,

[18] John Williams, *Digest of Welsh Historical Statistics, Vol. 1* (Cardiff: 1985), p. 300; Chris Williams, 'The hope of the British proletariat: the South Wales Miners, 1910–1947', in Alan Campbell, Nina Fishman and David Howell (eds), *Miners, Unions and Politics, 1910–1947* (Aldershot: 1996), p. 126.
[19] Quoted in Morgan, *Rebirth of a Nation*, p. 194.
[20] Barry Supple, *The History of the British Coal Industry, Vol.4: 1913–1946, The Political Economy of Decline* (Oxford: 1987), pp. 154–5.
[21] Francis and Smith, *The Fed*, p. 31.

despite repeated police attempts to retake the town.[22] After the dispute, the jailed miners became local folk heroes.

At the beginning of May 1926, the TUC called a general strike in defence of the miners. The results were unequivocal. The climbdown of the TUC just nine days into the General Strike – and the lock-out of the miners which followed it – was a total defeat from which the British labour movement did not recover for twenty years. During the dispute, the south Wales miners established effective control over the coalfield; in villages such as Bedlinog and Maerdy, their councils of action became virtual 'workers' governments' for their respective communities. Day-to-day survival focused around the Fed lodges, the miners' institutes and the chapels. These, together with their 'soup kitchens', enabled the miners and their families to survive without incomes for six months. Apart from the innumerable skirmishes, there were eighteen major battles involving police protection of strike-breakers. The invasion of the valleys by outside police forces worsened an already-embittered atmosphere. For Francis and Smith, in south Wales the events of 1926 'revealed an alternative cultural pattern which had no comparable equivalent in the other British coalfields. The totality of the commitment to the miners' cause was a form of class consciousness which translated itself into a community consciousness, so overwhelming were the miners in numbers and influence.'[23] Even after the strike, this remained etched on the collective memory of the region. As the poet Idris Davies put it: 'We shall remember 1926 until our blood is dry.'[24]

The eventual defeat of the SWMF in December 1926 was uncompromising and total. The new terms imposed included longer hours, lower wages and district-level agreements. Power shifted substantially towards the coalowners. Even before the new agreement had been signed, miners' leaders were being ordered off colliery premises in the Rhymney valley.[25] Mining employment fell steadily, from 217,989 in 1926 to 126,412 in 1936.[26] Additionally, the export-dependence of its coal industry meant that south Wales was devastated by the Depression. Between 1921 and 1936, 241 mines

[22] Hywel Francis, 'The Anthracite Strike and Disturbances of 1925', *Llafur*, 1/2 (1973), 58–62 (1972–5 compendium edition).
[23] Francis and Smith, *The Fed*, p. 55.
[24] Islwyn Jenkins (ed.), *The Collected Poems of Idris Davies* (Llandysul: 2003), p. 30.
[25] Francis and Smith, *The Fed*, p. 76.
[26] Williams, *Welsh Historical Statistics*, p. 300.

closed and by 1929 south Wales, which had once supplied one-third of world coal exports, now produced less than 3 per cent. By 1932 male unemployment in Wales averaged 39.1 per cent.[27]

The SWMF found itself fighting for its existence. Membership levels collapsed, from 136,250 to 72,981 during 1927.[28] Non-unionism became rife, with less than half of mineworkers being SWMF members between 1929 and 1932.[29] A potentially more serious threat was the South Wales Miners' Industrial Union (SWMIU), an explicitly 'non-political' union formed in 1926. The struggle against this company union preoccupied the Fed right up until the eventual disappearance of the SWMIU in 1938. Although relatively tiny, the SWMIU was entrenched in a few collieries where the SWMF's presence was minimal. The removal of the company union was essential because it undermined miners' unity, benefiting from the employers' anti-SWMF stance and organising unemployed miners to take the jobs of those involved in disputes. For Fed activists, company unionism was abhorrent because it rejected the principle of independent trade unionism, the workers' main defence against exploitation and repression. As Arthur Horner put it, 'Scab Unionism is fascism in embryo.'[30]

The Fed's fortunes began to revive in 1933–4, led by the anthracite miners in the west. Significantly, one of their agents, James Griffiths, was elected SWMF president in 1934. The anthracite miners played this role in this period because of their fortunate economic situation: south Wales anthracite production actually reached its maximum in 1934. Equally significantly, following their success in the anthracite strike of 1925 in defending the seniority rule, very few lodge officials had been victimised there after the defeat in 1926.

Building on this, in 1934 the SWMF structure was reformed along more democratic and centralised lines, making an elected executive council of rank-and-file miners the supreme executive authority within the Fed. The union's nineteen semi-autonomous districts – many of which had been devastated by unemployment and non-unionism – were replaced by eight larger, more efficient 'areas'. This reform enabled the SMWF to meet the challenge of company unionism.

[27]   Williams, *Capitalism, Community and Conflict*, p. 23.
[28]   Williams, *Capitalism, Community and Conflict*, p. 89.
[29]   Francis and Smith, *The Fed*, p. 117.
[30]   *Daily Worker*, 25 May 1936.

The most dramatic weapon used against the SWMIU was the 'stay-down' strike. These strikes, led by pro-Fed miners, took place in 1935 and 1936 in Nine Mile Point, Parc and Dare, and Bedwas, collieries that were SWMIU 'strongholds'. The ultimate success of this struggle was due to solidarity action shown by miners in surrounding pits and overwhelming community support within the south Wales coalfield.

The slow rebuilding of the SWMF and the struggle against unemployment were two prominent examples of a many-sided politicisation of the coalfield in the late 1920s and 1930s, which was also reflected in other ways. There was enthusiastic participation in the national hunger marches, with the main marches from south Wales to London in 1927, 1934 and 1936 expressing the community consciousness of a coalfield society that felt itself threatened with extinction. Even more dramatic were the demonstrations against the hated Means Test. On 3 February 1935, 300,000 people across south Wales marched in protest against the Unemployment Assistance Board Act, the biggest demonstration in Welsh history.[31] Wales, especially south Wales coalfield society, also gave extensive support to the republican government during the Spanish Civil War: collecting food, giving aid, establishing homes for Basque refugee children at Brechfa and Caerleon, holding countless meetings and rallies, and, most famously, supplying 206 volunteers to the International Brigade, thirty-three of whom died in the conflict.[32]

The Communist Party played an important role in the south Wales coalfield in the 1930s. Within the SWMF, its energetic work gave it an influence unparalleled elsewhere in British trade unionism. Electorally the Communists made some progress, particularly in the Rhondda: in the 1945 general election, they lost by only 972 votes in Rhondda East. Overall, though, they remained a long way behind Labour. No Communist was ever elected to parliament from the coalfield and the party made a significant impression only on a few local government bodies. Instead, Labour continued to dominate the politics in the region: it held the fifteen coalfield parliamentary seats

---

[31] Williams, *When Was Wales?*, p. 262; see also Neil Evans, 'South Wales has been roused as never before: Marching against the Means Test, 1934–36', in David Howell and Kenneth O. Morgan (eds), *Crime, Protest and Police in Modern British Society* (Cardiff: 1999).

[32] Hywel Francis, *Miners Against Fascism: Wales and the Spanish Civil War* (London: 1984; 3rd edn, 2012), pp. xiii, xiv, 248, 300–5.

without interruption, while further extending its control over the local authorities.

The harsh experiences of the late 1920s and 1930s inculcated in the south Wales miners a defiant resilience, which moulded the consciousness of successive generations. It was this tenacity which enabled them to survive the Depression and rebuild the Fed. By 1939 the SWMF could look to the future and concentrate on improving wages and conditions, rather than on simply surviving in the face of orchestrated hostility.

During the Second World War, the demands of the war economy meant an increased need for coal and men to mine it, thus reducing unemployment and increasing wages. Throughout the war, the SWMF leadership co-operated fully with the government's Joint Coal Production Committee. Nevertheless, the embittered interwar industrial relations climate continued to cast a long shadow: absenteeism, go-slows and unofficial strikes remained common-place.[33] From July 1940, strikes were illegal; nevertheless, between September 1939 and October 1944 there were 514 stoppages, mostly of short duration, in the south Wales coalfield.[34] The most significant unrest was the Porter Award strike of March 1944, when the south Wales coalfield, together with Scottish and Yorkshire miners, took unofficial strike action against the perceived inadequacy of the government's wage proposals.

The inability of the coal industry to meet wartime demands led to the government taking control of the mines in March 1942. For many miners, the next step was to implement complete nationalisation of the coal industry in order to overcome the crisis of production. Although Churchill's government rejected this, coal nationalisation became Labour Party policy – a key development, given Labour's sweeping victory in the 1945 general election.

The National Union of Mineworkers (NUM), formed on 1 January 1945, was closely involved in shaping the Coal Industry Nationalisation Bill. Many of the improved circumstances in the post-1947 industry were based on the 1946 Miners' Charter, drafted by NUM general secretary Arthur Horner. Horner's role here reflected a wider influence of the South Wales NUM on the government, via its sponsored MPs: James Griffiths was Minister of

---

[33]   See Keith Gildart, 'Coal strikes on the Home Front: miners' militancy and socialist politics in the Second World War', *TCBH*, 20/2 (2009), 121–51.

[34]   Francis and Smith, *The Fed*, p. 398.

National Insurance, Ness Edwards became Postmaster General and Aneurin Bevan was Minister of Health and Housing. It was Bevan who was the architect of the NHS, using his experiences of the Tredegar Medical Aid Society to build the greatest achievement of the Attlee government.[35]

Nationalisation on 1 January 1947 represented a landmark event in British coal-mining history. Although it had been an aspiration of the miners for a generation beforehand, it was the circumstances of the Second World War that demonstrated the practicality and the necessity of state control of the industry. Although by no means a panacea, nationalisation was widely applauded by south Wales miners, particularly after their interwar hardships.[36] Undoubtedly, nationalisation led to improved conditions in certain respects. Between 1947 and 1957, coal mining remained relatively well-paid, with weekly earnings about 25 per cent above the average for all industries.[37] The decade or so after 1947 was essentially a good period for the south Wales miners – particularly in contrast to what was to follow it.

Although formed as the result of an overwhelming vote by the miners for change, the NUM retained certain aspects of the MFGB's federalism. For south Wales, the continuity of federal union structures meant that the NUM South Wales Area inherited the substantial socio-political presence of its forerunner, the SWMF. The Area took an active interest in its members' well-being, maintaining the recreational, cultural and educational traditions of the valleys miners' institutes and its welfare movement, which reached its zenith in the mid-1950s. The Tredegar workmen's institute, with its silver band, operatic and choral societies, cinema and impressive library, was by no means untypical. In 1956, the union embarked on an ambitious expansion of its education system.[38] The South Wales NUM also continued the SWMF's medical care programme for its members, together with its Miners' Rehabilitation Centre (which was taken over by the Ministry of Health in 1951).[39] Undoubtedly, the

[35] Francis and Smith, *The Fed*, p. 434.

[36] Bill Jones, Brian Roberts and Chris Williams, '"Going from Darkness to the Light": South Wales Miners' attitudes towards Nationalisation', *Llafur*, 7/1 (1996), 96–110.

[37] William Ashworth, *The History of the British Coal Industry, Vol. 5: 1946–1982, The Nationalised Industry* (Oxford: 1986), p. 224.

[38] Alun Burge and Keith Davies, '"Enlightenment of the Highest Order": The Education Programme of the South Wales Miners, 1956–1971', *Llafur*, 7/1 (1996), 111–21.

[39] Francis and Smith, *The Fed*, p. 431.

Area union was a central institution in the day-to-day lives of its members.

Nationalisation brought about an uncharacteristic quiescence in industrial relations in south Wales until the early 1950s; after that, it recovered its reputation for militancy. Disputes in this period were characterised by the 'go slow' and brief, small-scale, unofficial stoppages. Year after year, more than 80 per cent of tonnage lost was in the Scottish, North East, and South West (that is, south Wales) Divisions, leading the industry's official historian to comment that 'it seems impossible to explain the contrasts [between these Divisions and the moderate coalfields] without reference to deep-rooted communal attitudes which long antedated nationalisation'.[40]

Disturbances in the early years of nationalisation should be kept in perspective, however; the 1950s were generally a period of calm before the arrival of mass pit closures. Coal remained in great demand as the low-cost fuel to power Britain's economic recovery. In south Wales, annual output hit 24 million tons in 1952 and maintained this level for the rest of the decade.[41] The prevailing optimism was encapsulated in 1957 by NCB chairman James Bowman's claim that 'Coal has provided the nation with the resources to weather the first critical decade of the post-war world. Even in an age of atomic energy, it will continue to be the mainstay of Britain's prosperity.'[42]

In 1957 the seemingly unlimited demand for coal ceased, owing to increasing use of oil and gas. Consequently, early in 1959 the NCB summarily closed thirty-six collieries, mainly in Scotland, south Wales and Cumberland. This was the beginning of a fundamental contraction of the industry that would continue throughout the 1960s. It was the growth of their opposition to this closure programme that propelled the south Wales miners back to their 'traditional' role at the forefront of the struggles of the labour movement.

*   *   *

This book explores the history of the south Wales miners between 1964 and 1985. The period covers the colliery closure programme

[40] Ashworth, *British Coal Industry*, p. 169.
[41] Williams, *Welsh Historical Statistics*, p. 308.
[42] Francis and Smith, *The Fed*, p. 448.

of the Wilson government, the growth of miners' resistance and the brief prospect of a secure future for them, through to eventual NUM defeat in 1985. The emphasis is on the dynamics of relations between the lodges, the South Wales Area and the national NUM, the Area's response to industrial and political developments, and also the impact on its relationship with the wider labour movement.

This book is essentially union-based labour history. Its main source material is the official records of the South Wales NUM; no other evidence type can produce a comparable level of detail. Crucially, though, care has been taken to avoid an unquestioning acceptance of the official viewpoint: wherever possible, verbatim conference records have been used to illustrate debate and potential discord within the Area. Oral history is invaluable in terms of shedding light on the experiences of individuals which would otherwise go unrecorded. It is also a useful tool for addressing issues of consciousness and opinion, important questions for the historian which are not readily accessible from institutional histories or through quantitative measurement.[43] As Hobsbawm states, however, oral history deals with 'personal memory, which is a remarkably slippery medium for preserving facts'; consequently, oral history evidence needs to be utilised alongside other primary sources and secondary literature, so as to provide a framework against which it can be measured.[44] This is the approach that this book has taken.

This type of labour history is not currently fashionable. The decline of the densely unionised heavy industries, together with the global hegemony of neo-liberalism, has encouraged neglect of the subject – though the working class has not disappeared even if more people in Britain now work in call centres and supermarkets than in collieries or steelworks. 'The [current] debility of labour studies . . . [stems from] the defeats and the consequent sense of demoralisation the labour movement has suffered from, as well as state policies and academic responses to them.'[45] Instead, historians have focused on the relationships between work, class, gender and community rather

---

[43] For a fuller discussion of this type of source material for coalfield histories, see Keith Gildart, 'Mining memories: reading coalfield autobiographies', *Labor History*, 50/2 (2009), 139–61.

[44] E. J. Hobsbawm, *On History* (London: 1997), p. 206.

[45] John McIlroy and Alan Campbell, 'Still setting the pace? Labour history, industrial relations and the history of post-war trade unionism', *LHR*, 64/2 (1999), 186.

than union-based histories. Nevertheless, the subject remains relevant both to the study of organised labour and to broader questions. McIlroy and others call for 'a history which situates unions within the complex web of community associations, parties, employers, economy and state. *Starting from* trade unionism as . . . the animating core of the labour movement . . . [remains] the most fruitful way to proceed.'[46]

A union-based labour history has significance. On a pragmatic level, unions are institutions which generate written records dealing with many issues that are central to the working lives of their members. Furthermore, this approach 'need not glorify organizations or their leaders, or ignore the problematic relationship that seems always to obtain between leaders and the rank-and-file . . . [R]esearch informed by an organizational perspective can make sense of a broader range of phenomena because it offers a common set of questions by which to relate them to one another.'[47] Recent coal-mining historiography includes several books which adopt this institution-orientated focus. Taylor, for example, in his two-volume history of the NUM, states that 'institutions matter . . . [because] they are the vehicles whereby interests are articulated and institutions encapsulate the processes whereby these interests are aggregated into behaviour'.[48] Similarly, in his study of the North Wales NUM, Gildart asserts that miners' class consciousness was rooted in their everyday experiences in the workplace, and that this informed their broader ideological outlook.[49] The organisational forms of class consciousness offer insights to the world of the miners, their families and communities.

A labour history sensitive to broader political and societal factors also has crucial insights to offer industrial relations studies, in terms of introducing the central explanatory dynamic of the agency-structure dialectic. As Gramsci states, '[t]he trade union is not a predetermined phenomenon. It *becomes* a determinate institution, i.e. it takes on a definite historical form to the extent that the strength

---

[46] John McIlroy, Nina Fishman and Alan Campbell (eds), *British Trade Unions and Industrial Politics, Vol. 2: The High Tide of Trade Unionism, 1964–79* (Aldershot: 1999), p. 12.

[47] James E. Cronin, 'Neither exceptional nor particular: towards the comparative study of labor in advanced societies', *IRSH*, 38/1 (1993), 73–4.

[48] Andrew Taylor, *The NUM and British Politics, Vol. 1: 1944–1968* (Aldershot: 2003), p. vii.

[49] Keith Gildart, *North Wales Miners: A Fragile Unity, 1945–1996* (Cardiff: 2001), p. 254.

and will of the workers who are its members impress a policy and impose an aim that define it.'[50] In any given case, this process occurs within a particular employment relations framework, which is itself affected by wider political and socio-economic considerations. Consequently, '[a]ny adequate interpretation of trade union development must . . . link theoretically the active initiatives of union members and representatives, the purposes and ideologies which inform their actions, and the external material forces which influence and constrain them.'[51] McIlroy and Campbell argue for a systematic consideration of industrial politics as a factor in trade union decision-making at every level, examining how developments in the workplace are contextualised within industry-wide or national political frameworks.[52] It follows that a historically-informed awareness of how political-economic processes and phenomena develop and interact is a prerequisite for understanding how unions operate.

The earliest research on the history of mineworkers in Britain was undertaken by activists such as Ness Edwards and Robin Page Arnot. Their work was 'largely institutional, inspirational, descriptive, etching the ascending fortunes of organization . . . into an iconography celebrating the irresistible rise of the working class',[53] a perspective characterised as 'the forward march of labour'. However, from an early twenty-first-century perspective, the element of inevitability in their assumptions is questionable. Similarly, this approach conceptualises the decision-making processes in the miners' union in a monolithic way, disregarding the potential for disagreement within and between its various echelons.

During the 1960s and 1970s, labour history was transformed by the rise of 'history from below'. Following the work of E. P. Thompson, this aimed to locate working-class organisations within their broader societies. In mining historiography, *Independent Collier* was the main early embodiment of this approach.[54] It portrayed

[50] Antonio Gramsci, *Selections from Political Writings, 1910–1920*, ed. Quintin Hoare (London: 1977), p. 265.

[51] Richard Hyman, 'Trade Unions: Structure, Policies, and Politics', in George Sayers Bain (ed.), *Industrial Relations in Britain* (Oxford: 1983), p. 61.

[52] McIlroy and Campbell, 'Still setting the pace?', 191.

[53] Keith Gildart, 'Cooperation and Conflict: Episodes from the North Wales Coalfield, 1925–35', *HSIR*, 12 (2001), 27–56.

[54] Royden Harrison (ed.), *Independent Collier: The Coal Miner as Archetypal Proletarian Reconsidered* (Hassocks: 1978).

an occupation subject to various economic, geographical and cultural influences, encompassing conflict and co-operation, which could only be understood by examining the realities of historical experience. Since *Independent Collier*, numerous local studies have underlined the diversity of mineworkers' experiences. This historiographical perspective is summarised by Geary, who shows how the state, company paternalism, the industrial relations system, geological conditions, ethnic and religious divisions, specific economic conjunctures, technology and differential pay systems, generational experience, migration and gender relationships all played key roles in determining levels of solidarity in coalfield societies. He concludes that 'industrial militancy was never a necessary consequence of being a miner'.[55]

Recent NUM historiography has reflected this emphasis on diversity and moderation. As Howell has commented, '[t]he National Union, in fact rather than aspiration, has never been . . . the solid militant politically radical union of legend'.[56] Similarly, Ackers and Payne argue that there has been an undue focus on 'peripheral' militant coalfields such as south Wales and Scotland and on the national strikes in 1926, 1972, 1974 and 1984–5.[57] This perspective has been enlisted in some quarters to argue that a lack of solidarity was normal in working-class politics. However, acknowledging the existence of complexity does not preclude the possibility that class solidarity might be constructed – a point first made in 1975 by John Williams.[58] An awareness of variability 'does not necessarily involve . . . rejection of an overarching conception of class and class struggle . . . [r]ather, such an approach is essential to an understanding of class formation and a prerequisite for examining the nature of collective action and division in mining communities'.[59] Moreover, accepting that a phenomenon is the product of a unique historical process does not mean that it is not

[55]   Dick Geary, 'The Myth of the Radical Miner', in Stefan Berger, Andy Croll and Norman LaPorte (eds), *Towards a Comparative History of Coalfield Societies* (Aldershot: 2005), p. 46.

[56]   David Howell, *The Politics of the NUM: A Lancashire View* (Manchester: 1989), pp. 213–18.

[57]   Peter Ackers and Jonathan Payne, 'Before the storm: the experience of nationalization and the prospects for industrial relations partnership in the British coal industry, 1947–1972 – rethinking the militant narrative', *Social History*, 27/2 (2002), 184–209.

[58]   John Williams, *Was Wales Industrialised? Essays in Modern Welsh History* (Llandysul: 1995), pp. 331–2.

[59]   Gildart, 'Cooperation and Conflict', 27–56.

part of a general pattern. Ackers and Payne regard the south Wales miners as an 'exceptional case' – but this does not mean that the miners' actions were not a concentrated expression of phenomena that existed commonly in more diffuse form elsewhere. As Dai Smith has pointed out, 'to be in advance of the column is not necessarily to be out of touch or even in the wrong place'.[60]

There were strong dialectical connections between politics, community and identity in coalfield societies.[61] As Howell comments, '[t]he distinctive self-image of each NUM Area was fundamental to the conduct of its internal affairs and to the character of its interventions in the National Union'.[62] Similarly, *Miners, Unions and Politics* utilises regional studies to exemplify how miners' institutions were shaped by the varying patterns of interaction between the labour process and the historically-derived structures of mining communities, with the potential for widely divergent outcomes. Consequently, '[t]he centrality of the union for miners could vary accordingly. In occupationally monolithic South Wales, the lodge could be central to communal life; in Lancashire, with its diverse occupational structure, commuting miners and workplace branches, the union was inevitably more marginal.'[63]

Throughout the twentieth century, the south Wales miners were one of the most militant sections of the British workforce:

> In South Wales, the [SWMF] . . . became much more than a union. Its Workmen's Institutes spread through the coalfield, ran leisure and cultural events, . . . laid on medical schemes and built libraries for their members. Moreover the 'Fed' had the abolition of capitalism written in to its rulebook in 1917. Much later, no other group of workers contested Thatcherism more obviously than the colliers of South Yorkshire, South Wales and Scotland.[64]

A recurrent feature in discussions about the south Wales miners is the extent to which their union was an integral feature of valleys society.[65] There are unmistakable echoes here of Kerr's and Siegel's

---

[60] Dai Smith, *Aneurin Bevan and the World of South Wales* (Cardiff: 1993), p. 15.

[61] For a recent case-study of the interactions between class and community in coalfield society, see Hester Barron, *The 1926 Miners' Lockout: Meanings of Community in the Durham Coalfield* (Oxford: 2009).

[62] Howell, *The Politics of the NUM*, p. 215.

[63] Campbell, Fishman and Howell, *Miners, Unions and Politics*, p. 6.

[64] Geary, 'The Myth of the Radical Miner', pp. 44–5.

[65] This point was reaffirmed on numerous occasions during interviews conducted by the author with mineworkers and support group activists.

characterisation of mining communities as 'isolated masses, almost a "race apart". They live in their own separate communities [with] . . . their own codes, myths, heroes, and social standards[, in which strike action] . . . is a kind of colonial revolt against far-removed authority', particularly their statement that '[t]he union becomes a kind of working-class party or even government for these employees, rather than just another association among many'.[66] As Church, Outram and Smith point out, in coalfields where coal was dominant and the union held an important societal role, this situation could indeed 'produce social practices, beliefs and actions which are in turn necessary conditions for high levels of strike activity'.[67]

Although south Wales mining historiography has retained the class-based analysis of the Page Arnot paradigm, it has adopted a less teleological view of political behaviour and demonstrated an enhanced awareness of complexities. The pre-eminent work on this subject, *The Fed*, by Hywel Francis and Dai Smith, uses its focus on the SWMF 'to write about the principal institutions used and devised by the South Wales miners within, and for, their society'.[68] Furthermore, its breadth of source material facilitates access to a variety of intra-union viewpoints, thereby illuminating the internal debates and strategic choices made as the Federation attempted to recover from the disaster of 1926. *The Fed* concentrates mainly on the first half of the twentieth century, although there is a brief discussion of the post-1945 period. Following in Francis's and Smith's footsteps, the chronological focus of this present book is in large measure a reflection of its aspiration to provide a similarly cogent analysis of the south Wales miners' history in the later twentieth century.

In recent years, however, *The Fed* has not escaped criticism: Lieven has censured its 'heroic' class-orientated perspective, while Zweiniger-Bargielowska has questioned the extent of miners' militancy in south Wales.[69] It is true that there are always exceptions

---

[66] Clark Kerr and Abraham Siegel, 'The Interindustry Propensity to Strike – an international comparison', in Arthur Kornhauser, Robert Dubin and Arthur M. Ross (eds), *Industrial Conflict* (New York: 1954), pp. 191–5.

[67] Roy Church, Quentin Outram and David N. Smith, 'The "isolated mass" revisited: strikes in British coal mining', *Sociological Review*, 39/1 (1991), 78.

[68] Francis and Smith, *The Fed*, p. xv.

[69] Mike Lieven, 'A "New History" of the South Wales Coalfield?', *Llafur*, 8/3 (2002), 89–106; Ina-Maria Zweiniger-Bargielowska, 'Miners' Militancy: a study of four south Wales collieries during the middle of the twentieth century', *WHR*, 16/1 (1993), 356–89.

to general patterns; however, the historian should not forget that the south Wales miners were consistently amongst the most militant workers in Britain for most of the twentieth century, whether this is measured by strike activity or support for radical socialist politics. This is not to say that this was inevitable. Rather, it was the consequence of the myriad interactions between individual miners, the lodges and the Area structure within a specific socio-economic and political framework that changed over time.

Zweiniger-Bargielowska has studied miners' militancy by analysing industrial relations in four south Wales collieries in the mid-twentieth century. Her conclusion is that 'militancy at colliery level was determined by a combination of local pit conditions, the balance of power between lodge and management, the degree of lodge leaders' control over the rank-and-file membership, and managerial strategies'.[70] This is an incontestable assessment; however, her very focus militates against sustainable generalisations about the South Wales NUM. A detailed study of selected collieries in the 1940s and 1950s, a period of relative prosperity, is less well-placed to afford comment on the turbulent history of the south Wales coalfield in the later twentieth century, particularly since the miners' main problems were industry-wide. In contrast, the present approach is to examine the south Wales miners as a whole through the prism of their union, while retaining an awareness of the potential for diversity within the overall framework.

One of the central elements of the industrial politics of trade unions is the interrelationship between activists, the official leadership and the broader union membership. While cautioning that '[t]he "ordinary member" should not be ignored', McIlroy and Campbell comment that '[t]he active minority's importance lies precisely in its immense significance to the development and sustenance of consciousness and action among broad groups of workers. What made unionists and what motivated them, as well as the complex processes of interaction (in the workplace and beyond), between members, representatives and officials, are central to understanding trade unionism.'[71] Similarly, the overall left-wing orientation of the South Wales NUM was readily apparent, but this should not conceal the complexity of its internal relations.

---

[70] Zweiniger-Bargielowska, 'Miners' Militancy', 383.
[71] McIlroy and Campbell, 'Still setting the pace?', 193.

Important strategic questions could be a source of fierce controversy at crucial junctures in the history of the south Wales miners. Consequently, the interactions between the various levels of the Area structure are a key focus of attention in this book.

Union policy and strategy provided the environment within which the membership, lodge activists and the leadership interacted. Hyman observes that several unions experienced active rank-and-file movements that emerged in the late 1960s but had declined or disintegrated by the late 1970s, suggesting that they were out-manoeuvred by the official leaderships and became isolated as the unrest of the early 1970s subsided.[72] Taking a different approach, Lyddon asserts that events of this period proved the effectiveness of mass strike action, that unofficial action could aid official union objectives, and that secondary solidarity action by other workers could make the difference between success and failure.[73] These issues are considered throughout the pages that follow.

A key debate has been over 'rank-and-filism', the attempt to write non-institutional histories of industrial relations that focus on economic and social processes. Hyman has stated that an awareness of the perennial potential for conflict of interest between grassroots members and full-time officials is an essential prerequisite for understanding the complex internal dynamics of trade unions.[74] Developing this theme, Campbell and others caution that union politics cannot be reduced to a polarisation between militant rank and file and moderate bureaucracy. Instead, they present a picture of 'competing interest groups within the membership and multi-layered levels of lay- and full-time officials, whose strategies were the complex outcome of personal attributes, ideological commitments, material status, and organisational loyalties and routines, and which were constructed within the constraints of widely divergent coalfield economies'.[75]

In the context of the south Wales miners, Zweiniger-Bargielowska's discussion of 'rank-and-filism' postulates a dichotomy between a radical activist/leadership minority and a passive majority – an

[72] Hyman, 'Trade Unions', pp. 51–2.
[73] Dave Lyddon, '"Glorious Summer", 1972: the High Tide of Rank and File Militancy', in McIlroy, Fishman and Campbell, *British Trade Unions and Industrial Politics*, p. 344.
[74] Richard Hyman, 'The Sound of One Hand Clapping: A comment on the "Rank and Filism" Debate', *IRSH*, 34/2 (1989), 309–26.
[75] Campbell, Fishman and Howell, *Miners, Unions and Politics*, p. 5.

inversion of the customary historiographical perspective. This question is examined in the period from the rapid decline of the south Wales coal industry in the 1960s through the struggles of the 1970s to the miners' eventual defeat in 1985. There was always the possibility of tension between the official leadership, lodge activists and the broader membership, particularly during phases of acute crisis. The results of the present study deny a simple or consistent distinction between 'radical leaders' and 'passive miners'.

More broadly, the historical events and processes analysed in this book address wider questions about politics and economics. One theme which emerges strongly is that economics is inherently political and that politics has direct economic effects. As Tenfelde has commented, 'Labour and working-class history . . . does not take place in a sphere free of politics.'[76] The separation of politics and economics in hermetically-sealed spheres, a common practice among both economists and political scientists, is a major impediment to understanding the decisions and activities of individuals, organisations and governments. In this respect, the present study strikes a chord with economic discussions about the coal industry that stress the political factors that informed actual decision-making, such as *The Coal Question*.[77] The collapse of coal under the Thatcher regime has generated several pertinent contributions, particularly that by Parker. His comparison of the differing situations in Britain and Germany is illuminating. During the 1980s and 1990s, the rapid contraction of the relatively efficient British industry contrasted starkly with Germany's continued subsidisation of its high-cost industry coupled with gradual consensus-led adaptation. He convincingly asserts that this disparity cannot be understood except in political terms.[78] Similarly, Golden concludes that the 1984–5 strike was provoked by forces external to the coal industry as part of a broader political imperative aimed at a transformation of the British industrial relations system.[79] The conclusions that follow concur with this analysis, both in terms of

[76] Klaus Tenfelde, 'On the History of Industrial Relations in Mining', in Gerald D. Feldman and Klaus Tenfelde (eds.), *Workers, Owners and Politics in Coal Mining* (Oxford: 1990), p. 9.
[77] Ben Fine, *The Coal Question: Political Economy and Industrial Change from the Nineteenth Century to the Present Day* (London: 1990).
[78] Mike Parker, *The Politics of Coal's Decline: The Industry in Western Europe* (London: 1994), p. 72; M. J. Parker, *Thatcherism and the Fall of Coal* (Oxford: 2000).
[79] Miriam A. Golden, *Heroic Defeats: The Politics of Job Loss* (Cambridge, 1997), p. 144.

Golden's specific contention and, more generally, in demonstrating that the economic struggles of the south Wales miners cannot be separated from the political context in which they occurred.

The aim of this book is to provide a socio-political study of the south Wales miners in the later twentieth century. They played a key role in industrial south Wales during these years: their history raises issues of importance for the historian and sheds light on investigations by other social science disciplines. The story of the south Wales miners, with its struggles, achievements and setbacks, is indeed a significant one.

I

THE POLITICS OF THE SOUTH WALES MINERS

Throughout modern British history there have been few trade unions with as strong an engagement with political activism as the NUM South Wales Area. The focus of investigation in this chapter is on the constituent aspects of the politics of the south Wales miners: the effect of the Area's structure, geographical considerations, the role played by the various hues of activist within the South Wales NUM, together with the interaction of all these factors.

Union Structure

The politics of the South Wales NUM can be understood as the product of the interaction of the leadership and the rank and file. Organisationally, the Area inherited the structures established by the reorganisation of the SWMF in 1933, and which were designed to put as much power as was practicable in the hands of the rank-and-file miner.

The colliery lodges were the basic framework through which the miners were organised and it was through these that collective rank-and-file opinion could be expressed, articulated via elected lodge committees. Lodge leaders could wield considerable influence. Although they never attained high-ranking office, men such as Cyril Parry (Morlais), Bryn Williams (Cwm), Mike Griffin (Penrhiwceiber) and Tal Walters (Bargoed) were prominent figures within the Area and important advocates at conferences of their particular political viewpoints (which ranged respectively, in these examples, from communism to right-wing Labour loyalism). In addition to this, lodges had a significance within their community derived from the fact that the miners looked to their union as the first point of contact for resolving their work-related grievances. Consequently, the local prestige of someone like Bill King, who was Merthyr Vale lodge secretary from 1962 until 1985, was considerable – and his position was by no means unique. In the view of one former lodge official, 'I think the leadership was very good in south Wales, because each pit had a recognised leader . . . And one person that stick out tremendous is Mike Griffin. From Penrhiwceiber . . . [They were] good orators, they could *speak* – and . . . they was *genuine trade unionists* and they fought hard in what they believed in.'[1]

The district committees operated in the space between the Area leadership and the lodges. According to Area rules, these committees met every two months to receive reports from the respective miners' agent for the district. Although it was not their ostensible purpose, they provided a ready-made forum for any combined activity between their constituent lodges; throughout this period, the Aberdare joint lodges committee was generally the most active in this respect. These district meetings were valued by the lodge committees, as a way of both obtaining a more detailed picture of the wider situation within the coalfield and also providing a forum for developing the next generation of lodge leaders. Nevertheless, they were never as significant a sphere of influence in the workings of the South Wales NUM as the executive council, the Area conferences, or the individual lodges themselves.

The supreme policy-making forum of the Area was its annual conference, held in the late spring. Additionally, special conferences could be convened as appropriate, to take the key decisions facing the Area. The voting in these conferences reflected the mandates given to the lodge representatives by their respective committees, to whom they were accountable. In this way, voting patterns reflected the balance of opinion in the coalfield reasonably accurately. Nevertheless, there were a few occasions when this proved conspicuously not to be the case, for example, the grassroots rejection of conference decisions to strike in February 1980 and March 1984.

The central governing body within the Area was its executive council (EC). It was composed of rank-and-file union members elected, on a triennial basis, to represent one of the Area's five districts: Swansea, Maesteg, Aberdare-Rhondda-Merthyr, Rhymney Valley, and Monmouthshire (later Gwent). Each district was represented by two executive members (or three if its membership exceeded 18,000 – a situation which rapidly ceased to be the case anywhere as the 1960s progressed). Given that each was of approximately equal size, this did not cause disparities; it also meant that no single district could dominate decision-making within the Area.

---

[1]   Interview with Colin Thomas, 14 January 2004.

The most senior figures were the Area officials: the president, general secretary, vice-president, and the miners' agents.[2] With the exception of the vice-presidency – which was decided triennially by a mandated card vote at the Area Annual Conference – these posts were all full-time and were elected via a membership ballot, after which their incumbents stayed until they retired or stepped down. Although these were the leaders of the south Wales miners, the Area's structure ensured that they were not able to dominate policy-making without securing the support of the EC, a body directly in touch with and responsible to the membership.

POLITICAL GEOGRAPHY

The large number of lodges within the south Wales coalfield, together with the relatively small number of men who were Area officials or EC members, makes it problematic to generalise about the influence of individual lodges within the South Wales NUM as a whole.[3] Typically, most lodges only provided one individual who became an Area leader during the period studied here, not least because of the geographically-based representation of the executive structure. There were exceptions to this pattern though, and these help to characterise some of the more significant lodges in the coalfield, whether by size, political influence, or both. Measured thus, some of the key south Wales lodges in the later twentieth century (together with their leaders) were: Maerdy (Emlyn Williams, Haydn Matthews, Arfon Evans), Coedely (Don Hayward, Ron Saint, Mike Banwell), Lady Windsor (Will Fortt, Emlyn Jenkins), Oakdale (Dan Canniff, Gary Woolf), Brynlliw (Evan John, Terry Thomas, Eric Davies), Fernhill (Cliff True, George Rees), Celynen North (Tom Jones, George Pritchard), and Cynheidre (Tommy Walker, Islwyn Rosser).

Although it is difficult to assess the influence of individual lodges within the Area, the picture is clearer when considered at district level. Ever since the formation of the SWMF in 1898, there was a

---

[2]   Initially there was one miners' agent for each of the five districts, although this number declined during the later twentieth century as the coalfield shrank.

[3]   There were ninety-five NUM colliery lodges and 76,500 mineworkers employed in south Wales at the beginning of 1964. Although much reduced, by the beginning of 1984 there were still thirty colliery lodges and around 23,000 mineworkers in the coalfield.

broad tendency for the leadership of the south Wales miners to be drawn from the central valleys of what became Mid Glamorgan. In the early twentieth century, almost all of the famous leaders had come from the Rhondda valleys: Noah Ablett, A. J. Cook, Arthur Horner and Will Paynter, 'intellectual giants in the trade union movement, of the highest political integrity and outstanding orators'.[4] There were exceptions, the most notable during the period studied here being Dai Francis, from Onllwyn in the Dulais valley. Similarly, Aneurin Bevan was the most high-profile exemplar of south Walian radicalism in British politics in the 1940s and 1950s and he hailed from Tredegar. Nevertheless, the general pattern was pronounced: for example, Will Whitehead, Emlyn Williams, George Rees, Des Dutfield and Don Hayward came from lodges in or around the Rhondda. The significance of this tendency becomes even more marked if we consider that all of these rose to prominence on the basis of their reputations as militants, whether as Communists or Labour left-wingers.

These people were products of their backgrounds. Consequently, it should not cause surprise that the majority of radicals in the broader Area leadership were generally from this part of the coalfield. Ron Saint and Emlyn Jenkins (EC members and lodge secretaries at Coedely and Lady Windsor respectively), for example, personified the personnel 'overlap' between the official leadership and the unofficial movement, providing a conduit from these lodges through the Area structure. At Area annual conferences throughout this period, it was lodges such as Fernhill, Coedely and Maerdy that submitted most of the militant and political motions for debate. Reflecting on this 'traditional radicalism', Emlyn Jenkins later commented that 'I'm probably very biased because I'm from the centre [of the coalfield], but I think all good things stemmed from the centre!'[5]

A corollary of the militancy of the geographical centre of the coalfield was the relative inclination towards moderation in its eastern and western regions. Although this too is a generalisation, it is confirmed by the weight of evidence, in terms of conference reports, Area minutes and oral history testimony. The explanation is the fact that the fringes of the coalfield had never been as completely

[4]   V. L. Allen, *The Militancy of British Miners* (Shipley: 1981), p. 121.
[5]   Interview with Emlyn Jenkins, 5 March 2004.

dependent on the coal industry as the central valleys had been, with steel manufacturing in Gwent and agriculture and tinplate in Carmarthenshire providing employment. The social consequence of this was that the lodges were never quite as hegemonic in their respective communities, so that the radicalism that characterised the Area as a whole was not as ingrained as it was elsewhere. Politically, most of the Gwent district could be characterised as right-wing Labour: this was the case with, for instance, Celynen South, Oakdale, Beynon, Abertillery New Mine, and Cwmtillery. Correspondingly, Gwent collieries were less strike-prone than other south Wales pits: for example, they were essentially unaffected by the unofficial strike-wave that swept large parts of the coalfield in 1969 and were reluctant participants in the Area-wide strike a year later, which they saw as 'unofficial' since it was not sanctioned by the national NUM. It was a similar picture with the west Wales lodges. There, industrial and political quiescence had been accentuated in the early 1960s by the influx of around a thousand men from Durham, to help to fulfil the manpower requirements of new 'super pit' projects. The main embodiment of these trends was Cynheidre. Ever since mining began there in the early 1960s, Cynheidre had had a reputation for 'moderation', a tendency reinforced by its 'receiver pit' role. Commenting on this, an executive member for the Swansea district (which included Cynheidre) later observed: 'I mean, the trouble with Cynheidre: it was a lodge of *mixtures*. *Historically* it wasn't a sound lodge . . . It was a mixture of people coming from different collieries that had closed down.' The other Swansea district EC member concurred, stating that 'they were a *bloody odd lot* down there . . . [T]here was a sort of an anti-[Area] . . . leadership element in Cynheidre colliery.'[6]

While this overall pattern persisted throughout the period studied here, there were variations. Although operating within the same general political, social and economic environment as other collieries in south Wales, the outlook of each lodge was also the product of its own mix of factors: geological considerations that could promote either pacific or militant industrial relations; the influence of charismatic or respected individuals; and the role of lodge tradition and history in creating a particular political milieu. Consequently, although the Rhondda traditionally had the highest proportion of

---

[6]   Interviews with Dane Hartwell (10 December 2003) and Eric Davies (30 January 2004).

left-wing lodges, it was not true that the district was everywhere a hotbed of radicalism: for example, Tymawr remained stead-fastly moderately Labour in outlook until its closure in 1983. Correspondingly, there were several militant lodges in west Wales, Brynlliw and Morlais for instance, while the upper Dulais valley was something of a Communist stronghold before the closure of its collieries in the early 1960s. Similarly, Six Bells had one of the few Communist lodge secretaries in Gwent; likewise, Celynen North was generally reckoned to be more left-wing than most other pits in that district, something which prompted a brief falling-out between it and neighbouring Celynen South over the latter's lack of enthusiasm for the 1970 strike.

The traditions described above were not immutable and were capable of change, given the appropriate circumstances. The main external catalyst for a shift in a lodge's outlook was the threat of closure. Throughout the period, there were occasions when lodges known for their pacific industrial relations and political moderation were spurred into an unofficial strike by news of the closure of their colliery. One of the most prominent examples of this was Coegnant in February 1981; it succeeded in galvanising the rest of the coalfield into action. The primary internal means of change was the election of lodge leaders who held markedly different views to those of their predecessors. One of the most notable examples of this was the replacement of the politically moderate Phil Stafford as lodge secretary of St John's in 1978 by the militant Ian Isaac. By the same token, it was only after Mike Richards replaced Tommy Lewis as lodge chairman at Lewis Merthyr in the early 1970s that the lodge began to be seen as a radical one.

POLITICAL PARTIES

The main point about the party politics of the South Wales NUM is that, as with the trade union movement in general, it retained institutional links with the Labour Party and most of its members who were politically active were Labour members. Consequently, the whole strategy of the Area was framed around Labour as the primary vehicle for effecting political change. In this respect, throughout the period the attitude of the South Wales NUM (indeed, that of the labour movement in Britain in the twentieth century) towards Labour was defined by a mixture of support for the Party and pressuring it to adopt the policies advocated by the Area. The relative prominence of these two strategic imperatives naturally fluctuated according to the broader context of the moment. When Labour was in opposition, the Area's principal political goal was the return of a Labour administration; once this was achieved, the focus was then to press the government to carry out the policies it wished to see implemented. In this way, the sharpest tensions between the Labour Party and the unions in this period emerged during the Wilson and Callaghan administrations in the 1960s and 1970s. Nevertheless, this reliance on the Party as the political wing of the labour movement prevented these disagreements from reaching crisis point. Whatever its disappointments and grievances with these governments, the South Wales NUM acknowledged that ultimately it had no other alternative but to continue to support Labour.

A key ingredient in the traditional radicalism of south Wales was the important historical role of the Communist Party. In sheer numbers, it was dwarfed by the Labour Party, which was a hegemonic political presence in most valleys communities. Nevertheless, there was a definite symbiosis between south Wales miners and the CPGB. The valleys were one of the few areas where the CPGB put down serious long-term roots; similarly, a clear majority of Communists in south Wales were also NUM members – whilst local miners' leaders such as Allan Baker, Ron Saint and Cliff True were long-term stalwarts of the Party's Welsh Committee throughout this period.[7] By the 1960s, the CP was not as potent a social force as it had been in preceding decades, largely as a consequence of the Cold War.[8] Despite this, south Wales remained a Communist stronghold. In the view of one lodge activist and former CP member, 'the South Wales NUM was more or less run by members of the Communist Party . . . [T]he Labour Party members would say that's wrong, but if you look at the officials you had at the time . . . they were all members of the Communist Party'.[9] Whilst this is an exaggeration, a sizeable proportion of the Area's leaders were in the CP, for example, Will Whitehead and Dai Francis (Area president and general secretary,

---

[7]   *WM*, 27, 28 March 1962; CP Welsh Committee papers, 1943–79 [PHM, CP/CENT/ORG/11/1–2].

[8]   See Kevin Morgan, 'Harry Pollitt, Rhondda East and the Cold War collapse of the British Communist electorate', *Llafur*, 10/4 (2011), 16–31.

[9]   Interview with Mike Richards, 27 January 2004.

respectively). Indeed, as the *Western Mail* commented, '[i]t is as traditional that a Communist be president of the South Wales NUM as it is that the chairman of the Cheltenham Women's Institute be a Conservative'.[10] However, the significance of the CP presence in the Area leadership was not so much in terms of numerical dominance as in their influence over the left-leaning Labour members on the EC, who shared many of the political viewpoints of the Communists. Throughout the later 1960s, for instance, Labour men such as Will Woods and Ben Davies, from the Rhondda and Dulais valleys respectively, were keen supporters of the campaign for increased wages and a tougher line against colliery closures.

The Communists' prominence within the Area hierarchy was not an infiltration of the organisation by 'shadowy subversives' but reflected the position in a significant minority of lodges. Admittedly, CP members from the coalfield met periodically to discuss Area policy, although this was scarcely a secret and Labour caucuses operated in an identical fashion. In south Wales, the Communists were most prominent in lodges in the Rhondda area. In Coedely, for instance, the lodge chairman, secretary, compensation secretary and assistant compensation secretary were CP members; in Maerdy and Fernhill, the majority of committee members were Communists.[11] Beyond this, it was possible for there to be a Communist presence even in the more moderate lodges: for example, Jim Morgan was a CP member and lodge secretary at Coegnant until 1966, during which time the lodge bought the *Daily Worker* and distributed it in the canteen. Similarly, Brian Elliott was Penallta lodge secretary from the mid-1970s until after the 1984–5 strike and also a CP member.[12] In many cases, the relative popularity of Communists reflected their perceived staunch defence of miners' rights. Their profile in the Area gives credibility to the claim of one former activist that the CP were 'a small force but we were a very influential force . . . [W]e were presenting policies and resolutions which would enhance the miners' case . . . The miners themselves recognised that Communist miners' leaders were men of integrity.'[13]

[10] *WM*, 29 March 1962.
[11] Interviews with Mike Banwell (9 March 2004), Kevin Williams (25 March 2004) and George Rees (8 December 2003).
[12] Interview with Verdun Price, 15 March 2004; Brian Elliott SWML interview (AUD/123).
[13] Interview with Arfon Evans, 1 April 2004.

Trotskyism does not feature prominently in the historiography of coal-mining trade unionism.[14] This is mainly because much academic work has focused on the early twentieth century, when there was only a miniscule number of Trotskyists in Britain. The first occasion when a Trotskyist party contested a parliamentary election occurred in the south Wales coalfield in May 1945, when the Revolutionary Communist Party (RCP) contested the Neath by-election. The long-term gains from this foray proved to be minimal. The RCP itself collapsed in 1950 and Trotskyism failed to put down sufficient roots to be able to present a serious challenge to the CP in the coalfield.[15] This situation changed during the 1970s and 1980s, however, with some miners either becoming members of the various emerging leftist organisations or acquiring an ideological affinity with them. Militant and the Socialist Workers Party (SWP) were to assume a greater prominence during the 1984–5 strike when, according to Blaenant lodge chairman Phil Bowen, '[w]e were playing out the Russian Revolution again, just about, in Wales!'[16] In the post-strike recriminations within the NUM, it was the organisation of these groups as the Broad Left Organising Committee which was the driving force behind the re-election of Arthur Scargill as president in 1988.

At no stage did the various Trotskyist groups active within the South Wales NUM ever form more than a very small percentage of the total union membership. Nevertheless, off-the-record comments made to the author indicated that members of the SWP and Militant were able to get elected to senior lodge positions from the 1970s onwards. The most prominent indicator of the growing influence of the extra-Communist Left was the election onto the Area executive council in August 1983 of Ian Isaac, the St John's lodge secretary and the leading Militant activist in the coalfield.[17] As with Labour and the Communists, these groups maintained a network of contacts throughout the coalfield, meeting occasionally to discuss issues pertinent to the NUM and the coal industry and to decide on policy.[18]

---

[14] From a south Wales perspective, one noteworthy recent exception to this general pattern is Ian Isaac, *When We Were Miners* (n.p., 2010), being the memoirs of the leading Militant activist in the South Wales NUM during the 1980s.
[15] John McHugh and B. J. Ripley, 'The Neath By-Election, 1945: Trotskyists in West Wales', *Llafur*, 3/2 (1981), 68–78.
[16] Interview with Phil Bowen, 26 March 2004.
[17] EC, 9 August 1983.
[18] Interview with Ian Isaac, 2 and 8 April 2004.

Not only is it very difficult to identify people who were card-carrying members of the Trotskyist Left; it is also the case that levels of workforce combativeness can be a misleading guide to formal party affiliation. For instance, staunch Labour supporter Tyrone O'Sullivan (Tower lodge secretary from 1969 onwards) consistently called for a militant policy of opposition to colliery closures, arguing for the continuation of the south Wales-led strike of February 1981, supporting the spread of industrial action via picketing in March 1984 and vehemently opposing the decision to return to work a year later.

PIT CLOSURES UNDER A LABOUR GOVERNMENT, 1964–70

The election of the Wilson government in 1964 was seen by the miners as an opportunity to safeguard the future of the industry. The Labour Party's policy of an annual coal output of 200 million tons was supported enthusiastically by the NUM, which thereafter used it as a benchmark figure for its various plans for expansion of the industry. Consequently, the rapid acceleration of the colliery closure programme that ensued was not what the miners expected. As the 1960s unfolded, growing grassroots uncertainty about the future of coal developed into outright pessimism, with thousands of miners leaving an industry which was contracting significantly as a result of government policy. The Area leadership reflected this view-point: even though both Will Whitehead and Dai Francis were Communists, neither believed that industrial action could solve the problem, or that the membership would support it.

Prospects of a showdown between the south Wales miners and the Wilson government of 1964–70 were reduced further following the election of staunch Labour loyalist Glyn Williams as Area president in 1966. NUM loyalty towards Labour remained an important factor in how the Area faced the situation in the 1960s. In interviews conducted years afterwards, key figures in the Area recounted candidly that conscious choices were made not to create a furore over pit closures that might jeopardise the stability of the first Labour government for thirteen years.[19] The same held true for the wages

---

[19]   Glyn Williams, SWML interview (AUD/113); interview with Dan Canniff, 17 February 2004.

question. Although Area annual conferences in the mid- and late 1960s typically carried denunciations of the government's incomes policy, there were always delegates who argued forcefully that the labour movement had a duty to help the Labour administration to implement this policy.

The policies of the Wilson government of the 1960s did provoke a reaction from the south Wales miners, even though this was slow to gather momentum. Rank-and-file resentment of declining relative wage levels and the colliery closure programme built up gradually as the decade wore on, leading to the emergence of groups of lodges which advocated action. By the late 1960s, the militants had secured representation on the Area executive council, thereby reinforcing the position of other activists (such as Emlyn Williams) who already held official posts. The crises over surfacemen's hours and wages, in 1969 and 1970 respectively, precipitated a struggle between this unofficial movement and the Area leadership, in which the former sought to make the latter adopt more combative policies. As one leading activist pointed out at the time, '[t]he miners' leaders in South Wales have said in the past that they were prepared to lead but they did not have an army. Well, we've provided the army. And we want them to win the battle.'[20]

In many respects, the Communist Party provided the lead: many of the leading south Wales militants were CP members, while the lodges in the vanguard of the unofficial movement were generally 'Communist lodges'. The situation was not simply one of Communist versus Labour, however; for instance, Emlyn Williams was a Labour member and also one of the most important radical figures within the Area at that time. Moreover, the surge of unrest that had developed across the coalfield by 1969 would not have had the significance that it did had it not struck a chord with the Area membership, who were also generally Labour supporters.

The whole thrust of the CP's post-war industrial policy was aimed at mastering the machinery of existing trade unions and using these to effect change, rather than creating new ones. Instead of pitching rank-and-file organisations against the unions' official leaderships, as the Minority Movement had done in the 1920s, the CP now aimed to build from the shop floor to secure its candidates for office. As part of this, during the winter of 1964–5 the CP leadership resolved on a

[20]   *The Miner*, No.10, November 1969.

new general tactic: the Broad Left.[21] The Broad Left amounted to a recognition of the need for left-wing allies and the necessity for more open CP organisation within the unions. The model of this type of Communist-Labour alliance by the late 1960s was the NUM, where the Broad Left was led by former Communists (Lawrence Daly), Communists (Mick McGahey, Dai Francis) and Labour leftists (Emlyn Williams). In 1967, following earlier campaigning work by South Wales and Derbyshire, this established the Miners' Forum as a way of co-ordinating the activity of the left-wing Areas within the NUM.[22] In south Wales, where there had been a CP presence amongst the leadership since the days of Arthur Horner, this was by no means a completely new phenomenon. This success fed into the second strand of the CP's industrial strategy: campaigning for wage militancy in the unions. In this way, the CP became a key factor in defining the whole tenor of industrial relations in Britain during the turbulent early 1970s.

In many respects, the rise of the Broad Left within the NUM has strong parallels with the emergence of the unofficial movement in the south Wales coalfield in the later 1960s. Both were, generally speaking, initiatives led by the Communist Party. Both shared the same basic objectives: wage militancy, opposition to the Wilson government's incomes policy, and strike action to defend the industry from the colliery closure programme. Furthermore, certain individuals – such as Emlyn Williams – were active in both. Despite these similarities, the activities of the unofficial movement in this period were not simply reducible to being those of the 'South Wales branch' of the Broad Left, for several reasons. First, lodge activists in the Cynon and Rhondda valleys had been working to galvanise coalfield-wide industrial action against pit closures since 1964, before the inception of the Broad Left. Secondly, rooted as it was within a number of militant lodges, it retained a significant independence of action: for example, by attempting to organise unofficial strikes against the closure of Rhigos in 1965 and Cambrian in 1966 and defying the Area officials by appealing to conferences to support this action. Consequently, even though it had supporters at every level in the Area's structure, it could be characterised more as a rank-and-file 'ginger group' than anything else. Thirdly, despite Dai Francis's status

---

[21] John Callaghan, 'Industrial Militancy, 1945–79: The Failure of the British Road to Socialism?', *TCBH*, 15/4 (2004), 395.

[22] Allen, *Militancy of British Miners*, pp. 8–9, 126–35.

as the most senior member of the Broad Left in south Wales, he had no input into or control over the unofficial movement in the coalfield. Indeed, by late 1969 he was being openly critical of what he saw as its divisive activities; Coedely and Cwm lodges, which were in the vanguard of the movement, responded by passing votes of no confidence in him.[23]

By the late 1960s, therefore, the CP's dual strategy of encouraging grassroots militancy and securing influential positions in the union hierarchy had led to the situation in south Wales whereby Communist lodge activists (such as Ron Saint and Cliff True) were clashing directly with the most senior Communist in the Area over a fundamental tactical issue. In this respect, the attitudes of individual CP members in the Area to particular strategic courses of action were conditioned primarily by the logic of the pressures placed upon them by their own positions in the union structure. Francis's role as a member of the NUM national executive committee (NEC) meant that he was obliged to argue the NEC case at Area level; in contrast, the rank-and-file status of Saint and others put them in the vanguard of unofficial militancy.

THE WAGES STRUGGLE: THE 1970S

The strikes of 1969 and 1970 in south Wales and several other coalfields provided the scenario against which the rank-and-file alliance of Communists and Labour militants was able to bring about a significant shift in Area policy. During the 'surfacemen's strike', unofficial action begun by Yorkshire miners spread until it affected Scotland, south Wales, Derbyshire, Kent, Nottingham and the Midlands.[24] This strike demonstrated that a significant proportion of the south Wales miners was prepared to take industrial action provided they were given an unambiguous lead – even if this did not come through official channels. Building on this, the following year the lodge activists and their supporters on the EC were able to overturn the opposition of the Area leadership to a unilateral strike in south Wales following the national ballot defeat on the wages question, and they even managed to get the strike declared official

[23]   EC, 14 November, 2 December 1969; ASC, 18 November 1969.
[24]   Allen, *Militancy of British Miners*, p. 156.

there, contrary to the wishes of the Area officials. Rank-and-file activism had succeeded in galvanising the South Wales NUM into a more militant pursuit of its objectives.

By the early 1970s, this process had been completed to a significant degree. Consequently, south Wales delegates to national conferences were in the forefront of pushing for the wage increases necessary to restore the relative earnings position of mineworkers, backed by the prospect of industrial action if necessary. Following the government's refusal to back down, this led to the strikes of 1972 and 1974. As Brynlliw lodge secretary Terry Thomas pointed out at the time, 'this strike was brought about by the militant action of the rank and file in 1970[, which] . . . showed the leadership that if they did not take the lead, the rank and file would have taken the lead out of their hands'.[25] The successful outcome of these strikes for the miners consolidated the rise of militancy in south Wales. By the mid-1970s, the majority of the official Area leadership were radicals or men who had risen to prominence during the upsurge of the preceding few years.

Beginning around 1969, the combination of the growing prominence of certain 'leading lights' in the unofficial movement, together with the responsive and participatory nature of the Area's structure, meant that there began to be a blurring of the distinction between 'official' and 'unofficial' within the South Wales NUM. Generally speaking, the leading militants of the 1960s had become the Area's leaders by the 1970s: the career of George Rees illustrates this point perfectly. This was not a simple process of 'selling out' – in most respects quite the opposite, since it represented the fulfilment of one of the central tenets of the CP's industrial strategy. Furthermore, the overall effect was for the official Area policy to become more robustly militant with regard to such issues as wages and colliery closures. This development in south Wales occurred simultaneously with developments in other coalfields across Britain and could be seen in the national strikes of 1972 and 1974, together with the conversion of Yorkshire into a left-wing Area.[26] However, the inevitable consequence of the effective 'take-over' of the Area leadership by these people was the disappearance of the unofficial

---

[25]   *Militant*, 11 February 1972.
[26]   For more on the left-wing 'take-over' of the Yorkshire Area, see Allen, *Militancy of British Miners*, pp. 137–40.

movement as a distinct entity, together with an increasing tendency among Communist miners to look to the official union machinery as the best vehicle for their activities.

Events of the 1970s brought about a greater affinity between the positions of Labour and the NUM regarding the coal industry. During the 1972 and 1974 strikes, official Party policy was one of supporting the miners' struggle for improved wages and conditions.[27] Thereafter, given the context of the international energy situation, the Labour governments' policies towards the coal industry in the 1970s were predicated on the assumption that coal would play an expanded role in seeking energy self-sufficiency for Britain. This was more in keeping with the aspirations of the south Wales miners and more closely represented the approach that they wished to see implemented.

The pull of Labour loyalism was not as conspicuous in the 1970s as it had been in the 1960s, partly because the government was not implementing a colliery closure programme and partly because there was a stronger mood of militancy among the south Wales miners than had existed a decade previously. Consequently, there was a greater readiness to speak out against aspects of Labour policy with which the Area disagreed. The Area president Emlyn Williams, a long-standing Labour Party member, exemplified this trend clearly. In his speech to the 1976 Area conference, for instance, his call for £100-a-week wages for faceworkers was an unequivocal rejection of the Callaghan administration's Social Contract.

PIT CLOSURES UNDER A CONSERVATIVE GOVERNMENT: 1979–83

By the early 1980s, South Wales faced similar problems to those of the 1960s: an unfavourable economic situation and a government committed to a pit closure programme. The stakes were now higher, since there were far fewer collieries by this time, there was little prospect of alternative employment and the Thatcher administration set to its task with unprecedented zeal. The South Wales NUM reacted to the threat much more proactively than it had done in the 1960s, in no small measure because many of its leading figures were men who had been in the forefront of the unofficial movement's

---

[27] See, for example, *Labour Weekly*, 14 January 1972 and 1 February 1974.

struggle against closures fifteen or so years before. In the early 1980s, the Area leadership worked to prepare the membership for a showdown with the government over colliery closures.

Notwithstanding its disagreements with the government in the later 1970s, South Wales continued to support essentially the same coal policy as Labour Party Wales, that is, of demanding an expansion of the industry. Throughout these years, both maintained their call for an annual national coal output of 200 million tonnes, stating their total opposition to colliery closures, 'except where reserves are exhausted, and then only where alternative jobs are available with equivalent pay and conditions'.[28]

Given its strong tradition of left-wing Labourism, it is not surprising that the rise of Bennism in the early 1980s struck a chord with the South Wales NUM. In May 1981, its annual conference endorsed Tony Benn's campaign to become Labour Party deputy leader, contrary to the stance taken by the Wales Labour Party as a whole, which backed Denis Healey. In the 1981 and 1982 annual conferences, Emlyn Williams argued for a radicalisation of the Parliamentary Labour Party (PLP) and the enforcement of its accountability to the broader Party. Similarly, in June 1983 the Area was one of the first unions to call publicly for Neil Kinnock to be the next Labour leader, since he was at the time seen as a left-winger.[29] As part of this outlook, South Wales was an enthusiastic supporter of the Alternative Economic Strategy, the policy of radical state intervention in the economy espoused by the Bennite left. Between 1979 and 1983, every annual conference of the south Wales miners called for far-reaching solutions to the crisis, ranging from demands for a break with monetarism to the implementation of a socialist economic strategy and a commitment by the next Labour government to a major programme of re-nationalisation. During the depths of the recession, the Area leadership even began to discuss measures that went beyond the PLP. At the 1981 annual conference, for instance, Emlyn Williams advocated 'extra-Parliamentary action', calling on the TUC to take its own steps to rectify the situation, such as taking over factories to prevent their closure, controlling use of redundancy payments and organising its own import controls.

---

[28]   Labour Party Wales EC Annual Conference Report 1979, p. 14; see also Labour Party Wales Annual Conference Report 1979 and 1984.
[29]   EC, 19 May 1981, 26 June 1983; ASC, 18 July 1983.

Despite the increasing climate of uncertainty in the coal industry and the enhanced likelihood of a clash with the government over pit closures following Thatcher's general election victory in 1979, Communist input in the affairs of the South Wales NUM began to dwindle from the later 1970s onwards. The main underlying cause of this was the organisational decline of the CP (with national membership falling from 28,378 in 1974 to 20,599 by 1979) and the consequent faction fighting which developed between the *Morning Star* supporters and the Eurocommunists, whose most prominent publication was the journal *Marxism Today*.[30] In terms of representation in the Area hierarchy too, from around the mid-1970s (say, following George Rees's election as Area general secretary in 1976) the CP began to lose ground. Whereas the 1960s had seen a reasonably significant minority of Communists among the leadership which had increased in the late 1960s and early 1970s, this process effectively came to a halt. With the sole exception of Arfon Evans, all of the new executive members elected in the late 1970s and early 1980s were Labour members.

This did not mean that the Communist Party became irrelevant to political developments within the Area. Indeed, in the early 1980s CP members in south Wales remained ready to criticise the monetarist policies of the Callaghan and Thatcher governments and to organise support for lobbies and 'Day of Action' protests against them. The 1979 Welsh Party Congress called for 'a Broad Alliance of all anti monopoly and democratic forces potentially uniting the overwhelming majority of the Welsh people against monopoly capitalism'. Communist miners also continued to support strike action against the colliery closure programme. Building on this approach, in September 1980 Allan Baker (a member of the CP's Welsh Committee and the Oakdale lodge secretary) stated: 'We need to get the South Wales miners to take a decisive stand against the whole concept of the rundown of the coal mining industry . . . and in the process involve the South Wales communities and through them hopefully have a political influence on the rest of Britain.'[31]

---

[30] Callaghan, 'Industrial Militancy', p. 404.
[31] *MS*, 1976–83 passim; AAC and ASC, 1976–83 passim; CP Welsh Committee papers, 1976–82, PHM, CP/CENT/ORG/11/2–3; *Marxism Today*, September 1980, p. 23.

THE 1984–5 STRIKE

The miners' strike of 1984–5 was one of the important industrial disputes of twentieth-century British history, a titanic year-long struggle pitting the NUM and its supporters against the combined weight of the state.[32] The strike began amidst some confusion, ended in defeat for the miners, and remained controversial throughout. Nevertheless, the decision to take action in March 1984 was not a strategic aberration. It must instead be viewed in the context of miners' recent experiences and their perception of the most effective means of combating the government's colliery closure programme.

Given the gravity of events and their eventual outcome, Labour's attitude towards the 1984–5 strike inevitably became a contentious issue. Different strata of the Party responded very differently to the challenge presented by the situation. At a local level, rank-and-file Labour members were a fundamental part of the bedrock on which the miners' support groups were built. The Labour Party Wales annual conference in Tenby in May 1984 opposed all colliery closures except on the grounds of exhaustion and called on the Labour NEC to formulate a national fuel policy based on coal, oil and gas. The MPs of the south Wales coalfield were also generally supportive, whether through attending picket lines in a symbolic show of solidarity or, in the case of Bridgend MP Ray Powell, offering his constituency office as a base for the local support group. Furthermore, in June of that year the Welsh Parliamentary Labour group met the Area leadership to give its endorsement to the strike – though its members were more circumspect about making strident public declarations to that effect.[33]

In contrast, the national Labour leadership showed a distinct reticence about supporting the miners' struggle, preferring instead to call on the government to negotiate a speedy resolution to the dispute.[34] This approach provoked strong criticism from some miners, with some of the bitterest attacks on Labour leader Neil Kinnock

[32] For a national perspective, see Andrew Taylor, *The NUM and British Politics, Vol. 2: 1969–1995* (Aldershot: 2005), pp. 173–234.

[33] *Labour Weekly* 25 May 1984; Hywel Francis and Gareth Rees, '"No Surrender in the Valleys": the 1984–5 Miners' Strike in south Wales', *Llafur*, 5/2 (1989), 58; EC, 8 June 1984.

[34] David Howell, '"Where's Ramsay McKinnock?"': Labour leadership and the miners', in Huw Beynon (ed.), *Digging Deeper: Issues in the Miners' Strike* (London: 1985), pp. 181–98.

coming from south Wales members. In the view of the Six Bells chairman, he 'deliberately kept his distance from us. He was no help whatsoever.'[35] As MP for Islwyn, he addressed an Oakdale lodge meeting in December 1984 and attended a Celynen South picket line in January 1985, though these seemed to many to be an exercise in tokenism. By late 1984 the EC had written to him to condemn his handling of the dispute. At the end of the strike, Emlyn Williams attacked Kinnock, stating: 'His utterances were tragic. He sat on the fence but in the end he fell the wrong way . . . He should have come out for us from day one.'[36] This stance, of continuing identification with Labour together with a persistent dissatisfaction with many of the policies adopted by the Party leadership, epitomised a recurrent and unresolved tension within the politics of the south Wales miners during the later twentieth century.

In March 1984, once the miners had begun their strike in opposition to the colliery closure programme, Communists in the NUM swung into line behind the resolution of the CP's executive committee, 'to work for maximum solidarity with the miners and other trade unionists in action in defence of jobs, wages and conditions, developing broad left activity wherever possible'.[37] In the first two months of the dispute – contrary to its later stance – the CP as a whole endorsed the picket-based strategy used by the NUM to spread the strike.

Throughout the dispute, the extra-CP Left was resolute in its support for the decision to take action, together with a strategy of spreading the strike via picketing and appeals to union solidarity. In the south Wales coalfield, the Militant perspective was stated unambiguously by Ian Isaac, who declared: 'The only unity now possible is that of direct action. At this stage in the dispute, there can be no question of a national ballot; the momentum must be developed . . . The majority have already made it clear where they stand.' He reaffirmed that '[t]he task of the striking majority now is to convince the non-striking minority of the need to fight . . . We are confident that all non-striking pits will listen to the class appeals of their brother miners and join the fight to stop pits being closed.'[38]

[35]   Interview with Jim Watkins, 18 February 2004.
[36]   *The Guardian*, 5 March 1985; EC, 6 November 1984.
[37]   CP EC minutes, 10–11 March 1984 [PHM, CP/CENT/EC/20/05]; *MS*, 12 March 1984.
[38]   *Militant*, 23 March, 6 April 1984.

Nevertheless, by May 1984 doubts were being expressed by the Eurocommunist-dominated CP leadership about the efficacy of the NUM strategy. That month, the Party's industrial organiser, Pete Carter, claimed that the strike 'could make a positive contribution towards building a broad alliance around the miners', but warned that '[i]t would be dangerous and sectarian to think that a major dispute of this character can be won by industrial muscle alone, even in the face of hostile public opinion'.[39] According to this perspective, the strike was primarily a struggle against government policy, as opposed to being a straightforward traditional strike. The main contention was that the miners would not win purely on a 'syndicalist' basis of industrial action but required a policy of concerted inter-action with the wider political process via a series of 'broad democratic alliances'. In south Wales, the main advocates of this 'popular front' policy were miners such as Allan Baker and prominent supporters such as Hywel Francis, with the latter spelling out his views on the subject in an essay in *Marxism Today* in February 1985 entitled 'Mining the Popular Front'. In a later interview, Baker reiterated his view that the focus of the NUM's strategy on mass picketing was too narrow and that a broader campaign of mass demonstrations and public meetings was needed to isolate the government from mainstream British political opinion. According to him, the strike 'was conducted as one of the last great nineteenth century industrial struggles by "the powers that be" . . . in the Union. Whereas we were in the . . . late twentieth century, fighting a radically different type of [government] policy.'[40] However, the ultimate conclusions of this line of argument did not represent majority opinion amongst the south Wales miners during the strike. Furthermore, there was a massive difference between this assessment of the strike and the stance taken by CP rank-and-file activists, such as Glyn Roberts of Tower lodge, who were (and remained) committed supporters of the methods used by the miners in 1984–5.[41]

The most distinctive contribution of the CP in Wales during the strike was to attempt to form its own 'broad democratic alliance', the Wales Congress in Support of Mining Communities.[42] Encompassing a

---

[39]   CP EC minutes, 12–13 May 1984 [PHM, CP/CENT/EC/21/01]; *MS*, 14 May 1984; see also Pete Carter, 'Striking the Right Note', *Marxism Today* (March 1985), 28–31.

[40]   Interview with Allan Baker, 13 February 2004; ASC, 29 August, 29 October 1984.

[41]   Interview with Glyn Roberts, 19 March 2004.

[42]   CP Welsh Committee papers, 1984–8 [PHM, CP/CENT/ORG/11/4]; Hywel Francis, 'Mining the Popular Front', *Marxism Today* (February 1985), 12–15.

diverse array of organisations extending beyond the labour movement, the WCSMC was launched in the autumn of 1984 with the aim of consolidating the 'alternative welfare state' built by the miners' support groups. The Congress also established several local branches and organised public meetings and demonstrations, helping to maintain the solidity of the strike during its final months. Its organisers envisaged it developing into a multi-issue pressure group and a Welsh 'popular front' against Thatcherism; however, the effective lifespan of WCSMC did not extend much beyond the struggle that had given it birth.

In south Wales, a key role in bringing the strike to an end in 1985 was played by a number of CP members. 'For all the images of fiery Welsh Communists which history provides, it was [they] . . . who quietly suggested . . . a return to work without a settlement . . . [After] Christmas [1984] . . . the majority of the Communist miners at Maerdy pit were talking about "broad alliances" and the possibility of an orderly return to work with "dignity and honour".'[43] Among the main advocates were Kim Howells (the Area's research officer), Arfon Evans (EC member and Maerdy chairman) and Peter Evans (Merthyr Vale chairman), who discussed a return in such isolated locations as a pub in Llanwonno, in the hills above Ynysybwl.[44] This plan was unpopular with other left-leaning activists who were aware of it: one lodge secretary later commented, 'there was a cabal then of Communist Party members and fellow travellers, with Kim Howells and the rest of them, they got together, to *end* the strike. And I thought that was a terrible thing.'[45] Nevertheless, it was this type of development which ensured that talk of an organised return-to-work had begun to circulate within the Area by early 1985.

Towards the end of the strike, the disparity of viewpoints held by south Wales CP members regarding how or whether to maintain the struggle makes it misleading to look for a coherent 'party line' in the Area. Instead, various Communists were advocating a series of positions that reflected the various options open to the Area: some were in favour of ending the strike by a return to work without a

[43] Raphael Samuel, Barbara Bloomfield and Guy Boanas (eds), *The Enemy Within: Pit Villages and the Miners' Strike of 1984–5* (London: 1986), pp. 163–4.

[44] Arfon Evans interview. For a damning criticism of this plan, see Tyrone O'Sullivan, with John Eve and Ann Edworthy, *Tower of Strength: The Story of Tyrone O'Sullivan and Tower Colliery* (Edinburgh: 2001), pp. 128–9.

[45] Interview with Bill King, 4 March 2004; *SW*, 12 January 1985.

settlement; others preferred an immediate negotiated agreement; others still wanted to continue the fight until the government was forced to concede terms. Ultimately, at the end of the February, faced with a deteriorating situation across the various coalfields, the South Wales leadership decided to recommend adoption of the policy of calling for a return to work without a settlement. In this way, fittingly, the Area's Communists, who had played a central role in defining the traditional radicalism of the south Wales miners in the twentieth century, were an important factor in the decision that signalled the end of an era in the history of their coalfield.

The decision in March 1985 was inevitably an extremely controversial one. Despite the adverse circumstances facing the NUM, six lodges – Penrhiwceiber, Tower, Cwm, Nantgarw, Merthyr Vale and Trelewis Drift – opposed the recommendation made by the South Wales leadership at the Area conference on 1 March to call for an organised return to work without an agreement.[46] Once the dispute was over, the key concern for activists became the reinstatement of all miners who had been sacked during the strike. In this respect, together with the inevitable wave of recriminations that followed from the defeat, leftist opinion was reflected throughout the mainstream of the South Wales NUM. Some blamed the Nottinghamshire Area for not joining the strike; others agreed with Emlyn Williams and castigated the Labour leadership and the TUC for not doing more to assist the miners.[47] Here, as throughout this period, radical politics was at its most influential in the coalfield when it accorded with the broader outlook of the south Wales miners as a whole.

CONCLUSION

Several conclusions can be drawn about the politics of the south Wales miners in this period. First, the overall effect of the democratic structure of the South Wales NUM facilitated the promotion of policies and individuals who reflected the requirements and

[46] The glaring exception to this list was St John's. However, at the conference, Ian Isaac (who had been sacked by the NCB a few weeks before) and Charlie White supported the recommendation, pointing to the prospect of the NCB encouraging the formation of rival unions and using these to break the NUM if the dispute continued for much longer.

[47] *The Guardian*, 5 March 1985.

aspirations of the broader membership. In this way, the historically-created and culturally-reinforced traditional radicalism that emanated primarily from the central valleys lodges came to play the defining role in the Area. On a party-political level, the basic outlook of the south Wales miners was 'left Labourism'. Not only did an affinity with Labour define the general ideological milieu within which they operated; it was also the case that some Labour leftists such as Emlyn Williams were amongst the Area's most influential radicals. Within this broad 'labourist' framework, other left-wing activists contributed to the overall tone and direction of politics in the coalfield, working towards a more militant policy on the questions of wages, conditions and colliery closures. While the Communists were the most prominent militants in the Area for the first part of the period studied here, from the later 1970s their position in the political vanguard had been encroached upon by lodge activists who were more inclined to be Trotskyist in their outlook. Overall, it was the combination and interaction of these factors that brought about the distinctive political radicalism of the south Wales miners.

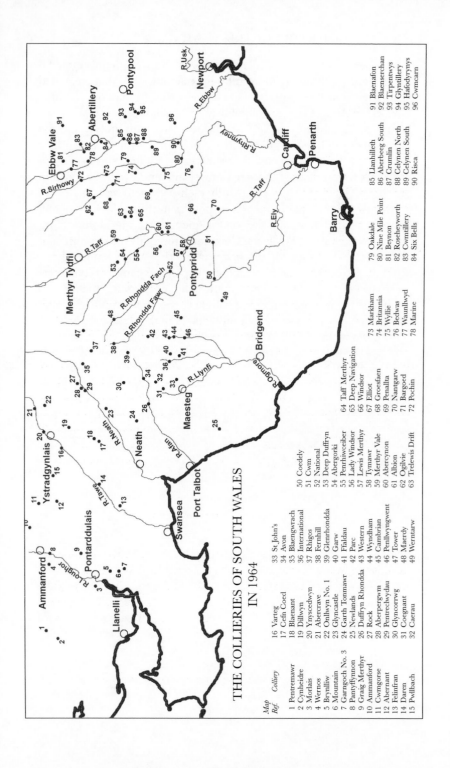

THE COLLIERIES OF SOUTH WALES
IN 1964

Map
Ref. Colliery

1 Pentremawr
2 Cynheidre
3 Morlais
4 Wernos
5 Brynlliw
6 Mountain
7 Garngoch No. 3
8 Pantyffynnon
9 Graig Merthyr
10 Ammanford
11 Cwmgorse
12 Abernant
13 Felinfran
14 Daren
15 Pwllbach

16 Varteg
17 Cefn Coed
18 Blaenant
19 Dillwyn
20 Ynyscedwyn
21 Abercrave
22 Onllwyn No. 1
23 Glyncastle
24 Garth Tonmawr
25 Newlands
26 Duffryn Rhondda
27 Rock
28 Aberpergwm
29 Pentrechwydau
30 Glyncorrwg
31 Coegnant
32 Caerau

33 St John's
34 Avon
35 Blaengwrach
36 International
37 Rhigos
38 Fernhill
39 Glenrhondda
40 Garw
41 Ffaldau
42 Parc
43 Western
44 Wyndham
45 Cambrian
46 Penllwyngwent
47 Tower
48 Maerdy
49 Werntarw

50 Coedely
51 Cwm
52 National
53 Deep Duffryn
54 Abergorki
55 Penrhiwceiber
56 Lady Windsor
57 Lewis Merthyr
58 Tynawr
59 Merthyr Vale
60 Abercynon
61 Albion
62 Ogilvie
63 Trelewis Drift

64 Taff Merthyr
65 Deep Navigation
66 Windsor
67 Elliot
68 Groesfaen
69 Penallta
70 Nantgarw
71 Bargoed
72 Pochin

73 Markham
74 Britannia
75 Wyllie
76 Bedwas
77 Waunllwyd
78 Marine

79 Oakdale
80 Nine Mile Point
81 Beynon
82 Roseheyworth
83 Cwmtillery
84 Six Bells

85 Llanhilleth
86 Aberbeeg South
87 Crumlin
88 Celynen North
89 Celynen South
90 Risca

91 Blaenafon
92 Blaenserchan
93 Tirpentwys
94 Glyntillery
95 Hafodyrynys
96 Cwmcarn

II

CLOSURES: 1964–1970

The 1960s brought pessimism and frustration for the south Wales miners. Looking back, Dai Francis (Area general secretary, 1963–76) felt that it was 'one of the most difficult periods that I can remember in my fifty years with the Union'.[1] Far from the security which they believed they had obtained following the nationalisation of coal in 1947, this decade was characterised for the south Wales coalfield by a dramatic colliery closure programme, which attained its maximum speed under the Wilson governments of 1964–70. Britain was not the only industrialised country whose coal industry shrank in the 1960s, though this trend was amplified by the energy policy decisions of successive governments. Coal's nationalised status, together with a Labour administration in office, led the NUM to attempt to mitigate the effects of this decline rather than to challenge the entire policy – a perspective with which South Wales generally agreed. As the decade unfolded, however, it became clear that an increasing proportion of the membership was dissatisfied with this approach. Although it was not immediately apparent at the time, the rapid contraction of the industry set in motion interconnected tensions and processes, both economic and political, which had a profound impact not just on the south Wales miners but on industrial relations in Britain.

CONTINUITY AND CHANGES

For south Wales and the other coalfields, there were broad continuities in this period of dramatic change. The National Coal Board remained the biggest employer in south Wales: in 1962, its 88,000 mineworkers comprised 14 per cent of the total labour force.[2] Moreover, the South Wales NUM retained its important social role in the lives of its members. In the cultural sphere, this was most

---

[1]   SWML interview with Dai Francis (AUD/131).
[2]   Gerald Manners (ed.), *South Wales in the Sixties: Studies in Industrial Geography* (Oxford: 1964), p. 75.

noticeable in the Miners' Gala (established in 1953) and the Miners' Eisteddfod (which began in 1948).

Before the advent of affordable foreign holidays, the Miners' Gala was a major highlight of the social calendar in south Wales. Held in Cardiff every June, the Gala reached the zenith of its popularity in the mid-1960s. Colliery lodges organised free buses to take people to the Galas and convoys of them descended on Cardiff from all round the coalfield: over 30,000 miners and their families attended the 1965 Gala, for instance. The scale of events in a Gala was striking. Brass bands played an important role: in the 1960s, it was not uncommon to have up to fifteen bands there. In addition to music, there were art and craft exhibitions, rugby, soccer and tug-of-war tournaments.[3] The defining feature of the Gala was its successful blend of politics and entertainment. In addition to criticising government policy and calling for better pay and conditions for mineworkers, a recurrent feature of resolutions passed at Galas in the 1960s was a call for the end to the Vietnam war. Internationalism remained a key theme, with Czechoslovak and Hungarian miners invited in 1964 and 1969. The Galas' main guests were often those at the forefront of the struggle against fascism or imperialism abroad, such as Greek seamen's leader Tony Ambatielos in 1964 and a North Vietnamese delegation in 1970.

The Miners' Eisteddfod was a unique cultural event and a source of pride for many miners. The only festival of its kind to be sponsored by a British trade union, it stimulated numerous cultural activities, particularly choral music. The Eisteddfod was very popular, mainly with people from the predominantly Welsh-speaking western coalfield, many of whom would spend the whole day there. Held annually in Porthcawl, its prestige was sufficient to prompt a visit from TUC general secretary Vic Feather in 1969. The Eisteddfod – and also the Gala – was seen to be important in helping to maintain cultural standards and solidarity with miners in other coalfields and countries, in the face of the adversities facing their industry.

May Day provided another focus for community self-expression, underlining the ready synthesis in mining areas of social activities, politics and sporting events. One of the biggest May Day celebrations was held at Aberdare. In 1966, this included a march, speeches by Will Paynter (NUM national general secretary, 1959–68, and former

---

[3]   *WM*, 21 June 1965.

president of the south Wales miners), Glyn Williams (Area president, 1966–73) and Dai Francis, in addition to a programme of sports competitions. Reporting in the Area's newspaper, Penrhiwceiber lodge secretary Mike Griffin observed that '[a]ll the threads of the speeches and events seemed to weave a fabric that socialism holds the prospect of Peace, Prosperity and Happiness . . . [L]odge members went away tired, but yet invigorated for the tasks ahead.'[4]

Despite such expressions of community solidarity, in the 1960s south Wales miners found that their daily lives were being increasingly disrupted by changes in their industry. Colliery closures were the most notable feature here. Although these generally led to transferrals to other pits rather than redundancies, they nevertheless caused problems. Moving to a new pit often meant increased travel-to-work time, with men having to get up at 4 a.m.; a nominal working day of eight hours could often mean one of over eleven hours.[5] This development inevitably affected miners' family and social lives. Transferral typically presented the challenge of a bigger and more anonymous working environment, where it was more likely that new and unfamiliar coal-cutting machinery would be in use. More significantly, men were often downgraded when they moved to a different colliery. In this context, it was possible for the seniority rule – a vital trade union defence against victimisation – to lead to a form of 'tribalism', as men sought to retain their status in the face of newcomers. In September 1964, for instance, there were problems at Marine colliery, owing to the NCB's decision to transfer men there from nearby Waunllwyd.[6] Men were reluctant to transfer to other collieries and often chose to leave the industry instead. As one miner who experienced transferral observed, 'every colliery's different. When you go to a strange colliery . . . you're not going to have the same sort of status as you had when you're in your pit before – *and a lot of men finished . . .* They just couldn't handle it.'[7]

Transferrals had almost as significant an effect on the 'receiver pits' as on the men who were displaced. In some cases, it was feared that an influx of manpower without a corresponding increase in

[4]   Mike Griffin, 'Aberdare Miners Celebrate May Day', in *The Miner*, No.3, May/June 1966.
[5]   Interview with Emlyn Jenkins, 5 March 2004; Stephen W. Town, *After the Mines: Changing employment opportunities in a South Wales Valley* (Cardiff: 1978), pp. 91–2.
[6]   EC, 15 September 1964.
[7]   Interview with Gordon Bartley, 22 January 2004.

output per man-shift (OMS) could make the receiver pit itself
a target for closure. Transferrals also led to an increasingly
'cosmopolitan' workforce. As opposed to miners at a pit living in the
adjoining village, by the 1960s men were being drawn from further
afield. Some pits experienced this phenomenon to a greater degree
than others. Cwm colliery, in Beddau, employed men from as far
away as the Garw valley and even had men transfer from Scotland
and Derbyshire – in contrast to 'village pits' such as Maerdy in the
upper Rhondda Fach. Penallta, in the Rhymney valley, was similarly
'cosmopolitan'. Although most of its workforce lived locally, some
men commuted from Merthyr Tydfil, Senghenydd and Cardiff.
Penallta successfully integrated men from several nearby collieries in
this period.[8] Mass transferrals of this type could have a variety of
effects on the union leadership of a receiver pit. At Cwm, the lodge
officials – mainly men from local villages – remained in post, despite
the influx of newcomers.[9] Conversely, transfers could sometimes
help to galvanise a lodge leadership. Following the closure in 1967 of
International colliery, Blaengarw, transferral of its workforce to
nearby Ffaldau led to the effective replacement of its lodge officials
by the more politicised ex-International men.[10]

Despite the upheavals of the 1960s, the strong links between
collieries and communities remained. 'It was a totally different
experience then to today . . . [N]early everybody was involved in the
colliery . . . whether they were miners, whether they were women
working in the canteen. The small shops in the area all revolved
around it . . . [E]verybody seemed to be involved.'[11] Given this
closeness, it was not surprising that pit closures had serious
repercussions in the valleys. Will Paynter wrote: 'I wonder sometimes
if those who decide policies to precipitate the contraction of the coal
industry have any idea as to what a pit closure means to the
community built around it . . . Closure . . . represents a disaster as
poignant and harrowing as a death in the family.'[12] One of the areas
worst affected was the practically mono-industrial upper Afan valley,
which lost its last pit – Glyncorrwg – in 1970. Its miners either

[8]   SWML interview with Brian Elliott (AUD/123).
[9]   Interview with Eddie Thomas, 17 March 2004.
[10] SWML interview with Berwyn Howells (AUD/21).
[11] Interview with Kay Bowen, 14 April 2004.
[12] Will Paynter, 'We Can't Let A Vital Industry Be Strangled', in *The Miner*, No. 12,
November/December 1967.

moved away or travelled elsewhere to work. Local trade declined, the infrastructure withered and socio-economic problems increased. The valley's railway was pulled up, its tunnels filled in. Cultural life inevitably suffered. When its pit was open, Blaengwynfi had a drama group, a brass band, a library and a debating society. All went when the colliery closed in 1969, since they were supported through miners' financial contributions.

'THE PRAETORIAN GUARD OF THE TRADE UNION MOVEMENT'

One of the distinctive historical features of the culture of the south Wales miners was self-education, mainly via their institute libraries. Although these were generally established in the late nineteenth and early twentieth centuries, they were by no means moribund in this period. Indeed, as late as the 1970s, Blaengwrach lodge was establishing its own library devoted solely to political literature. Miners' ideas were sharpened through debate. As one lodge secretary later reflected: 'the south Wales miners were well-informed [and] . . . very much aware of their own *history* . . . I think that's what *made* them as they were . . . [S]ome of the debates that went on underground, . . . they'd be a *damn sight better* than . . . "Any Questions"! . . . [T]hey'd be *far more* interesting . . . *All* those things would be discussed underground.'[13]

The Area's bi-monthly newspaper, *The Miner*, was a product of this outlook. It reported on developments in the industry and the union and also frequently carried articles on pertinent political or historical topics: for example, the centenary of the TUC in 1868, the history of the Chartists, the fiftieth anniversary of the Russian Revolution, and the need for solidarity with South African workers in their struggle against apartheid. It was not uncharacteristic of *The Miner* to feature an article in which one of the Area's leaders argued that 'socialism can come into being only by the . . . toppling of the capitalist system from below . . . it involves the direct and formidable class action of the workers in the mass'.[14]

While it is true that by no means all south Wales miners were radicals, they generally had a much more politically developed

[13] Interview with Dane Hartwell, 10 December 2003.
[14] Trevor James, 'The Labour Government – What Next?', in *The Miner*, No. 15, May/June 1968.

outlook than many of their contemporaries. 'I think that you could say that we were one of the most radical [Areas] of the . . . [NUM] – or of *any union*, in fact . . . I mean, south Wales miners were *known* for that. We were involved in everything. On the anti-apartheid scene, in South Africa. *Every* issue, there was an involvement.'[15] Miners generally attributed this trait to historical and geological factors: a legacy of the struggle to get a living wage from obdurate coalowners, in conditions unsuited to high productivity. Undoubtedly, many south Wales miners were proud of their reputation as 'the praetorian guard of the trade union movement'.[16]

A consequence of the politicised outlook of the south Wales miners was their keen engagement with contemporary political issues. Enoch Powell's racism was condemned unanimously at their 1968 annual conference, while the 1967 conference spelt out its opposition to joining the European Common Market. In May 1966, the EC supported the strike by the NUS, donating £1,000 to their strike fund and inviting them to address the 1966 Gala.[17] The executive criticised the 'anti-working class' nature of the 1968 budget, while the annual conference that year condemned government education and health policies, particularly the introduction of prescription charges. Dai Francis was a persistent critic of the Wilson government's economic policy, calling instead for 'socialism, the only system under which the problems we face today can be solved'.[18] He was by no means alone in advocating such measures. In 1966, the Area conference demanded the re-nationalisation of the steel industry; the previous year, it had called for the nationalisation of private monopolies as a step towards a planned economy.

1964: THE COALFIELD AT A CROSSROADS

At the start of 1964, the south Wales coalfield was at a crossroads. Although the industry had been in gradual decline since the late 1950s, there were signs that this trend might be about to be reversed. This ambiguous picture was reflected in the statistics. On one hand,

---

[15] Interview with George Rees, 8 December 2003.
[16] Interview with Ray Lawrence, 11 March 2004.
[17] EC, 17 May, 14, 28 June 1966.
[18] Dai Francis, 'Curing The Country's Ills?', in *The Miner*, No. 18, November/December 1968.

the outlook seemed gloomy. In 1963–4, the NCB South Western Division (south Wales and a few Somerset pits) lost 4,564 men and made operational losses of £1,798,879, or 1s. 6d. per ton. Absenteeism was 2.5 per cent above the national average, with unofficial stoppages about twice the equivalent British figure. Mechanisation levels were 72 per cent across Britain but only 50 per cent in the Area; national OMS was 34.6 cwt, compared with 23.9 cwt in south Wales.[19]

From another perspective, however, there were grounds for cautious optimism. Annual saleable output in the coalfield had recovered from a low of 17.4 million tons in 1961 to 18.9 million tons by 1964. An increasing percentage of output was coming from new or updated facilities and many major post-nationalisation projects – including Brynlliw, Hafodyrynys, Cwm and Abertillery – were soon due to reach full production. By some calculations, even allowing for further closures of older workings, the coalfield was capable of reaching an annual output of 25 million tons by 1965.[20] OMS levels, although low by British standards, were increasing consistently, whilst mechanisation was being successfully introduced in coalfaces where it had formerly been thought impractical. In the west, anthracite production was at its highest level for twenty-five years.[21] Following initial geological problems, the two new anthracite 'super pits' – Cynheidre and Abernant – were gearing up production and were expected to boost output significantly. The coal-fired Uskmouth 'B' power station opened in 1963, to meet the booming demand for electricity. Furthermore, the opening of Llanwern steelworks in 1962 seemed to assure the region's coking-coal pits of a secure long-term market.

The south Wales miners did not share this appraisal of the situation. In May 1964, Will Whitehead and Bert Wynn (the Derbyshire Area secretary) published a pamphlet called *A Plan for the Miners*: this criticised NCB policy and the NUM's non-confrontational attitude towards it, calling for immediate improvements in wages and conditions in order to halt the numbers of men leaving the industry. At roughly the same time, the first concerted attempt to make a stand against pit closures occurred, over the proposed closure of Nine Mile Point colliery, Cwmfelinfach. Although initially against the closure, after a fruitless meeting with the NCB the EC decided that it could

[19] EC, 22 September 1964; ASC, 5 November 1964.
[20] Manners, *South Wales in the Sixties*, p. 91.
[21] *WM: Commercial and Industrial Review*, 22 January 1964.

not pursue the matter further. A few weeks later, this was overturned at the annual conference, which demanded that Nine Mile Point stay open. The Board was unyielding, however. Consequently, in June 1964, a further conference decided not to oppose the closure, provided that it caused no redundancies – a reaffirmation of official NUM policy. Ray Beacham (Nine Mile Point lodge secretary) warned of the dangers of not resisting closures and observed that at 'some time in the not too distant future this policy would have to be drastically revised'.[22]

THE WILSON GOVERNMENT AND THE PIT CLOSURE PROGRAMME

The election of a Labour government under Harold Wilson in October 1964 was welcomed by miners. There was an expectation that there would be a reversal in the fortunes of the coal industry; as one miner later recalled, 'we thought Harold Wilson would be the answer to our problems'.[23] It should not be a surprise that Wilson was seen in this light: he had been one of the architects of coal nationalisation and had stressed the importance of promoting miners' welfare at the 1960 Party conference. In December 1964, the Area leadership met the new Secretary of State for Wales, James Griffiths, to discuss its concerns about the industry's problems. The south Wales miners' proposed solutions were outlined at their 1965 annual conference: a government-guaranteed output target of 200 million tons, a halt to pit closures except through exhaustion, and substantial improvements in wages and conditions to attract more manpower. In February 1966, the NUM issued a plan for government assistance for the coal industry, with proposals ranging from retention of the current fuel oil tax to a call for greater use of solid fuel by local authorities and government departments.[24]

Labour's pro-coal policy had been spelt out clearly in Opposition, with a pledge for an annual output of 200 million tons forming part of its 1964 manifesto. Despite this, by February 1965 Fred Lee (the Minister for Power) was refusing to be bound by this promise. When it was unveiled later that year, the National Plan envisaged a coal

[22]   EC, 24 March, 28 April 1964; ASC, 22 June 1964.
[23]   Emlyn Jenkins interview.
[24]   WM, 19 December 1964; *The Miner*, No. 2, March/April 1966; ASC, 11 March 1966.

output of no more than 170–180 million tons by 1970. Dai Francis attacked this as 'a betrayal' and said that 'the plan brings the coalfield face to face with one of the greatest crises in its history'.[25]

The precipitous decline in the fortunes of coal was part of a wider process in which governments in the 1960s sought to maximise use of nuclear power, gas and oil. Will Paynter attributed this outlook to the government's wish to expand nuclear power for military purposes, coupled with the tremendous political pressure wielded by the oil corporations.[26] Oil was also cheaper in the short term (despite its adverse effect on the balance of payments), an important factor in an increasingly 'free market' situation in the energy sector. Another point to consider is the influence of civil servants on energy policy. Between 1961 and 1971, there were ten different ministers of power: the only continuity came from the civil servants, who ensured that fuel policy remained the same. When they met miners' leaders to discuss policy, ministers would be completely reliant on the brief prepared for them by their civil servants – often seemingly reading from it directly. Paynter's view was that '[i]t was so obvious that they weren't masters in the department that they were supposed to be in charge of'. Lord Robens (NCB chairman, 1961–71) stated: 'In Opposition, Labour had the right policy for the coal industry; in office, it ran away from it because the civil servants were too persuasive and determined for the Ministers Harold Wilson appointed'.[27]

The Wilson administration saw a sharp acceleration of the process of colliery closures which had begun in the late 1950s. Thirty-three pits closed in south Wales between 1959 and 1964; forty-four closed in the five years that followed. More significantly, while many of the earlier closures were because of geological factors, a notable feature of many collieries shut between 1964 and 1970 was that they had been formerly considered long-life 'showpiece' units. As Ben Morris (Area chief administrative officer, 1964–72) later observed, 'Then in 1964–66, [the closure programme] . . . started really in earnest – Elliot closed . . . then you had Groesfaen. Big units now, I'm talking about . . . And gradually you had this position of a substantial qualitative change taking place in the coalfield.' In

[25] *The Miner*, No.2, March/April 1966; *WM*, 5, 10 February, 17 September 1965; *The Times*, 4 November 1965.
[26] SWML interview with Will Paynter (AUD/105).
[27] Will Paynter SWML interview; Lord Robens, *Ten Year Stint* (London: 1972), p. 170.

November 1965, the NCB announced that twenty-five pits – including twenty-one in south Wales – were now classed as 'short-life' units. Both Paynter and Alfred Kellett (NCB South Western Division director) asserted publicly that the main force behind this closure programme was the Ministry of Power.[28]

The unwillingness of the government to stick to its former policy made miners' leaders realise the extent of the crisis facing their industry. In April 1965 Paynter addressed a meeting in Pontycymer, warning that coal was facing the greatest crisis it had ever known and that only a national fuel policy could safeguard its future.[29] Will Whitehead struck a similarly apocalyptic tone at the 1965 Area annual conference when he stated that 'if the situation continues to deteriorate . . . then there will be no mining industry in South Wales as we know it inside ten years'. In April 1965, the Divisional NCB informed the EC that saleable output had dropped to 18.44 million tons, 900,000 tons less than the equivalent figure the previous year. Annual operating losses for the Division had leapt to £3 million and OMS had actually fallen (a stark contrast with the national trend of rising productivity). A central factor here was the runaway increase in manpower drift from the industry. The first twenty-three weeks of 1965 saw 186 miners per week leaving the coalfield – a rate which, if it had continued, would have finished coal-mining in south Wales by 1971. External developments did little to improve prospects. In September 1965, an Area conference called to discuss the region's poor performance was dealt additional hammer-blows by the news of the discovery of North Sea gas and the prediction that nuclear power would be cheaper than coal and oil by 1970.[30]

One of the most striking features of the Wilson government's pit closure programme was the relative lack of protest which it provoked from the NUM. This was mainly because it was a Labour government and therefore could obtain acquiescence for policies which would otherwise have been opposed. Senior Labour members within the Area leadership in the 1960s later recounted that party loyalty was an important factor when deciding how strongly to resist closures or fight for better wages. As Dan Canniff, an executive member at the time, candidly put it: 'We bent over backwards for the Labour

---

[28] Ben Morris SWML interview; *WM*, 22 November, 13 September 1965.
[29] *WM*, 26 April 1965.
[30] EC, 13, 27 April 1965; ASC, 22 September 1965.

government'.[31] Throughout this period, Glyn Williams argued that, despite the miners' various complaints, it was still a priority to ensure that Labour was re-elected.

Instead of confronting the Wilson administration, official Area policy in the 1960s kept within the overall NUM strategy of trying to persuade the government to halt the colliery closure programme. In February 1966, a south Wales contingent led 1,500 miners on a march through London to meet Fred Lee and lobby parliament. Additional lobbies, of parliament and the Welsh Office, were arranged for February and September 1967 respectively. Local MPs could be supportive of the miners' case: Donald Coleman (Labour MP for Neath), for instance, addressed a mass meeting of Cefn Coed lodge, pledging to assist their campaign. Meetings with Welsh Office ministers were unhelpful, merely serving to emphasise that all the governmental decision-making power lay with the Ministry of Power. In September 1966, Ben Morris told George Thomas (Minister of State for Welsh Affairs) that 'the Union is not prepared to accept . . . that there can be any wisdom in the unholy haste to close pits . . . [T]he Government were not creating a sound and healthy heart to the industry, but were in fact doing the exact opposite.' At the meeting with Cledwyn Hughes (Secretary of State for Wales) in December 1966, Dai Francis stated: 'Frankly we have not had much change out of previous meetings and it is no understatement that we are deeply disturbed with the present position. We do not want a perpetuation of Tory policy . . . It is my personal opinion that this Government is intent on creating a pool of unemployment.' Hughes appealed to the Minister of Power, Richard Marsh, on behalf of the miners – but nothing was forthcoming.[32]

Although the Ministry of Power made the strategic decisions about the coal industry, their plans were implemented by the NCB. Consequently, for many miners, it seemed as if the Board was determined to close the south Wales coalfield. In early 1966, Whitehead expressed the view that 'All Welshmen realise there is a strong anti-Welsh lobby at Hobart House [NCB national headquarters]'. Paynter later said: 'I don't think south Wales featured very high in

[31] Glyn Williams SWML interview (AUD/113); interview with Dan Canniff, 17 February 2004.

[32] The Miner, No. 1, January/February, No. 2, March/April 1966; EC, 10 September, 20 December 1966, 7 February, 30 August 1967.

the consideration of the Labour government as a coalfield to be preserved or expanded', agreeing that the Board had an anti-Welsh attitude.[33]

At pit level, it often seemed to miners that the NCB made a point of closing collieries with strong traditions of militancy. As Emlyn Williams, a key activist in the coalfield in this period, saw it:

> [T]he intent [of the NCB was] . . . to slaughter the Welsh coalfield. Because what is significant during that period was, the militant pits that closed like Seven Sisters [in 1963], Rhigos [in 1965] . . . I believe that these pits were deliberately selected for closure because [of] . . . this militancy that had grown up there . . . [T]he pits that were closed were the pits that were doing the clamouring to fight, people that were saying, 'We should resist closures'.[34]

The decisions made by the management at certain collieries had a central bearing on whether they stayed open. Ben Morris felt that the Board 'undoubtedly' manoeuvred circumstances in pits which they wished to close so as to make them uneconomic, for example, by the withholding of investment or conducting unnecessary exploratory work. Rhigos colliery was closed midway through an extensive construction programme of new surface buildings, an experience shared by several other pits. The closure of Llanbradach colliery in the Rhymney valley in 1961 was an early example of this phenomenon. Llanbradach had received substantial investment and had a good workforce and plentiful reserves. However, the management's attitude to industrial relations meant that the best workers decided to leave the industry and work at Llanwern instead. 'The Board always had an unhappy knack of putting square pegs in round holes . . . They could spoil a good pit almost overnight by moving a good manager, promoting him and putting an inferior or incompetent manager into the pit.'[35]

THE 'SUPER PIT' POLICY

The NCB's development strategy for the south Wales coalfield in the 1960s was based on concentrating resources in fewer and bigger

---

[33] *The Miner*, No. 1, January/February 1966; Will Paynter SWML interview.
[34] SWML interview with Emlyn Williams (AUD/161).
[35] Quotation taken from Ben Morris SWML interview; Dane Hartwell interview.

collieries. Between 1960 and 1965, the NCB planned for annual investment to increase to £16 million, the second highest figure for any British coalfield. This reflected the geological importance of south Wales, which had by far Britain's biggest reserve of special quality coal types. The Board employed around 88,800 in south Wales in 1960 but planned that 90–94,000 men would be needed by 1965. Consequently, it was one of only four coalfields where the minimum output estimated for 1965 was higher than the 1958 output. In addition to the opening of new anthracite projects – the 'super pits' at Cynheidre and Abernant, and Pentreclwydau, Blaengwrach and Cwmgwili – there was extensive redevelopment at more than eighteen collieries. This coalfield-wide reconstruction programme was expected to be largely completed by 1965.[36]

It is undeniable that this capital expenditure improved the performance of the coalfield in the period 1964–70. There was further investment, in Deep Navigation, Merthyr Vale and Coegnant. Treforgan, a new drift mine near Crynant which opened in 1966, was one of the most modern pits in Britain at the time. By 1964, the best OMS figures were achieved by selected pits in the Swansea district, with Brynlliw attaining an output of 48 cwt. A few years later, Cwmgwili had set an OMS record of 107 cwt and become the most profitable mine in Britain, while several pits were operating at an OMS of around 40 cwt.[37]

In several important respects the 'super pit' strategy did not deliver the success that was anticipated. The 'flagship' collieries of Cynheidre and Abernant were very ambitious undertakings: Cynheidre had been expected to produce one million tons a year of saleable coal (almost double the output of its six immediate neighbours), while Abernant, at a cost of £10 million, was one of biggest, deepest and most expensive collieries in Britain. One of the main problems they experienced was a shortage of manpower, which affected output significantly. In 1964, for instance, Abernant had a workforce of 960, over 400 fewer than the required number. These difficulties were compounded by other factors: Cynheidre was plagued by geological hazards; at Abernant, the management's wish to get production started as soon as possible meant that retreat

---

[36] *WM*, 1 June 1960.

[37] Hywel Francis and David Smith, *The Fed: A History of the South Wales Miners in the Twentieth Century* (London: 1980), p. 461; Manners, *South Wales in the Sixties*, p. 95; *WM*, 4 October 1967; *WM: Commercial and Industrial Review Pt.II*, 17 January 1968.

mining methods were not introduced, thereby compromising the pit's long-term profitability.[38]

The most conspicuous failure of the 'super pit' strategy was at Pentreclwydau, near Glynneath. Opened in the late 1950s at a cost of several million pounds, it was expected to be the long-term replacement for the older pits in the area. This did not turn out to be the case: Pentreclwydau was closed in 1967. A telling indicator of the underlying problems there occurred when its closure was announced. The unofficial movement in the coalfield decided to organise strike action, only to be informed that the lodge had agreed to accept closure.[39] A former collier at the pit reflected: 'I think men were glad to see that place shut . . . There wasn't a happy atmosphere down there at all. What had happened, you had The Rock colliery, Glyncastle, Aberpergwm, Rhigos, coming into Pentreclwydau – and they all had *different customs*. It was a *job* to weld them together.'[40] Events at Pentreclwydau showed that the NCB's failure to heed miners' grievances could have serious implications for its whole strategy for the coalfield.

MANPOWER DRIFT

The biggest problem facing the south Wales coal industry in the 1960s was the increasing numbers of men choosing to leave the pits and work elsewhere. As early as 1962, it was becoming apparent that this manpower drift meant that the coalfield was becoming less likely to hit the Board's 1965 output targets. As Whitehead observed in 1964, 'What started in 1959 as an involuntary contraction when the [NCB] . . . closed seven pits, has ended up with a voluntary contraction because . . . men . . . no longer have any faith in continued employment in the industry . . . It is the policy of the Board . . . which has brought this situation about.'[41] This exodus

---

[38] In the traditional advancing method of mining, a coalface was worked outwards away from the main underground roads, with its supporting roadways being cut concurrently. In contrast, with the retreat mining method, the roadways were driven out first and then the coalface retreated back between them. This resulted in greater efficiency and productivity. *WM*, 27 February 1962, 21 May 1964; SWML interview with Ron Williams (AUD/115).

[39] SWML interview with Haydn Matthews (AUD/134).

[40] Interview with Harry Samuel, 20 January 2004.

[41] *The Times: Survey of Wales*, 31 January 1962; *The Miner*, Vol.12, No. 4, July/August 1964.

became even more serious after 1964. South Wales manpower levels declined at an accelerating rate: 1,800 overall left the industry in 1961, 2,500 in 1962, 4,000 in 1963, 5,000 in 1964 and 8,240 in 1965. Across Britain, between 600 and 800 miners a week were leaving the industry by 1966.[42] Since those who went were more likely to be craftsmen and the younger workers, this manpower drift had a detrimental effect on the composition of the workforce. In 1962, the average age in the industry was 41, with 30 per cent of miners aged over 50; by 1970, only around 12 per cent of mineworkers were under 25, whereas nearly 40 per cent were over 50 years old.[43]

The manpower drift in south Wales in the 1960s was caused by the growing uncertainty about the coal industry's future and the increasing availability of more stable and less arduous employment elsewhere. There was a wide variety of choices open to ex-miners, including Ford in Swansea, BP at Baglan Bay, Borg Warner at Port Talbot, Metal Box at Neath, Cam Gears in Resolven, British Nylon Spinners in Pontypool, Hoover at Merthyr Tydfil and the Llanwern and Port Talbot steelworks. These jobs were generally better-paid than coal mining. As one colliery electrician later pointed out: 'wages . . . hadn't kept pace with outside . . . and consequently men started to drift from the pits . . . They would say, "why stay in the mines? There's no money there".'[44]

In many respects, the NCB's 'super pits' policy exacerbated the manpower drift. Many older workings, some of which were far from being geologically exhausted, were closed specifically to transfer their labour to 'long life' collieries. Garngoch No. 3, for instance, was closed purely to increase manpower at nearby Brynlliw. From a pit-level perspective, this policy could appear lacking in rationality. Pantyffynnon and Wernos were shut (in 1969 and 1966 respectively) for this reason, despite the anthracite shortage and the fact that they had been modernised successfully.[45] The most glaring failure was the case of Glenrhondda, in the upper Rhondda Fawr, one of the

[42]   WM: Commercial and Industrial Review, 19 January 1966; WM, 5 July 1966; The Miner, No. 2, March/April 1966.
[43]   Manners, South Wales in the Sixties, p. 91; Michael P. Jackson, The Price of Coal (London: 1974), p. 128.
[44]   Gordon Bartley interview.
[45]   Terry Thomas interview; EC, 23 July 1968; Town, After the Mines, p. 38; WM, 17 December 1968.

coalfield's biggest profit-makers. In 1966 the NCB decided to close Glenrhondda to redeploy its manpower to Cwm, despite lodge warnings that the workers would not accept this. The closure went ahead, and, as the lodge predicted, the overwhelming majority of the men opted to take redundancy.[46]

During the Wilson government's years, coal's industrial exodus meant that the process of decline developed its own momentum. As Cliff True (an EC member) noted:

> During 1964 . . . [f]or the first time the Board decided to close pits because of a lack of manpower when hitherto the reasons had been either coal exhaustion or the pits were too uneconomical to work . . . One of the main reasons for men leaving the industry at this rate is the feeling of insecurity that has been engendered in the industry by the Coal Board with its policy of closing pits.[47]

The report presented to the 1964 Area conference argued that the policy of shutting pits itself led to further closures due to the manpower shortage created by the feeling of insecurity in the industry: 'Not only are pits closing falsely on economic grounds but, worse still, mining communities are concluding that the industry is finished and here lies the great danger.'[48] Even high-productivity collieries could find themselves losing money – or eventually closing – because of a lack of manpower. This process inevitably raised questions about the viability of the entire coalfield. One of the clearest examples of this was the ill-fated Blaentillery Drift mine, near Blaenafon. This highly mechanised pit was scheduled to open in August 1967, but did not do so due to manpower shortages. Although the NCB preferred to think of the project as being 'delayed' rather than 'abandoned', four years later it conceded that it was unlikely that the pit would ever begin production.[49] Ironically, by insisting that all priority in the south Wales coalfield be given to its designated 'long life' projects at the expense of many other collieries, the NCB created a 'vicious circle' of closures and manpower losses, in which even the success of the 'super pits' was far from guaranteed.

[46] EC, 15 February, 5 April, 12 July 1966; *WM*, 1 October 1980.
[47] *The Miner*, Vol.13, No. 1, January/February 1965.
[48] Area Executive Council Annual Report 1964; *WM*, 6 May 1964.
[49] *WM*, 20 October 1967, 30 January 1974.

The South Wales NUM had a simple solution to the problem. As Dai Coity Davies, the Area's social insurance officer, later explained: '[t]he way to solve a manpower problem is not to bleed one colliery to get another. The way to solve a manpower problem is to improve the conditions and wages of the men in the pit . . . Men *will* go into the pit, but you've got to recompense them properly for it.'[50] In the union's view, this was the only way to break the industry's cycle of perpetual decline. The 1965 Area conference reiterated this point, with Whitehead stating there that: 'What is killing this industry is its failure to attract manpower because the wages it is offering are miserable.'[51]

WAGES

The inadequacy of wage levels remained a grievance for miners throughout the 1960s. Overall, after price movements, taxes and social benefits are taken into account, the net income of an average miner with a wife and two children was 22 per cent above the average for manufacturing workers in 1957, but two per cent below by 1969.[52] The Wilson government's incomes policy was a particular focus of resentment, with strongly-worded condemnations of it becoming a staple feature of Area conferences. This policy was a source of further controversy within the NUM in September 1966, when the NEC accepted the wage freeze, contrary to the National conference's decision to oppose it.[53]

Throughout the period 1964–70 in south Wales, talk of action to improve wage levels simmered in the background, seemingly without prospect of boiling over. The more radical lodges in the coalfield – such as Coedely, Morlais and Fernhill – advocated industrial action to further the miners' case. The 1964 annual conference called for the NUM to take industrial action in support of a claim for a 5s. per week pay rise for daywagemen, with the Area leadership striving to restrain the demand for a strike. The election of the Wilson government did not lead to a lessening of calls for wage improvements but it did generally mean an increased reluctance to consider action to

[50] SWML interview with Dai Coity Davies (AUD/382).

[51] AAC, 1965.

[52] William Ashworth, *The History of the British Coal Industry, Vol. 5: 1946–1982, The Nationalised Industry* (Oxford: 1986), p. 304.

[53] EC, 13 September 1966; ASC, 26 October 1966; *WM*, 3 September 1966.

achieve them. Regardless of these demands, the main trend in the
1960s was for national ballots to accept whatever wages the Board
was prepared to offer. On the occasions that the South Wales
membership opposed these minimal increases, their opinion was
outweighed by the more moderate Areas. As a collier who began
work in this period later commented:

> Well, my overriding memory . . . of it all was in the Sixties was that the
> Union was the ones that wasn't prepared to upset the apple-cart in any way,
> because some of the wage increases we had then were . . . ludicrous to say
> the least . . . [W]e used to always to accept it because we were persistently
> reminded that we were a subsidised industry, and if we rocked the boat, then
> . . . it could affect the livelihood of pits. So I can never remember any
> industrial sort of agitation in them years at all.[54]

In spite of this lack of progress on the wages question, the 1960s
ironically witnessed one of the most significant achievements of the
NUM in its history – the establishment of the National Power
Loading Agreement in 1966. The central feature of the NPLA was
that, for the first time, daywages were to be paid to faceworkers.
As its name implied, it was a spin-off of increased mechanisation:
daywages were seen as more feasible than a national piecework
system. Under this scheme wage parity was introduced gradually,
with a uniform national rate being achieved by December 1971.
Paynter was the key figure in making the NPLA a reality. He later
recalled that certain sections of the NUM (particularly high-output
Areas such as Nottinghamshire and also many faceworkers) were
initially opposed to it, since it would limit their earning potential.[55]
However, by the early 1970s, the NUM had come to realise the
virtues of the NPLA: it enshrined the principle of equal pay for
equal work and led to increased unity. For south Wales, the principal
benefit of the NPLA was that it meant a significant 'levelling up' in
the basic wages of faceworkers, with the weekly rate increasing from
£17 10s. 0d. to £22 10s. 0d.[56] Equal pay at a fixed rate meant miners
were less likely to take short-cuts with safety and would foster a more
'team conscious' spirit. Some collieries even experienced an initial
increase in output following the introduction of the NPLA.

---

[54] Interview with Ron Stoate, 2 December 2003.
[55] Will Paynter SWML interview.
[56] AAC, 1966.

The elimination of piecework had far-reaching effects on coal-mining industrial relations. One side-effect of a guaranteed wage for colliers was that it reduced some of the unofficial powers of patronage wielded by the management and overmen in the pits. Ironically, the NCB's policy of manpower transferral amplified the effect of this, by undermining localised traditions of deference within collieries. It was not surprising that many south Wales miners came to feel that the introduction of the NPLA 'was one of the finest things that ever happened' in the industry.[57]

A standardised wage for faceworkers also affected the entire pattern of disputes within collieries. With piecework, by far the most common forms of unrest were localised unofficial strikes, owing to disagreements about the price-lists by which men were paid. The NPLA shifted the focus of the wages struggle from pit-level to national level, reducing the basis for these frequent, small-scale strikes. Consequently, the total number of disputes in the south Wales coalfield fell from 582 in 1965–6 to 130 in 1972–3 (the first full year of NPLA parity).[58] A more significant development for the future was that it strengthened the bonds between the various NUM Areas, creating the unity that was the basis of the miners' victories in the 1972 and 1974 strikes.

ABSENTEEISM

If the south Wales miners had very clear ideas about what should be done about wages, absenteeism was a far more thorny issue. In 1964, absenteeism in the Area was 2.5 per cent above the national average. The situation worsened during 1965–6 and in 1969 south Wales had the worst absentee record in Britain.[59] Attempts by the Board to use this to explain the coalfield's poor performance were rejected by Area officials. In September 1965, Whitehead stated bluntly: 'My organisation does not condone unwarranted absenteeism, but to say that certain pits are closing because of it is a deliberate lie.'[60] Nevertheless, Area leaders were concerned about the problem, with

---

[57] Interview with Bill King, 4 March 2004.

[58] David Ingli Gidwell, 'Philosophy and Geology in Conflict: The Evolution of a Wages Structure in the South Wales Coalfield, 1926–1974', *Llafur*, 1/4 (1975), 204.

[59] ASC, 5 November 1964; AAC, 1969; EC, 19 April 1966.

[60] *WM*, 13 September 1965.

Glyn Williams publicly attacking 'excessive absenteeism' as 'a source of danger and irritation to the regular workers'.[61] Lodge committees also took steps to remedy the situation. Newlands lodge, for example, held pithead meetings in January 1968 to boost attendance, as part of their campaign to keep their colliery open. Another proposal to tackle absenteeism, suggested by Coedely lodge, was a plan to pay a bonus to men who attended regularly.[62]

While it might be easy, from a twenty-first century perspective, to condemn miners in the 1960s for absenteeism, the context for their actions should be appreciated. Mining was physically arduous and dangerous work, often in adverse conditions. Holidays were few and far between: the 'miners' fortnight' in the summer, and bank holidays (which did not then include New Year's Day). The fact that pits seemed to be closing regardless of how hard men worked was a further disincentive for regular attendance. There was also the increase in the average age of the workforce: it was still conceivable that men sixty years old (or even older) would be expected by the Board to work full shifts cutting coal by hand. George Rees, who was a lodge secretary in this period, later pointed out the potential injustice in this system:

> Another thing which we had was the absentee committee. Having men appear before management, having to explain why they weren't in work. And when you look back, you think, 'Christ'. They were fetching a man of sixty-two in . . . 'cause he'd lost work – and he was still clearing his stent of bloody coal. *What right did we have to do things like that*, y'know? . . . [W]hy should I sit in judgment on a man who've given his lifetime in the industry? Well, I wasn't there in judgment; I was there to try to safeguard his job.[63]

Absenteeism was not so much a cause as a symptom of the underlying problems facing the south Wales coalfield in the 1960s.

MECHANISATION

The south Wales miners experienced a great deal of change in the day-to-day realities of mining in the 1960s, possibly more so than in any other equivalent period. At the turn of the decade, many

[61]   Area, *President's Address by Glyn Williams* (1967), p. 10.
[62]   EC, 16 January 1968, 18 February 1969.
[63]   George Rees interview.

collieries were being worked via methods essentially identical to those employed in the early twentieth century. Pit ponies were still used in some places and it was not compulsory to wear a helmet underground, so some older men continued wearing cloth caps. The majority of coalfaces were 'hand-filled', that is, colliers cut their own designated 'stent' (a length of approximately five yards) of coal by hand, using pneumatic picks – 'punchers' – and shovelling it onto a conveyor belt. There was a world of difference between old-fashioned and modern colliery workings. Ferndale No. 5 colliery, for example, used horses and hand-filling, whereas nearby Maerdy had underground locomotives, mechanised coal-cutting ('power loading') and a pithead baths.[64] In this respect, in 1960 most pits in the coalfield were more like Ferndale No. 5 than Maerdy; by 1970, investment and technical developments meant that Maerdy was more representative of the average south Wales colliery.

An increasing level of mechanisation was one of the most significant features of coal-mining in south Wales in the 1960s. The Area leadership supported this wholeheartedly, since it removed some of the physical hardship of the work and they believed it would help collieries to avoid closure. Only 6 per cent of the coalfield's output was cut mechanically in 1955, a figure which had risen to 36 per cent by 1961. By the end of 1964, power-loading was responsible for half of total output in south Wales. The remainder of the decade saw this process continue, with mechanisation increasing to 80 per cent by 1970.[65] The 'second phase' of mechanisation in south Wales began in 1965, when a ROLF installation began production at Marine colliery. By 1967, with the NCB pressing ahead with the introduction of ROLF machinery and hydraulic roof supports, Glyn Williams was predicting that half of the industry's total output would be coming from remotely-operated coalfaces by 1970–1.[66]

The success of the mechanisation of the south Wales coalfield was readily apparent by the end of the 1960s but it had not been achieved without difficulties. As one miner observed: 'in the beginning . . . they were trying to introduce methods of working

[64] Interview with Ivor England, 27 February 2004.

[65] *The Times: Survey of Wales*, 31 January 1962; ASC, 5 November 1964; *WM: Growth of a Nation Pt. 1*, 23 June 1970.

[66] EC, 19 January 1965; *WM: Commercial and Industrial Review*, 20 January 1965; Area, *President's Address by Glyn Williams* (1967), p. 5.

which were successful in the flat coalfields of Yorkshire and Nottingham . . . And it *didn't work*, because of the undulations in the geology of the south Wales coalfield . . . But eventually . . . they were designing mechanisation and conveyor systems to suit the difficult conditions.'[67] There also remained the perennial obstacle of agreeing on a reasonable level of output for each mechanised coalface. Negotiations revolved around the specific geological conditions, the relative strength of lodge and management at the colliery, and various logistical considerations. Localised disputes about the establishment of power-loading norms were far from uncommon in this period, for example, at Markham colliery in October 1964 and Brynlliw in June 1965. In time, miners came to appreciate the advantages of power-loading. This can be seen, for instance, in the threat in October 1968 by Fernhill lodge of strike action unless the NCB introduced mechanisation at their colliery.[68]

For colliers, mechanisation brought fundamental changes. In addition to making work less arduous, it led to a greater reliance on teamwork at each coalface. Power-loading also introduced a variety of new logistical problems: for example, the need to co-ordinate coalface advances with advances in the supply-road and tail-road, and the extra work required to install all the relevant machinery in the face. It also made the coalface potentially a more dangerous place, due to the presence of powerful machinery in confined spaces. As a Maerdy collier pointed out, 'progress' could seem far more ambiguous when viewed from the coalface: 'The coal board go on about the improved conditions. It's only the conditions [for] . . . the machines . . . that have improved. Conditions for the men are just the same as they always were – hot and dirty. In fact, conditions are probably more dangerous now because all the time you have to compete with the speed and efficiency of a machine.'[69]

DISASTERS

In a decade already characterised by depressing developments for the south Wales coalfield, the 1960s saw valleys communities also having to endure three major disasters. 'All of these disasters

---

[67] Dane Hartwell interview.
[68] EC, 13 October 1964, 29 June 1965, 8 October 1968.
[69] Quoted in *WM*, 30 September 1970.

attracted massive press coverage, often bordering on melodrama. By contrast, rarely was there a mention of the miners who died in ones and twos at the coalface or slowly and painfully of dust diseases, at home, mourned only by their families and friends.'[70] The first two were underground explosions at collieries; the third struck a village whose name has subsequently become synonymous with tragedy.

On 28 June 1960, the worst explosion in south Wales since 1927 occurred at Six Bells colliery, near Abertillery, killing 45 men. Five years later, 31 miners died and 13 were injured in a blast at Cambrian colliery, near Clydach Vale, on 17 May 1965. Those who died had had no chance of survival: 'The thirty-one took the full force of the . . . blast in a coal face only 2ft 8in. high. The men were identified by the numbers on their lamps.' The official report into the explosion was published six months later, which led to the NCB improving methods of checking for firedamp and better procedures for testing electrical equipment underground.[71]

On 21 October 1966, tragedy struck Aberfan when a coal tip on the hill above the village slid, engulfing the local school and several houses. Of the 144 people who died, 111 were children. Shortly afterwards, Merthyr Vale miners arrived to lead the rescue effort. They were later joined by the emergency services and men from collieries throughout the region, in a massive rescue operation which lasted several days. Thousands of miners subsequently attended the funeral service for the victims of the disaster.

The subsequent Tribunal of Inquiry found the NCB formally responsible, in that it lacked any policy about tipping and was indifferent to the need for safety measures. It noted that 'much of the time of the tribunal could have been saved if . . . the NCB had not stubbornly resisted every attempt to lay the blame at their door'.[72] On 24 October 1966, for example, the South Western Division's chief geologist stated that the disaster was caused by a spring appearing within the tip, claiming: 'As far as we can say no water course existed on the site before the tip was started . . . I have never known anything like this before.'[73] This argument was fundamentally flawed: the springs over which waste was tipped – which caused the slippage – are on an Ordnance Survey map of 1919 and a

---

[70] Francis and Smith, *The Fed*, p. 458.
[71] *WM*, 17 May, 26 November 1965.
[72] Quoted in *WM*, 4 August 1967.
[73] *The Times*, 24 October 1966.

Geological Survey map of 1959. In addition to this, there had been a tip slide further down the valley (in which no-one was injured) in December 1939, while the Aberfan tip itself was reported to have moved in 1959 and 1964.[74] In September 1966, Merthyr Vale lodge secretary Bill King noticed that it looked unstable, later recalling that it looked 'like a huge shovel had taken a scoop out of the heart of the tip'.[75] He raised the matter with the management at a consultative committee meeting and the following day they sent a bulldozer to shore up the base of the tip. It was impossible that the NCB could have been unaware of the potential threat which loomed over Aberfan. As the inquiry report noted, 'the disaster is a terrifying tale of bungling ineptitude'.[76]

The NUM had warned the management about the potential for a tip slide at Aberfan on several occasions before it occurred. However, the tribunal said that it would be unfair to blame it for doing no more than it did before the disaster occurred. The report decided that '[t]he union lacked easy access to expert knowledge; they were completely reassured by men whom they were entitled to look to and rely upon; and they were doubtless influenced, though unconsciously, by the thought that their livelihood was involved'. The EC endorsed the report and called on the government to adopt its recommendations fully.[77]

Subsequently, tip safety understandably became a key concern for valleys communities, to which the Board responded by introducing a new system of coal tip inspection and stabilisation. It was a harsh irony that it required a disaster of the scale of Aberfan to prompt the NCB to begin the process of removal and landscaping of the tips which had blighted the valleys for so long.

LOCALISED DISPUTES AND THE 'SWEAR WORD STRIKE'

Throughout the 1960s, sporadic small-scale strike action was a recurrent feature across the south Wales coalfield. Fernhill, a particularly militant colliery, was threatened with closure because

---

[74] Iain McLean and Martin Johnes, *Aberfan: Government and Disasters* (Cardiff: 2000), p. 29; *The Times*, 24 October 1966.
[75] Bill King interview.
[76] Aberfan Inquiry Report, p. 25.
[77] Aberfan Inquiry Report, p. 112; EC, 8 August 1967.

of its workforce's willingness to utilise unofficial action. The most likely cause of a local strike (in the pre-NPLA period) was the piecework pay-rate at the coalface; an example of this occurred at St John's colliery, Maesteg, in May 1964. Another common grievance was excessive managerial 'interference' in the running of a pit, typically through altering established customs: strikes occurred for this reason at Penallta in September 1964 and Parc and Dare in May 1965. The 'stay-down' strike was also employed occasionally, as a way of highlighting a perceived injustice. At Llanhilleth in September 1967, for example, nine men brought the pit to a halt in opposition to a 'productivity deal' which had duped men into accepting sub-NPLA rates.

Possibly the most unusual stoppage in south Wales in the 1960s was the 'swear word strike' of May 1965, which centred on Deep Duffryn colliery, Mountain Ash. The episode began with an altercation between an apprentice and a pit deputy. This led to unofficial action by the pit's 650 mineworkers in calling for the deputy and the apprentice to be moved to different sections of the colliery, which duly occurred.[78] NACODS members objected to this and struck in retaliation. Events escalated into a strike by the 3,500 south Wales pit officials, which halted production at 56 of the 85 mines. This was the single biggest coalfield disturbance in Britain in 1965–6, accounting for over 40 per cent of total lost output that year.[79] The miners themselves were opposed to the NACODS strike: speaking at NUM Area conference, Whitehead called it 'the biggest blunder since the charge of the Light Brigade'.[80] By early June, the Ministry of Labour had forced NACODS to back down, so ending the strike. The incident provides an insight into the undercurrent of tension between workmen and colliery officials during this period.

THE MINERS AND PIT CLOSURES IN THE 1960S

The one issue on which most south Wales miners remained relatively quiescent in the 1960s was the question of pit closures. There was a general acceptance of the NCB's argument that obsolescent

[78] *WM*, 27 April 1965; EC, 4 May 1965.
[79] Ashworth, *British Coal Industry*, p. 300; *WM*, 27 May 1965.
[80] *WM*, 27 May 1965.

workings had to be shut in order to concentrate production on more modern facilities, particularly since there were still enough collieries for men to be able to transfer to work somewhere nearby. While meetings were organised to oppose closures, they failed to make much headway. After initial protests, many lodges offered no significant resistance to the decision to shut their collieries. The main forum in which the need to fight the industry's contraction was expressed was the Area conferences. Even here, the dominant trend was for delegates to reaffirm the official NUM policy of not opposing colliery closures that did not cause redundancies.

This unwillingness to take direct action to defend their industry was due to a variety of factors. A key consideration was that many miners felt that decline was inevitable given the increasing competition from alternative energy sources, and they did not want to do anything which might hasten this process. Associated with this was the reluctance of some older miners, who remembered the dark days of the 1930s, to damage 'their' nationalised industry. The majority of the union's leadership in the 1960s – such as Paynter, Glyn Williams and Dai Francis – were of this generation, men whose experiences of earlier defeats had led them to believe that it was impossible for miners to achieve their aims through strike action.[81] Furthermore, any decision about making a stand against the closure of a particular colliery always ran into opposition from men whose own pits had been closed and who had transferred elsewhere, and who were resentful that a similarly combative stance had not been adopted in their own case. Press speculation about pits' viability also sapped miners' morale; in September 1966, the EC condemned this as 'insidious propaganda'.[82] All these coalfield-level impediments to action were compounded by the general British situation in the 1960s. The South Wales leadership felt that there should be a national campaign against closures; however, the official NEC position was that this was only a problem for a few Areas, which should therefore resolve it themselves. NEC inactivity reflected its domination by right-wing Areas and was a source of frustration to Paynter during his tenure as general secretary.[83]

Once the Board had announced a closure, the NUM was entitled to put the colliery through the NCB's review procedure if it felt there

[81]   SWML interviews with Glyn Williams (AUD/258), Ben Morris and Brian Elliott.
[82]   EC, 27 September 1966.
[83]   Glyn Williams (AUD/113) and Will Paynter SWML interviews.

was a strong argument for it to stay open. The Area leadership only proposed such cases as it thought stood a good chance of success; even so, its efforts were singularly unfruitful. Exasperation with this system led to expressions of no confidence in the NCB and calls from the south Wales miners for an independent review procedure. Not surprisingly, Area leaders came to see the appeals process as a waste of time. Glyn Williams later reflected that 'when you went up to London [to argue against a closure], you were just going through the drill – and you felt it'.[84]

For most of the 1960s, the Area's policy on pit closures mirrored that of the national NUM: closures were not to be opposed by industrial action unless they caused redundancies. According to this approach, lobbying parliament and demonstrations remained the main vehicles for protest. The policy was a recurrent subject of debate in executive meetings but was probably a fair reflection of the majority view in the coalfield, since conferences at this time regularly endorsed the leadership's standpoint. Despite this, the Area officials still felt the need to justify themselves. Speaking at the 1965 annual conference, Dai Francis argued that the leadership 'need not apologise for the role it has played in the policy of containment, which had results because there were no men on the road [made redundant]'. As the decade unfolded, however, this became a less convincing contention. In May 1966, for instance, 108 men were made redundant when Pwllbach was shut.[85] In none of these cases did the Area leadership call for action, thus demonstrating that the fundamental point underpinning this policy was a pessimistic assessment of the chances of success of any prospective strike.

THE UNOFFICIAL MOVEMENT AND THE REVIVAL OF RADICALISM

Not all the south Wales miners held this gloomy perspective about the efficacy of strikes. Beginning with the abortive campaign to save Nine Mile Point in 1964, sporadic attempts were made by some lodges to force a more radical policy. Throughout 1965 and 1966, the frequent discussion of colliery closures at Area conferences was due to this pressure. The necessity of a more combative stance was often stated bluntly. At the 1966 annual conference, for example,

---

[84] Glyn Williams SWML interview (AUD/113).
[85] EC, 10 May 1966.

Ron Saint of Coedely lodge argued: 'If *now* is not the time to strike, when is it?' In September 1965, a delegation of representatives from twenty-eight lodges attended an EC meeting and called for a harder line against pit closures. The 1965 annual conference saw several lodges speak out on this topic: Arthur Owen (Groesfaen) said that he 'could shed tears on the Executive Council's dilly-dallying over pit closures', while Charlie Blewett (Penallta) said that the Area officials 'are sincere and able men but you can have a kind of prudent inactivity which is close to death'. Cyril Parry (Morlais) summarised the radicals' viewpoint, stating that 'change is necessary if we are to stop the slaughter of pits in South Wales . . . Either the Executive Council must *lead* or let the rank and file do the job.'[86]

In the 1960s in south Wales, opposition to the closure programme was not led by the Area officials but by groups of lodge activists, a loose network known as the 'unofficial movement'. One of the leaders of this movement later reflected: 'Well, as far as the official leadership of the South Wales Area was concerned, there was no resistance whatsoever – campaigns, yes . . . but no positive resistance to pit closures'.[87] The movement centred on pits in the middle of the coalfield, traditionally the most radical region, with the Cwm, Maerdy, Fernhill, Tower, Coedely, Taff Merthyr and Lady Windsor lodges being collectively nicknamed 'the magnificent seven'.

The origins of the 1960s unofficial movement lay in the 'Shakespeare group', a network of activists who met in the Shakespeare Hotel in Neath. In 1951–2, this group instigated unofficial action against the threatened closure of Wern Tarw colliery, before a specially convened Area conference in May 1952 outlawed such unofficial bodies.[88] After the dispersal of this group, the movement practically disappeared – apart from in the Cynon valley, where unofficial organisation was retained under the aegis of the Aberdare May Day committee. This committee built up contacts with activists throughout south Wales and the other British coalfields in the course of its May Day organisational work but remained in being because it did not present any challenge to the Area leadership. Emlyn Williams (miners' agent for the Aberdare, Rhondda and Merthyr district) was a central figure in this movement. In December 1964,

[86]   AAC, 1965.
[87]   SWML interview with Emlyn Williams (AUD/33).
[88]   Francis and Smith, *The Fed*, pp. 442–5.

with EC permission, he organised a meeting to discuss the NCB's pit closures policy.

The gradual growth in the influence of the unofficial movement in south Wales in the later 1960s reflected increasing rank-and-file discontent and frustration at the official Area policy. One activist later recalled: 'There was a hell of a lot of turbulence through the Sixties . . . In the south Wales coal industry, there was a lot of pits closing, a lot of pits with uncertain futures.'[89] Much of this unofficial activity revolved around the central valleys, particularly the Cynon and the Rhondda, but other lodges elsewhere also participated, for example, the Garw Valley joint lodges committee, and the Amman grouping in the west of the coalfield.[90]

The relationship between these unofficial organisations and the official Area leadership was inevitably an ambivalent one. It was not necessarily antagonistic; as Emlyn Williams reflected, 'we were not a movement against the leadership . . . we were a ginger group trying to get some movement going in relation to pit closures and other matters in South Wales, particularly on wages.'[91] These groupings were tacitly recognised by the Area hierarchy: it was not uncommon for full-time officials to address meetings organised by joint lodge committees. There was also an overlap of personnel, with Emlyn Williams, George Rees, Don Hayward, Emlyn Jenkins, Will Woods and Evan John all key figures in the Area's structure and active supporters of the unofficial movement. Even so, the potential for tension remained. Glyn Williams later stated that he was not keen on the whole concept of unofficial groups within the union, while Dai Francis felt that they undermined NUM unity.[92] On one occasion, George Rees was threatened with expulsion from the executive by Glyn Williams for attending meetings which advocated unofficial strike action.[93] The role played by the unofficial movement remained controversial. At an Area conference in February 1965, after several speakers had called for strike action against pit closures, the Penllwyngwent delegate stated that the EC was the highest authority within the Area, not the unofficial movement. Similarly, several months later, Whitehead warned that there could be only one

[89]   Ivor England interview.
[90]   Berwyn Howells SWML interview; interview with Eric Davies, 30 January 2004.
[91]   Emlyn Williams SWML interview (AUD/161).
[92]   Glyn Williams SWML interview (AUD/113); Dai Francis SWML interview.
[93]   SWML interview with George Rees (AUD/140).

leadership in the coalfield.[94] By late 1969, the activities of the unofficial movement were being criticised by the Area officials and an Area conference, while Coedely and Cwm lodges passed votes of no confidence in Glyn Williams and Dai Francis.[95]

The strategy of the unofficial movement in the later 1960s was to attempt to pressurise the Area leadership into adopting more combative policies. Its activities were not confined to being a 'ginger group', however: on some occasions, it set about orchestrating unofficial strike action against colliery closures. This can be seen clearly in the campaign against the closure of Rhigos in 1965 and Cambrian in 1966.

The opposition to the closure of Rhigos colliery in 1965 was the first significant attempt by the unofficial movement at taking a stand. Events began in October 1964, when deputations from Rhigos and Glyncastle (which was also threatened with closure) met the executive in an unsuccessful attempt to persuade it to call for industrial action.[96] Despite this setback, the unofficial movement began preparations for action over Rhigos. By January 1965, Mike Griffin (chairman of the Campaign Against Colliery Closure Committee) was predicting that there would be a week-long strike by 10,000 miners from sixteen lodges in the Aberdare-Merthyr area. As it turned out, the only pits to take strike action were Penrhiwceiber and Rhigos. The reason for this climbdown was the NEC announce-ment that NUM policy was to call for a complete standstill on colliery closures until the Wilson government introduced a national fuel policy.[97] George Rees (Fernhill lodge secretary at the time) also later claimed that the strike had been launched pre-emptively by Mike Griffin, before other lodges had been able to discuss the matter.[98] In February 1965, an Area conference reaffirmed support for the NUM policy of calling for the government to guarantee an annual coal output of 200 million tons, but voted not to oppose the closure of Rhigos and Glyncastle. Following the failed strike bid, Whitehead went to Penrhiwceiber and told them that they must submit to the elected Area leadership. The militants realised that

[94] ASC, 9 February, 22 September 1965.
[95] EC, 14 November, 2 December 1969; ASC, 18 November 1969.
[96] EC, 13 October, 2 November 1964.
[97] *The Miner*, Vol.13, No. 1, January/February 1965; *WM*, 7, 12, 18 January 1965.
[98] George Rees interview; George Rees SWML interview.

they would need greater co-ordination if their campaign were to be successful.

The second major intervention by the unofficial movement centred on the struggle to save Cambrian colliery. In August 1966, the NCB announced that the pit would soon close. The Cambrian lodge was determined to resist, refusing to co-operate in arranging for men to be relocated to other pits and then going on strike in September 1966.[99] An Area conference was held on 15 September to discuss support for the lodge's action, with a large contingent of strikers travelling to Porthcawl to lobby the delegates. However, despite this and the fact that the majority of the speakers were in support of a strike, the conference voted not to oppose the closure. Although this was a setback for the unofficial movement, it never-theless proved that there were groups of miners active in the Area who were convinced of the need to confront the NCB over the run-down of the industry.

In addition to this campaigning work in their own Area, the unofficial grouping in the central south Wales valleys in the 1960s was a key component in the revival of radicalism in other British coalfields. The Aberdare May Day committee played an important role, with May Day celebrations used as a platform to establish contacts in other Areas. This unofficial movement grew, building up its resources until it was able to establish the Miners' Forum as a national focal point for left-wing activists in the NUM. The Miners' Forum, which met in Leeds, became an important means of communication between left-wing elements (mainly from Yorkshire, south Wales, Kent and Scotland) in the different Areas. The aim of the Miners' Forum was to change NUM policy on wages and pit closures, via conference decisions. It realised that Yorkshire (the largest Area) would have to be won over to the Left for them to stand any chance of making this a reality. Left-wingers on the NEC (including the south Wales representatives) also met to discuss union policy. Although formed in the late 1960s, the Miners' Forum would come to play a central role in the NUM a few years later, in the struggles of the early 1970s.

[99] EC, 9, 23 August, 13 September 1966; *WM*, 13 September 1966.

'Marsh Gas' and the Accelerated Closure Programme

Despite the campaigning of NUM activists, the mid-1960s seemed full of gloom for the south Wales miners. The pit closure programme reached maximum intensity in 1966–8 and the Area was faced with the prospect of inexorable industrial decline. Efficiency gains from mechanisation were outweighed by haemorrhaging manpower levels and increased absenteeism, leading to falling output. In August 1967, the coalfield discussed the unwelcome news that the government intended to reduce its overall annual coal output requirement, from 170 million tons to 155 million tons.[100] In September 1967, the NEC met Harold Wilson at the Labour Party conference in Scarborough, to call for a halt to the colliery closure programme. At the meeting Wilson – who was anxious to avoid adverse political repercussions – agreed to postpone all closures until the end of the year.[101] Paynter called this arrangement 'nothing but window dressing'; his assessment was proved correct when the closure programme resumed in earnest in 1968.[102] Between 1966 and 1970, the number of south Wales collieries fell from 77 to 52, with manpower dropping from 64,600 to 40,300.[103]

By the later 1960s, it seemed to many miners as though pit closures were inevitable. Consequently, one viewpoint focused instead on calling for new jobs to be brought into the valleys. The Area's annual conferences in 1966, 1967 and 1968 passed resolutions calling for alternative industries to be established in south Wales. In May 1967, Glyn Williams welcomed the relocation of the Royal Mint to Llantrisant and the decision to establish the National Motor Vehicle Registration and Licensing Centre at Swansea, demanding that they be augmented by a programme of government-directed factory building. In January 1969, the EC urged Minister of Power Roy Mason to reduce the rate of pit closures and bring additional employment to the coalfield.[104]

The coal industry's problems intensified after the appointment of Richard Marsh as Minister for Power in 1966 and the discovery of North Sea gas at roughly the same time. Marsh's 1967 White Paper

[100] ASC, 21 August 1967.
[101] TNA, PREM13/1610; EC, 26 September, 2 October 1967.
[102] As quoted in Robens, *Ten Year Stint*, pp. 168–9.
[103] John Williams, *Digest of Welsh Historical Statistics, Vol. 1* (Cardiff: 1985), p. 308.
[104] *The Miner*, No. 15, May/June 1968, No. 1; January 1969.

on Energy Policy consolidated the Wilson administration's views on the coal industry, confirming the miners' worst fears. While national coal output in 1966 had been 175 million tons, the White Paper said that this would fall to 155 million tons by 1970 (with a total of 135,000 miners to be displaced) and 120 million tons by 1975.[105] Paynter pointed out the folly of this policy: 'Concentration and rationalisation were preceding at a manageable rate until the Government called for an acceleration of closures in mid-1965 and forecast an intensive and continuous run-down to 1975 and beyond'.[106] He also made a far-sighted appraisal of the dangers involved in reliance on other forms of fuel, emphasising the safety risks from nuclear energy and highlighting the instability of supply of oil (owing to political upheavals in the Middle East) and its adverse effect on Britain's balance of payments. Paynter and Robens calculated that if the trends spelt out in the White Paper were to continue to 1980, there would be only 65,000 mineworkers left in Britain – a staggering loss of 320,000 jobs over a twelve-year period.[107]

BITTERNESS AND BACKLASH

In these circumstances, it is not surprising that the miners began to take a harder line against pit closures. In November 1967, 4,000 mineworkers lobbied parliament, the first national lobby since the formation of the NUM. A few weeks later, the Area leadership discussed the White Paper with the Labour MPs for south Wales. Here, EC member Will Woods called it 'a complete betrayal of the trust we reposed in the Government'.[108]

At the same time, the reaction to the crisis was causing significant shifts in official Area policy towards colliery closures. On 20 November 1967, the EC's left-wingers succeeded in convening an Area conference and recommending to it a national strike against the government's fuel policy. By the time the conference was held three days later, however, Britain had been hit by the major financial crisis which caused the devaluation of sterling. The government's

[105] *The Miner*, No. 12, November/December 1967; *WM*, 15 November 1967.
[106] *WM: Commercial and Industrial Review, Part II*, 17 January 1968.
[107] ASC, 23 November 1967.
[108] EC, 25 November 1967.

subsequent statement that it would re-evaluate its fuel policy meant that the EC resolution now deferred any talk of strike action until the terms of this reappraisal became known. Nevertheless, the implications of this change in policy were readily apparent. At the Area conference, speakers from several moderate lodges expressed concern at the new stance; the leadership justified it by stating that different circumstances required a different approach. The conference passed the EC's recommendation overwhelmingly, with Don Hayward expressing the majority viewpoint: 'If we don't stand and strike, then all we are saying is if pits close and men go to the road, there is nothing further we can do about it.'[109]

The first effects of the reappraisal of the Area's policy towards pit closures began to make themselves felt in early 1968. In March, an Area conference restated its opposition to NEC caution and underlined its support for a national campaign of 'guerrilla' strikes. Significantly, Glyn Williams stated that 'if we are going to take industrial action, we should take it now, not some time in the future when we would be considerably weaker', adding, 'I, too, believe we have reached the end of the road as far as talking is concerned.' Following this, it seemed quite possible that South Wales would lead a campaign of industrial action with the support of the Derbyshire, Kent, Scotland, Nottinghamshire, Durham and Yorkshire Areas – a prospect which alarmed the Secretary of State for Wales.[110] The fact that this did not occur was due partly to the narrow defeat of the conference's proposals by a ballot of the Area membership, by 24,050 votes to 21,550.[111] This result was a defeat for the EC's new policy, although the closeness of the margin indicated that opinions were changing within the coalfield. The 1968 and 1969 Area conferences underlined this shift, accepting the need for strike action to defend pits from closure.

The increasing willingness of the south Wales miners in the later 1960s to consider taking drastic action to halt the run-down of their industry was mirrored by a growing bitterness towards the Wilson government. Relations started to sour around 1967: in that year, Minister of Labour Ray Gunter had a very hostile response at the Miners' Gala in Cardiff to his suggestion that the miners should welcome the changes underway in their industry.[112] *The Miner* was

[109] ASC, 23 November 1967.
[110] *WM*, 19 March 1968; TNA, PREM13/2769.
[111] EC, 9 April 1968.
[112] *WM*, 12 June 1967.

equally scathing: 'The government has shown an arrogance totally out of keeping with the finest traditions of the movement. This arrogance can be best illustrated by the government's insistence (despite all warnings by the miners – and indeed, from the Coal Board) to accelerate pit closures.'[113] At rank-and-file level, men began to see that government policy was the cause of the pit closures. This attitude was reflected even at secure collieries: at Deep Navigation, for instance, one miner stated that '[t]he real villains as far as I'm concerned are the Government. They've let us down badly.'[114] In July 1968, in his final speech to the NUM National Conference before retiring, Paynter savaged the closure programme, saying that it had made him 'a very bitter man'. Labour supporters like Charlie Blewett viewed developments with dismay: 'In 1964 . . . [t]here was a great resurgence and great hopes. There is no such feeling today and the Labour Government has brought the Labour Party near to heartbreak.' This disaffection became sufficiently pronounced for some miners to raise the possibility of withdrawing the political levy from Labour.[115]

The most conspicuous backlash against the government by frustrated miners came in the series of shock by-election results in south Wales in the later 1960s. In Carmarthen in 1966, the success of Plaid Cymru was a product of discontent in the mining communities in the Gwendraeth and Amman valleys. Even more strikingly, by-elections in Rhondda West in 1967 and Caerphilly in 1968 saw impregnable Labour seats reduced to wafer-thin majorities by huge swings to Plaid. Glyn Williams described the Rhondda result as a 'massive protest vote' at the Wilson government's closure programme.[116] Following Labour's narrow victory in Caerphilly, the party's election agent commented: 'It is understandable that the miners wished to protest at the Government . . . They have a right to feel aggrieved.'[117]

By this time, miners' frustration at low wages and pit closures was becoming increasingly evident. The tone of the Area's 1968 conference, for instance, was one of simmering resentment. Reflecting

[113] *The Miner*, No. 11, September/October 1967.

[114] *WM*, 30 November 1967.

[115] *WM*, 5 July 1968; AAC, 1968; EC, 9 April 1968; *The Miner*, No. 11, September/October 1967.

[116] Area, *President's Address by Glyn Williams* (1967), p. 15.

[117] *WM*, 20 July 1968.

on this period, one miner observed: 'Bit by bit, on all sides, there was a spark . . . of fightback . . . against . . . the Board, against governments . . . Towards the end of that 1960 period . . . something was breaking out here and there. The resolutions to the national conferences started to get harder, firmer. It was a very slow growth. But you could see it. Looking back now, you could see how it was building up.'[118]

This bitterness was given direct expression in two events during 1968. In February, when the NCB announced the closure of Cefn Coed and Ynyscedwyn (despite a reprieve obtained as recently as October 1967) at the same time as Wilson was in Wales, Cledwyn Hughes was worried that the prime minister would be met by a 'mass movement of social protest'.[119] In fact, Wilson's itinerary took him through Cefn Coed, where he was met by a crowd of protesters. He decided not to stop, 'to the amazement of the local people and the television crews and reporters'.[120] Wilson later met lodge leaders, but the episode did little to allay miners' fears of government indifference to their plight. Another dramatic confrontation occurred in Blackpool in September 1968, when about 200 south Wales miners stormed the Labour Party annual conference in protest at pit closures, holding up proceedings and making 'a terrific impact' on the assembled delegates.[121]

An important factor underpinning this revival of South Wales militancy was the impact of the younger sections of the workforce. This was partly their response to the broader political and cultural context of the later 1960s, but it also reflected specific developments in the industry. As one miner (who started work as an apprentice in 1959) later explained: 'a *hell of a lot* of men left the industry at that time . . . but the men that remained, the younger men then, were hell-bent on changing things . . . [W]e had young ideas. And we weren't prepared to be pushed around.'[122] This generation of miners had never worked under the old coalowners and were generally less deferential towards the management, taking at face value the belief that nationalisation meant that the collieries were 'owned by the people'.

[118] Interview with Des Dutfield, 12 February 2004.
[119] TNA, PREM13/2769.
[120] Robens, *Ten Year Stint*, p. 171.
[121] *The Miner*, No.18, November/December 1968; *The Times*, 1 October 1968.
[122] Dane Hartwell interview.

The changing mood of the south Wales miners in the late 1960s was exemplified by a transformation of the Area's executive council in the elections at the end of 1968. Six new members were elected, the biggest change in personnel since the Area's structure was reorganised in 1933; one newcomer later reflected that '[t]here did seem to be a want of a clearing out of the old school, then, and new blood coming in'.[123] Furthermore, three of them – George Rees, Emlyn Jenkins and Evan John – were Communists. These, together with Emlyn Williams, Don Hayward and Will Woods, constituted a strong left-wing presence among the Area leadership. The effect of this was discernible at pit-level: one lodge secretary later recalled that 'You had a change of heart among the Executive. It seemed to put fire in their bellies again.'[124] The effect of this overhaul was soon apparent in the EC's call for an extra £5 a week for miners – an ambitious demand, given the low wages in the 1960s. Equally significantly, the militants in the leadership were able to strengthen the power of the rank-and-file EC, at the expense of the full-time Area officials and appointed officers.[125] While this caused minor ructions within the Area hierarchy, it ensured a greater level of democratic accountability in the union.

Although the dominant trend in 1969 in the south Wales coalfield was an exacerbation of the tensions which had been apparent throughout the 1960s, there was one noteworthy exception. For the first time during the Wilson government years, it was possible for a few pits which had been threatened with closure to avoid this fate. The two most interesting examples are Celynen South and Penallta, where miners used unorthodox strategies to save their collieries. At Celynen South, the lodge committee sided with the management in an attempt to reduce losses, becoming responsible for sacking persistent absentees. This was 'hugely unpopular' with the pit's work-force and also within the Area in general; it was, however, an important factor in the reprieve of the colliery in October 1969.[126] At Penallta, the lodge ran a waste minimisation campaign and hired a public relations firm to help them to argue their case. The story

---

[123] Emlyn Jenkins interview.

[124] Berwyn Howells SWML interview.

[125] George Rees interview; SWML interview with Don Hayward and Emlyn Jenkins (AUD/381).

[126] Ray Lawrence, *Celynen South, 1873–1985: A Short History to Commemorate the Closure of the Colliery* (n.p., 1985), p. 15; Ray Lawrence interview; EC, 7 October 1969.

attracted the attention of the national press and the consequent
boost to morale at the pit helped to raise production sufficiently to
escape closure. By June 1969, Penallta had been saved.[127]

One colliery which was shut in 1969 was Avon Ocean, Abergwynfi.
In this respect, it was no different from dozens of others in the 1960s.
What made it stand out was that it was the first time that the Area
leadership recommended strike action in opposition to a pit closure.
Avon (pronounced 'Afan') was an unlikely candidate for closure: its
OMS was considerably above the divisional average, it had one of
the youngest workforces in south Wales and a good absentee record.
However, the Board wanted to shut Avon because, it claimed, there
was no market for its coal, even though closure would increase local
unemployment to 15 per cent.[128] At an Area conference in June 1969
called to discuss the situation, Evan Jones (Ogilvie) said that: 'The
report on Avon is . . . most frightening . . . because few pits in South
Wales have outputs better than Avon'. Glyn Williams cautioned
against a strike; however, he found himself in a minority among the
Area leadership. In August 1969, urged on by its more militant
members and galvanised by widespread discontent on other issues in
the coalfield, the EC took the unprecedented step of recommending
strike action against the closure of Avon. At an Area conference
on 20 August, however, delegates rejected the strike call by 49
votes to 32. While some of those who opposed it criticised the
unconstitutional nature of such action, probably a greater number
were influenced by veiled NCB threats that pits which shut down to
participate in industrial action might never be reopened. This defeat
was underlined by a coalfield ballot held a few weeks later. In
December 1969, the Area leadership reassessed its policy in the light
of this experience. Despite having a radical position on many other
issues, it remained conscious of the difficulties of securing united
strike action in defence of a particular colliery. The closure of Avon
illustrated the deep-seated problems still facing the south Wales
miners.

[127] Interviews with Don Jones (23 February 2004), Gordon Bartley and Ron Stoate;
Brian Elliott SWML interview; *WM*, 18 April, 21 May 1969; *Daily Mirror*, 27 June 1969;
Fay Swain and Cory Williams (eds), *Penallta: A Brief History of Penallta Colliery in the Rhymney
Valley* (Ystrad Mynach: 1994), p. 58; Gareth Salway, *Penallta: A Pit and its People* (Abertillery:
2008), pp. 50–2.
[128] EC, 28 May, 11 June 1968.

THE SURFACEMEN'S STRIKE

Despite the despondency caused by the Avon Ocean closure, within weeks the coalfield was gripped by unofficial strike action on the question of surfacemen's hours. In some ways, however, it would be misleading to differentiate between these developments, since in both cases the driving force for action was the group of lodges in the Rhondda area. The subject of the strike was an emotive one, since surfacemen were the lowest-paid mineworkers and were often men who had been disabled by industrial accident or industrial disease. In many respects, the surfacemen's strike was the culmination of tensions which had built up over the preceding decade. As one activist later recalled:

> [I]t had all been leading up to something. You couldn't *squash* the feeling . . . it was a period of things were beginning to stir, then . . . And of course . . . the *major* action was the surfacemen's strike . . . [T]hat was a *much bigger* issue . . . in the coalfield. Although it burned out, in its place was a feeling that . . . although we've lost that, that things *will* change. There was a lot of radical feeling after that.[129]

The question of surfacemen's hours had been simmering for several years before 1969, being discussed in Area conferences from 1966 to 1968. In July 1968, Cwm lodge led protests at the NUM National Conference in Swansea, calling for a 40-hour week for surfacemen. Eddie Thomas, the lodge's chairman, stated: 'A 40 hour week was one of the reforms demanded in 1868 but we have not had it yet . . . [The NEC] are not even dragging their feet. They are anchored.' The Conference agreed to aid the surfacemen, calling for wage increases of 15–20 per cent for them. That month, Six Bells lodge wrote to the EC, suggesting industrial action on this subject.[130]

The Area conference in April–May 1969 increased the likelihood of a clash over surface hours. The motion which was passed, known subsequently as the 'Cwm resolution', was a clear declaration of intent: 'This Conference demands that the hours of surface workers be reduced to 36½; failure to achieve this just demand by 1st September, 1969, means that *we strike* [original emphasis]'. Interestingly, not one delegate spoke against this. Ron Saint observed:

---

[129] Dane Hartwell interview.
[130] EC, 9 July 1968.

'The Cwm Resolution contains the dreaded word "strike" . . . The wages and conditions of our people on the surface are a scandal and it is only because we refuse to use the strike weapon . . . if we don't fight on this issue, we won't fight on any!' In August 1969, the Area conference that rejected action over Avon colliery decided to postpone any strike on this issue until after a lobby of the Joint National Negotiating Committee in September. South Wales miners were enthusiastic participants in the lobby but it did not produce the desired results. In early October 1969, the executive agreed to a request for an Area conference; at the conference on 14 October, delegates backed EC proposals for an official national strike. However, a minority of delegates from the more radical lodges argued that this was insufficient since Yorkshire miners were already out on strike over surface hours and that the Area should join them immediately. Ron Saint warned that '[u]nless we . . . take . . . action, then some of the best lodges in the coalfield will . . . strike . . . in support of Yorkshire and the surface men'.[131]

The surfacemen's strike was the biggest stoppage since nationalisation, heralding the return of militancy to the industry. This unofficial strike involved 130,000 miners from 140 pits across Britain and lasted from 13 to 27 October 1969. South Wales played an important role, with 16,000 men from 24 pits becoming involved in the days immediately following the Area conference. Leading radicals later highlighted the spontaneous nature of this strike, with miners responding instantly to the strike call.[132] The strike was led by militant lodges from the centre of the coalfield which had been at the forefront of the unofficial movement, although some pits from further west, such as Brynlliw, also participated. The strike was spread through appeals for solidarity and picketing of other pits, which met with mixed results; similarly, repeated attempts by Don Hayward, George Rees and Will Woods to get the strike declared official were unsuccessful.[133]

Despite setbacks, the main significance of the surfacemen's strike was that the unofficial movement was able to channel a decade of frustration across the coalfield into decisive action on one particular issue. The strike's leaders expressed the popular mood concisely.

[131]　ASC, 14 October 1969.
[132]　Don Hayward and Emlyn Jenkins SWML interview.
[133]　EC, 20, 22 October 1969.

Ron Saint (Coedely) said: 'The rank and file have been waiting for a call like this for a long time . . . [The NCB] do not want us to have a victory which might give us confidence in the power of militancy.' Cliff True (Fernhill, chairman of the strike committee) stated: 'When you squeeze down a spring so hard it eventually explodes outwards . . . Morale amongst miners has reached rock-bottom, with everyone afraid of militancy in case their pit is closed. Now men are realising that pits will be closed whether they strike or not and we might as well get the best out of it while we can.'[134]

One of the most dramatic episodes of the strike occurred at an Area conference held on 22 October, when militants attempted to get the dispute declared official. Their central argument was that the Cwm resolution still applied. However, following the debate, Glyn Williams provoked uproar when he refused to allow a vote, on the grounds that the lodges' vote on the subject a few days previously (which had supported the EC's recommendation to call for a national conference to discuss national strike action) made a conference decision unnecessary. Afterwards, there were angry scenes as strikers mobbed him, calling for his resignation and also shouting abuse at the Area general secretary and vice-president.[135] Apart from making a good story for the local press the following day, this conference also provided an insight into the dynamics within the South Wales NUM by the late 1960s. The striving of the unofficial movement for an immediate stoppage had produced tensions with the Area hierarchy, which felt duty-bound to follow formal procedures. Nevertheless, this antagonism obscures the fact that all sections of the Area supported strike action; the disagreement was over how it should be achieved. The essential issue was one of tactics and democratic procedure, with the debate revolving around the respective imperatives of unity and action in taking the struggle forward. The dialectics of this process helped to revitalise the union, making it seem more vibrant and powerful than before.

The final issue during the surfacemen's strike was the NCB's 'package deal'. Although the focus of the strike had been surface hours, a subsidiary consideration was a general wage claim by the NUM. Consequently, the NCB bracketed together in one 'package' no change over surface hours and – unprecedentedly – a concession

[134] Quoted in *WM*, 22 October 1969.
[135] *WM*, 23 October 1969.

in full of the NUM's wage claim of an extra 27s. 6d. per week. The Board's aim was presumably to deflect miners' attentions from the original issue: consequently, both the Area leadership and a conference on 31 October 1969 were in favour of rejecting the proposed deal. Following campaigning against the package throughout the coalfield, the Area provided a quarter of all the British 'no' votes in the national ballot in November – although the overall result was a resounding acceptance of the deal.[136]

Despite its ambiguous conclusion, the surfacemen's strike provided the biggest wage increases in the history of the nationalised industry and put militancy back on the miners' agenda in a way that it had not been for decades. In May 1970, Ron Saint observed: 'Some say that the last October strike was a fiasco. I would liken it to John Reed's "Ten Days That Shook The World". It certainly shook a lot of people.'[137] The unofficial nature of the strike undoubtedly caused friction but it also had a greater significance, particularly in a coalfield like south Wales, where the dominant experience of the 1960s had been one of setbacks and closures. The dispute showed that industrial action could restore miners' wage levels and it popularised arguments about taking a stand against pit closures; it was seen as a victory for direct action methods. Emlyn Jenkins later reflected that the surfacemen's strike 'brought about the solidarity . . . [It proved] that something could be done by striking – because surface wages were *absolutely disgusting* . . . [I]t did achieve at the end of the day what we set out to do.'[138] This development was to have a fundamental effect on the south Wales miners in the 1970s.

CONCLUSION

Events of the 1960s provided an important development in the history of the south Wales miners, weakening significantly faith in the belief that the nationalised industry would ensure long-term employment. During this decade, the NCB responded to the shrinking demand for coal with a far-reaching closure programme, with which the NUM generally co-operated so as to lessen the blow. Even

---

[136] The overall result was 193,985 'for' and 41,322 'against'; in south Wales it was 18,594 'for' and 10,116 'against' [EC, 2 December 1969].

[137] AAC, 1970.

[138] Emlyn Jenkins interview.

though the mass transferrals of the 1960s were themselves a key factor militating against the development of resistance to this industrial change, the growth of the unofficial movement in south Wales and elsewhere nevertheless reflected an increasing sense of grassroots frustration. In an industry with an uncertain future, it became difficult for the NUM to play the positive role envisaged by its leaders when it had been nationalised. Consequently, by the end of the 1960s, the Area leadership had 'learned not to ask their men to make sacrifices for their industry and their country, and accordingly the "rank-and-file" did not disappoint them.'[139]

By the time the Wilson government left office in June 1970, a resurgence of NUM militancy seemed likely. Their experiences of the 1960s had led many miners to believe that only direct action could safeguard their livelihoods. Furthermore, Edward Heath had based his election manifesto on a draconian Industrial Relations Bill and suggested that the Conservatives break with their 'one nation' image; by the same token, miners were happier to confront the Tories rather than a Labour administration. Consequently, the years 1970 to 1974 were a period of disturbances comparable with the 'Great Unrest' of 1910–14. The 'industrial pyrotechnics' of the early 1970s were the explosive culmination of the pressures which had been building up in the coal industry during the preceding decade.

---

[139] Nina Fishman, 'Coal: Owned and Managed on Behalf of the People', in Jim Fyrth (ed.), *Labour's High Noon: The Government and the Economy, 1945–51* (London: 1993), p. 75.

III

STRUGGLE: 1970–1974

The period 1970–4 saw an explosion of industrial unrest among the
coal miners of Britain, sending shock waves around the entire
country. In 1972 and 1974, the NUM held the first national miners'
strikes since 1926 and, unlike in 1926, they were victorious on both
occasions. In 1974, the Heath government fought – and lost – a
general election under the slogan, 'Who governs?' These strikes
shattered the prevailing myth of the 1960s that Britain was no longer
reliant on coal. The NUM, with South Wales in the vanguard, was
back in the forefront of the economic and political life of the country.

THE 1970S: A BRIGHT FUTURE?

For the south Wales coalfield, the 1970s began much as the 1960s
had ended. At the Area conference in May 1970, Glyn Williams (the
president of the south Wales miners) stressed the wide variety of
useful coal types mined in the region and pointed out the dangers of
a too-rapid rundown of the industry. The coalfield was the least
technologically advanced in the country, accounting for the majority
of the 115 non-mechanised coalfaces in Britain in February 1971.[1]
Manpower drift was still a problem, with the number of south Wales
mineworkers falling from 46,300 in 1969 to 40,300 in 1970.[2] The
NCB spent £100,000 on a recruitment drive in the coalfield in 1970
but failed to address the underlying reasons why men were leaving,
namely, low wages and uncertainty about the industry's future. Many
faceworkers felt that the introduction of the NPLA in 1966 had led
to a decline in their wages, while surfacemen could be earning as
little as £11 a week after stoppages.[3] Furthermore, the failure of
Labour to adopt an integrated fuel policy and its subsequent defeat
in the 1970 general election made a secure future for the industry
seem remote.

[1]   EC, 23 February 1971.
[2]   John Williams, *Digest of Welsh Historical Statistics, Vol. 1* (Cardiff: 1985), p. 308.
[3]   *WM*, 30 September 1970.

Despite all this, changing trends in the global energy market meant that the early 1970s witnessed a renaissance for the British coal industry. Whereas in the 1960s the governmental attitude was that coal was a liability retained only because of the social cost of removing it completely, events showed that cheap alternatives could not be guaranteed. Following increases in oil prices, in February 1971 the NCB announced plans to boost annual output to 150 million tons. NCB chairman Lord Robens proclaimed: 'From now on we are going to ignore the (1967) White Paper's highly erroneous forecasts . . . The [NCB's] "five-year plan" . . . means no more closures . . . It means job security for the years ahead.'[4] Electricity generation was seen as the main market for the modern coal industry. In 1960 the CEGB was using 52 million tons a year; by 1979 power stations were consuming 89 million tonnes.[5] Britain continued to depend on domestic coal production, with about 75 per cent of its electricity generated in coal-fired stations.

The renewed prospects for coal in the 1970s meant that it was possible for the miners to view the future with cautious optimism for the first time since the 1950s. In the south Wales coalfield, the NCB planned a programme of increased investment at existing collieries and forecast an improvement in total annual deep-mined output from 11.4 million tons in 1970 to over 12 million tons within the next few years. Abernant was the first pit in south Wales to use high speed 'retreat mining' methods, while Treforgan's electronic remote control systems made it the most technologically sophisticated mine in the coalfield. Mechanisation levels in south Wales collieries had increased to 86 per cent by 1971. Several collieries showed significant increases in output per man-shift (OMS): Penallta and Britannia reached 43 cwt and 45.8 cwt respectively in October 1970, Taff Merthyr and Marine had 61.5 cwt and 64.7 cwt in June 1973, while Trelewis Drift showed the full potential of retreat mining techniques by hitting an OMS of 162.7 cwt.[6]

[4]   Coal News, February 1971.
[5]   Gerald Manners, Coal In Britain: An Uncertain Future (London: 1981), pp. 47–8.
[6]   WM, 30 October 1970; WM: Commercial and Industrial Review Pt.2, 23 January 1970; WM: Growth of a Nation Pt.2, 7 July 1971; The Miner, June 1973.

Wage structure reform

Further changes were at work in the organisation of the coal industry in the early 1970s. One of the long-term post-war trends had been towards a rationalisation of the wages structure which the NCB had inherited. The NUM was keen to establish the principle of equal pay for equal work, while the Board wanted a simpler system that produced fewer disputes. The most important steps were the New Daywage Structure in 1955 and the National Power Loading Agreement in 1966. This process was finalised with the introduction of the Third Wages Structure in 1971 and the new Craftsmen's Agreement in 1970.

The first moves towards a Third Wages Structure began in 1968, when the south Wales miners called for a new system for those not covered by existing national agreements. In June 1969, they learned that the NCB was looking at introducing a wage structure which would abolish the last remnants of piecework in the industry. Their main concern was that there should be parity within the new scheme and, consequently, in May 1970, the Area annual conference called unanimously for immediate parity within the Third Wages Structure. Following the Board's acceptance of the principle of standardised wage rates, however, the south Wales miners endorsed the proposed structure by a large majority.[7] After further improvements negotiated by the NUM leadership, the Third Wages Structure was introduced in June 1971. The new agreement gave national rates of pay to the remaining 44,000 workers in the industry still not on daywages, thereby removing the last traces of piecework from the industry. This did not mean that it was beyond improvement. In May 1972, for instance, an Area conference called for the abolition of the lowest grade – Grade C – of the Third Structure by its inclusion in Grade B.

The new Craftsmen's Agreement emerged along essentially the same lines as the Third Wages Structure. Six craftsman grades had been established under the New Daywage Structure of 1955 but this was subsequently deemed inadequate by the men themselves. As one colliery electrician later succinctly expressed it: 'craftsmen's wages was *rubbish*'.[8] This scenario – skilled workers on low wages – meant

---

[7]   ASC, 8, 16 March 1971; EC, 6 April 1971.
[8]   Interview with Gordon Bartley, 22 January 2004.

that craftsmen led the exodus from the coal industry in the 1960s. The Area leadership was keen to see this trend reversed. In May 1969, Glyn Williams told miners' delegates that 'We must . . . call for a substantial advance in the rates paid to craftsmen . . . which recognises the degree of technical proficiency required by them'.[9]

The NCB's new Craftsmen's Agreement proposals were discussed by the south Wales miners later in 1970. While the new scheme planned for three wage grades (essentially, fitters and electricians; skilled; and semi-skilled craftsmen), a minority of critics argued that there should be only two. Nevertheless, the NCB offer for top-grade craftsmen working on mechanised faces to receive the NPLA rate was supported unanimously by lodges across the coalfield. Despite some reservations about the actual proposed wage levels, the Area's lodges voted to accept the Craftsmen's Agreement in December 1970.[10] As the 1971 Area conference was well aware, though, there remained problems with the agreement. These difficulties mainly revolved around differentials, as between the various grades of craftsmen and between craftsmen and some categories of workers conditioned to the Third Wages Structure. Problems were reported in several pits, for example, at Abernant, Caerau and Deep Duffryn in September 1971 and Penrhiwceiber in June 1972. Area conferences in August and November 1972 discussed the pay-gap that now existed between coalface- and outbye-craftsmen, with Terry Thomas (Brynlliw) reporting that '[t]here is grave discontent in the ranks of the craftsmen in this coalfield, and if this vexed problem is not resolved in the near future, the craftsmen will solve it themselves.' The grievance was felt sufficiently strongly that in May 1973 the annual conference called for industrial action on the issue, to begin in November. As it transpired, by that time the miners had become engaged in a broader struggle on the wages question. Notwithstanding this, the issue of craftsmen's differentials remained unresolved. Area conferences in the later 1970s would regularly feature calls for improvements in craftsmen's pay and conditions, with the 1978 conference demanding a complete reconstruction of the Craftsmen's Wage Structure.

[9] *The Miner*, No. 5, May 1969.
[10] EC, 6, 20 October, 29 December 1970.

THE RISE OF NUM MILITANCY

The years 1970 to 1974 marked an upturn in the radicalism of the
south Wales miners and form an important chapter in their history.
Whereas the 1960s had been characterised by a defensive campaign
against colliery closures, the early 1970s saw the miners adopt a
more militant stance, owing to an increasing appreciation of the
need to fight to defend the industry and working conditions within
it. One area where this was most apparent was pit closures. In
December 1970, the EC reaffirmed that its policy was to oppose
the closure of any colliery (apart from on grounds of geological
exhaustion) while market demand for coal continued to exceed
supply.[11] This stance represented a clear step forward from the
strategy of the 1960s. The 1972 Area conference saw a further
hardening of attitudes. Here, a resolution was passed which called
for opposition to *any* closures that were not due to geological
exhaustion, with the use of industrial action to enforce this, if
necessary. Speaking in support of the resolution, EC member
George Rees said: 'The myth of strikes decimating the coal industry
has been smashed . . . Over the years many people said industrial
action would destroy the mining industry. We did not take action and
the industry was massacred.'

An insightful barometer of the increasing radicalism in the Area
during this period is the combative stance adopted by some lodge
officials known for their political moderation. A good example is
Charlie Blewett, lodge secretary at Penallta. Speaking about wages at
the 1970 Area conference, he stated: 'Let us say in cold blood that
we would be considering strike action, and I know that delegates will
applaud to know that Charlie Blewett in these present circumstances
is advocating strike action'. This statement prompted Ron Saint, a
leading militant, to observe that 'when you can get Charlie Blewett
talking about strike action, then I think we are well on the way to
reaching our goal'.[12]

This upsurge of NUM militancy in the early 1970s is inexplicable
without an understanding of the context of the widespread bitterness of the late 1960s, which was harnessed successfully by unofficial
forces in the union and channelled into causes from which the miners

[11] EC, 29 December 1970.
[12] AAC, 1970.

could benefit. At a national level, the Miners' Forum – or Broad Left, as it was also known – was a very important factor, facilitating communication and co-ordination between the left-wing elements in the various Areas. The leftwards shift in the centre of gravity within the NUM in this period was due largely to the conversion of Yorkshire into a left-wing Area. In south Wales, the years 1969 to 1974 saw the zenith of the unofficial movement, although its activities were not without their controversies. In the aftermath of the 'surfacemen's strike', in late 1969 and 1970 several lodges criticised the unofficial movement (which centred on Coedely, Fernhill and Cwm lodges) and called on it to disband.[13] Tensions were still apparent in August 1970: Glyn Williams told members to abandon the unofficial movement, while Area vice-president Emlyn Williams asked militants not to jeopardise the NUM's new-found commitment to strike action over wages by any pre-emptive sectional action. The movement's leaders remained unrepentant, however. Ron Saint (Coedely) dismissed suggestions that they should join the official campaign on wages, stating: 'I would reject [the] . . . invitation to come inside the Organisation and fight because you cannot fight effectively with your hands tied behind your back'.[14]

Following the unhappy experiences of the unofficial movement in south Wales in the 1960s in trying to get strike action over colliery closures, by the early 1970s the Miners' Forum had realised that the best prospects for united national action were on the question of wages. As one activist later recalled: 'We built it up as a result of forming the Miners' Forum for the British coalfield . . . coming back here, building up the Miners' Forum in South Wales, sending out emissaries, particularly in pits we thought were doubtful. And I would say that it took us two years to build up the kind of force that we felt we would need for '72.'[15] The growing influence of the unofficial movement in south Wales can be seen by comparing the strikes of October 1969 and November 1970. In the former, the majority of the EC was opposed to unofficial action; in the latter, the executive declared the strike to be official in south Wales, contrary to the wishes of the Area officials. For the first time for nearly fifty years, the prospect of widespread strike action appeared on the NUM agenda. Retrospectively, both an Area official and a

[13] EC, 14 November, 2 December 1969, 24 August 1970.
[14] ASC, 25 August 1970.
[15] SWML interview with Emlyn Williams (AUD/33).

rank-and-file activist could agree that the roots of the successful
national strike in 1972 lay in the rising tide of grassroots militancy
between 1969 and 1971.[16]

THE WAGES STRUGGLE

A key issue facing the south Wales miners in 1970 was wages. At
their annual conference in May 1970, delegates voted unanimously
for a £5 a week wage increase for all grades, with weekly minima of
£21 for underground and £20 for surface work. Significantly, the
resolution – moved by Coedely – called for a national strike if these
increases were not forthcoming. As Ron Saint commented, '[t]he
Resolution uses the word "strike" deliberately because my lodge is of
the opinion that one hour's strike is worth a year's talking'. The
NCB's seeming reluctance to stick to the agreement to introduce
complete NPLA parity by 31 December 1971 also concerned delegates
sufficiently for them to support talk of strike action to achieve this
goal. The South Wales wages resolution was narrowly accepted by
the National Conference in July 1970. Official NUM policy was now
to call for wages of £20 surface, £22 underground and £30 NPLA,
with the threat of a strike if these were not forthcoming – a scenario
that could not have been more different from the union's cautious
bargaining during the 1960s.

Although the NUM was formally committed to strike action over
wages, the south Wales miners were keen to ensure that there was no
backtracking. In September 1970, they lobbied the NEC in
opposition to the NCB's wage offer. The NEC agreed that the offer
was inadequate, calling unanimously on the membership to vote for
strike action. As EC member Will Haydn Thomas stated at the time:
'Miners . . . certainly don't want a strike, but without a struggle there
can be no hope . . . Since 1959, we have slipped down the wages
table from 2nd to 16th, and this is because we failed to struggle.'
The significance of the national leadership's changed stance was not
lost on the Area's radicals. Bryn Williams (Cwm) commented,
'Who would want unofficial action when the [NEC] . . . are now
unanimous for strike action. Our aim since last July has been to bring
some life to this coalfield and Union where hitherto it was dead . . .

[16] SWML interviews with Dai Francis (AUD/131) and Haydn Matthews (AUD/134).

There is going to be a struggle, and it will not be easy, but let us have the courage to face it.'[17]

The lead-up to the national ballot in October 1970 was a tense time. Heath had raised the stakes by suggesting the need for a showdown over wage levels in the nationalised industries, which prompted threats from NUM general secretary Lawrence Daly of a general strike. Robens did little to pacify the situation, suggesting that the NCB might not stick to its agreement to introduce NPLA parity by the end of 1971 and calling on mineworkers to reject their union's advice.[18] In south Wales, the Area leadership campaigned vigorously, organising pithead meetings across the coalfield to galvanise support. The national ballot result did not dispel the controversy. A clear majority (55.5 per cent) had voted for strike action but this was less than the two-thirds majority stipulated by the NUM constitution. This result prompted outrage in south Wales, where 83 per cent voted for a strike – the highest proportion of any Area.[19] On 29 October, Glyn Williams and Area general secretary Dai Francis (who were obliged to argue the new NEC line of acceptance of the NCB's wage offer) found themselves overruled by the rank-and-file EC, which decided to recommend that South Wales strike unilaterally. The following day, an Area conference backed the EC's recommendation for strike action from 9 November.

The strike of November 1970 was much more broad-based in south Wales than the 'surfacemen's strike' the previous year. Unofficial action pre-empted the arranged start-date: by the time an Area conference was called on 4 November, half the coalfield was already out. At this conference, delegates voted overwhelmingly for a strike in south Wales – the first complete stoppage since 1926. By 9 November, 130,000 miners, mainly from south Wales and Scotland, had stopped work.[20] On 12 November, a large contingent of south Wales miners – led by Emlyn Williams – travelled to London to ask the NEC to reject the NCB's pay offer. At an Area conference on 14 November, the EC's call for the strike to be escalated was carried. Despite this, the collapse of support in other Areas inevitably limited the room for manoeuvre in south Wales. The decision by several lodges to return to work signalled the

[17] ASC, 23 September 1970.
[18] *WM*, 26, 29 September 1970; EC, 6, 29 October 1970.
[19] *WM*, 24 October 1970.
[20] EC, 10 November 1970.

beginning of the end of the strike and was a cause of local bitterness at the time.[21] Although attempts were made to picket these pits, the Area leadership decided to end the strike in an organised manner. Consequently, Area conferences on 19 and 21 November resolved to return to work but to campaign against acceptance of the Board's proposed pay offer.

One of the most significant aspects of the strike was the politicised context in which it occurred. Robens set this tone by alleging that it was the work of 'avowed Communists' in south Wales and Scotland. While it is true that Communists were active in the NUM in calling for a full implementation of the union's official policy on wages, their arguments would have carried little weight if they had not been in accord with the attitudes of the majority of miners. As Charlie Blewett (Penallta) observed, 'Everyone who voted at the delegate conference at Porthcawl last week was mandated to do so. Most of those who voted are members of the Labour Party. There is no question of a small handful of bogeymen influencing events.'[22] Ultimately, this 'Red scare' served only to close ranks within the NUM.

As it transpired, the strike was a controversial episode in the Area in its own right. For those who saw the NUM principally as a national union, the strike was still unofficial despite EC backing. At Area conferences held during the strike, this clash between National and Area loyalties produced some bitter exchanges. Mike Griffin (Penrhiwceiber) was one of the fiercest critics, labelling the strike a 'fraud that has been perpetuated on the members' and calling on the Area's leaders to resign.[23] In the weeks following the strike, several lodges condemned the way Glyn Williams and Dai Francis handled the matter. The spectrum of views ranged from those who felt that the Area officials had acted unconstitutionally in calling the strike to those who argued that they should have campaigned more vigorously at NEC level in opposition to the NCB's wage offer.[24]

Despite these disagreements, the November 1970 strike was far from being a disaster. Even though it was not a national stoppage or an outright victory, it secured the biggest wage advances in the industry since 1947: an extra £3 for daywagemen, £2 16s. 0d. for

---

[21]   WM, 16, 18 November 1970; EC, 16 November 1970.
[22]   WM, 10 November 1970.
[23]   ASC, 19 November 1970.
[24]   EC, 7, 24 November, 15, 29 December 1970.

craftsmen and £2 7s. 6d. for NPLA workers, and improved conditions for surface workers.[25] At the 1971 Area conference, it was clear that miners had begun to think about the strategic lessons that could be learned from the episode: some delegates stressed the need for national-level action, while others pointed to the increased confidence within the union as a result of rank-and-file activism and the virtues of sustained campaigning on the wages issue. In this respect, it provided a platform for further action. Emlyn Williams later observed: 'the 1970 run-off – that was an exercise to see how far we could go. But what was encouraging about that was that South Wales was the only coalfield that came out under leadership and returned, although defeated, under leadership. They and the Yorkshire panel were the last two to go back.'[26] Fundamentally, the strike highlighted the need to combine radicalism with discipline, thereby laying key foundations for the subsequent victories of 1972 and 1974.

The enthusiasm among the south Wales miners to fight for improved wages and conditions in their industry was matched in the early 1970s by a willingness to campaign on wider socio-economic issues. The increasing unemployment in Britain was a subject close to their hearts, given their experiences in earlier decades. The EC protested to the government at the unemployment figure of 750,000 in January 1971, viewing with alarm the increase to 814,000 three months later.[27] The 1971 conference condemned rising unemployment levels unanimously and called for 'a truly Socialist Government' as a solution to the problem. South Wales miners also took part in demonstrations against unemployment in 1971 in London, Merthyr Tydfil and Cardiff, culminating in a lobby of parliament in November 1971.

THE HEATH GOVERNMENT AND THE 'SECOND GREAT UNREST'

The Heath government presided over a period of intense labour unrest comparable with the 'Great Unrest' of 1910–14, polarising opinion along class lines far more than had its Labour predecessor.

---

[25] Hywel Francis and David Smith, *The Fed: A History of the South Wales Miners in the Twentieth Century* (London: 1980), p. 469.

[26] Emlyn Williams SWML interview.

[27] EC, 26 January, 20 April 1971.

The south Wales miners showed their solidarity with other workers engaged in the struggle. In January 1970, the EC publicly backed the teachers' pay claim; they also supported strikes by the dockers in July 1970 and by postal workers in January 1971. Two UCS shop stewards addressed an Area conference in August 1971; subsequently, the Area donated £1,000 and made arrangements for a regular levy from members to be sent to them. In addition to this, the south Wales miners gave financial support to the UCATT building workers' strike and made a donation to the British Leyland Occupation Committee in September 1972. Further examples of the Area's solidarity with other unions occurred in March 1973, when they offered support to NUPE, COHSE, TGWU and NUGMW in various local disputes and agreed to restrict coal movements in support of a strike by ASLEF.

A central reason for the upsurge of strike activity during these years was Heath's attempt to 'prove his strength' by taking on the unions. Although subsequent experiences of Thatcher changed popular perceptions about what a hard-line Conservative government looked like, it must be remembered that Heath was elected after promising to take a more combative stance on industrial relations issues and to implement an Industrial Relations Bill aimed at restricting trade union activities. This policy provoked a strong union response, with few workers being more determined opponents than the south Wales miners.

In south Wales, opposition to the Industrial Relations Bill began in December 1970, when the EC sent representatives to a lobby of parliament. Later that month, an Area conference discussed how best to combat the Bill, which several speakers described as being 'the first steps towards a Corporate State'. While most delegates wanted a National Conference convened to co-ordinate industrial action by the NUM and the trade union movement in opposition to it, a minority of radicals called for immediate protest strikes. After this, the Area leadership sought to increase rank-and-file awareness about the threat posed by the Industrial Relations Bill by distributing information leaflets and anti-Bill petitions across the coalfield. In February 1971, 200,000 trade unionists (including about 2,000 Welsh miners) demonstrated in London against the Bill.[28] The following month, the south Wales miners lobbied the TUC conference

---

[28] *The Miner*, No. 26, March 1971; ASC, 31 December 1970.

on the subject on 18 March. The 1971 Area conference condemned the Bill and by November that year the NUM had de-registered from it, in accordance with instructions. In May 1972, miners' delegates criticised the harsh treatment meted out to the TGWU in the light of the Industrial Relations Act and called on the labour movement to defeat this legislation. Events took a dramatic turn after the imprisonment of five dockers (the 'Pentonville Five') under the terms of the Act. In July 1972, a deputation from Wern Tarw, Cwm, Coedely, Ogilvie, Maerdy and Fernhill discussed the matter with the EC, which voted unanimously to bring the coalfield to a halt in protest.[29] The following day, an Area conference called for a strike – although nine lodges had already stopped work. As it turned out, the prospect of a general strike prompted the release of the Pentonville Five two days later. Although this development represented a significant victory, the south Wales miners kept up the pressure on the government, calling for the repeal of the Act at their 1973 annual conference and supporting the AUEW in its opposition to it.

THE ROAD TO 1972

For the Area, an entirely different type of obstacle emerged in May 1971, when Joe Gormley became the new national president of the NUM. Gormley was a 'moderate' from Lancashire; in contrast, South Wales had nominated Mick McGahey (a Communist from Scotland) as president and Emlyn Williams as vice-president. In the election, McGahey's votes came mainly from the more radical Areas: South Wales, Scotland, Kent and Yorkshire. South Wales voted for McGahey by 21,035 votes to 6,127 – the highest proportion of any Area, apart from Scotland.[30] Although McGahey was subsequently elected national vice-president in 1973, Gormley's victory meant that the most powerful post in the NUM stayed in the hands of the right-wingers.

Despite the election of Gormley, the National Conference in July 1971 saw a consolidation of the radicalism that had been developing within the union during the preceding two years. Delegates called for significantly increased wages: £35 per week for NPLA workers,

---

[29]   EC, 24 July 1972.
[30]   *The Miner*, No. 29, June 1971.

£28 for underground workers and £26 for surfacemen. An important constitutional development was the conference's adoption of a South Wales motion to alter Rule 43, bringing the necessary majority for national strike action down from 66 per cent to 55 per cent. The significance of this should not be underestimated: the ballot mechanics of the NUM structure could have a pivotal role in shaping political events. In 1970, for instance, over 55 per cent of the membership had voted for strike action which had been denied by the NUM's constitution. Without this change to Rule 43, the ballot result would have been insufficient for national strike action in 1972, and the subsequent history of the NUM would have been completely different.

Wage levels were the main focus of the south Wales miners in 1971. At their annual conference, an EC resolution was passed calling for a £5 per week wage increase 'across the board', and a national strike if the Board failed to concede this. Emlyn Williams expressed concisely the miners' viewpoint:

> [S]ome leaders would prefer wage negotiations without the threat of industrial action, but wage negotiations in the present climate to succeed must have teeth. Last year was the only year we made any real progress because of the threat of industrial action. The cost of living since 1970 has skyrocketed, and this new claim, if conceded in full, will only allow us to remain in the same position . . . [W]e warn the Government on the issue of [NPLA] parity [that] . . . we see this as a deep rooted principle from which we are not prepared to depart. The failure of the Government . . . to recognise this will lead to mass industrial action.

Following the National Conference in July 1971, the NUM's wage demands were spelt out clearly; equally apparent was the refusal of the NCB, directed by the government's incomes policy, to give serious consideration to them. This impasse prompted the NEC to introduce an overtime ban from 1 November 1971 and to arrange a strike ballot. The overtime ban worked effectively in south Wales, reducing total output by around 15 per cent during its first week.[31] More importantly, it made miners conscious of their low rates of basic pay and prompted them to look to strike action if the ban did not produce the desired results.

[31] EC, 9 November 1971.

The overtime ban sharpened the resolve of NUM members to obtain a better deal and consequently they voted for national strike action, to begin on 9 January 1972. Across Britain there was a 58.8 per cent majority; in south Wales, 65.5 per cent voted in favour.[32] Both the NCB and the government were surprised at this, since they had expected Gormley's influence to dampen militancy. In fact, all Areas supported the strike fully once it was underway. Nevertheless, the press was convinced that the miners would lose. The *Daily Mail*, for example, claimed that 'There's plenty of coal in stock . . . A fight to the bitter finish would . . . end in a defeat for the miners as abject as their last official strike in 1926.'[33]

These over-confident predictions failed to appreciate the significance of the wages issue for the NUM. In one respect, the miners' wish to see full NPLA parity by the end of 1971 explains their sense of urgency. As one lodge secretary later recalled, 'There is no doubt that parity in '71 was one thing . . . We were afraid we wouldn't get there, very much afraid. I believe quite sincerely that unless that pressure was on we *wouldn't* have had parity in '71.'[34] Furthermore, national wage parity was itself a powerful factor in uniting the Areas into a coherent force. As George Rees later commented, 'if it wasn't for the [NPLA] . . . we wouldn't have had the national strikes of '72 and '74 . . . [I]t was the [NPLA] . . . that brought everyone together . . . And *that* was the main reason why we were successful.'[35]

THE 1972 STRIKE

The 1972 miners' strike was their first national stoppage since 1926. It occurred at a time when the Heath government was determined to force the unions into submission, having defeated the Post Office workers and the electricity workers in 1971. The NUM was convinced of the justice of its case. At the start of 1972, the basic weekly wages for surfacemen and underground workers were £18 and £19 (approximately £16 net pay), but the government's official subsistence level was also £18 a week. Emlyn Williams expressed the

---

[32] *WM*, 3 December 1971.
[33] Quoted in V. L. Allen, *The Militancy of British Miners* (Shipley: 1981), p. 207.
[34] SWML interview with Berwyn Howells (AUD/21).
[35] Interview with George Rees, 8 December 2003.

point concisely: '[T]his is a strike for a decent living wage . . . Today [the miner] . . . is well down the wages league. As his income has dropped in relation to other workers, the miner has more than doubled productivity in South Wales.'[36] The enthusiasm with which the south Wales rank and file – particularly the younger miners – responded to the strike call impressed both lodge activists and Area leaders. As the Area vice-president at the time later put it, 'The miners were of the view they were in the gutter and they intended to come out of it.'[37]

The miners' main advantage in the 1972 strike was the scale and unanimity of their action. This provided the necessary critical mass and also enabled the left-wing Areas to engage in successful militant activity. In south Wales, the detail of picket organisation was carried out by district-level committees, subject to overall control from the Area office. At Area level, Emlyn Williams and the miners' agents allocated picketing duties to the lodges, on the basis of information gathered by Dai Francis. The scale of the operation was impressive, with south Wales miners picketing targets in, for example, Didcot, Aberystwyth, Basingstoke and Southampton.[38] This task was made easier by the flying picket, a new tactic made possible by increasing levels of car ownership. Mass picketing was another effective means by which the miners were able to garner support for their cause.

Once the strike was underway, a central priority was to prevent unauthorised movement of coal. For the south Wales miners, this involved monitoring and picketing docks as far afield as Plymouth. The key to success here was support from TGWU dockers. One of the most notable victories was achieved in persuading Cardiff dockers not to unload two coal ships.[39] Lodges also persuaded local coal merchants to make only essential deliveries, to schools, hospitals and old people's homes. As a result of this solidarity, the miners soon controlled all coal movement in south Wales. Ironically, for those on picketing duty, this success meant that the day-to-day reality of the strike could be 'really boring'. As one Blaenant worker later commented, 'In south Wales, once somebody said they were on strike,

[36] *WM*, 11 January 1972.
[37] Emlyn Williams SWML interview.
[38] Dai Francis SWML interview; EC, 17 January 1972.
[39] *WM*, 14 January, 18 February 1972.

nothing moved . . . You'd do your turn at picketing – [but] what's to picket? Nobody would move anything.'[40]

Having secured control of the movement of coal, on 13 January picketing operations were expanded to include the south Wales power stations, the steelworks, and all other major coal users. Miners kept up twenty-four hour surveillance of power stations in the coalfield and also in the west of England. An important factor was the secondary action by the NUR and ASLEF in preventing the transport of coal and oil supplies. Round-the-clock picketing began at south Wales steelworks on 18 January and was soon having an effect on output. At Port Talbot, Ffaldau lodge was able to persuade steelworkers to stop all coal movement within three days of picketing.[41]

The NUM success in 1972 was due almost entirely to the physical solidarity of other trade unionists. This level of support meant that miners often found that they only needed token pickets. South Wales dockers agreed to 'black' coal imports and in some cases refused to handle coal even before the appearance of NUM pickets. Lorry and train drivers did not cross picket lines, shutting off supplies to the power stations. Across south Wales, from Llanwern steelworks to Carmarthen Bay power station, miners found that they were well received by the workers whom they were picketing. At Pembrey power station, a NUM 'mole' telephoned the local lodges to warn them of any imminent attempts to deliver oil.[42] As the Oakdale lodge chairman later observed, 'In essence, it wasn't the miners who won the [1972 and 1974] strikes; it was the support from the other trade unionists in the country'.[43]

Trade union solidarity generally made picket-line confrontations unnecessary; even the south Wales NCB praised the orderliness of Welsh pickets. Despite this, a few flashpoints did occur. In south Wales, most disturbances involved COSA, the NUM's white-collar section. On 15 January, COSA joined the strike and picketed their fellow office workers who were members of CAWU (the clerical workers' union). CAWU had promised to respect picket lines but did not uniformly do so. NUM members had some success in picketing

[40]   Interview with Phil Bowen, 26 March 2004.
[41]   *WM*, 13, 19, 25 January 1972; *The Miner*, 7 February 1972; *Area President's Address by Glyn Williams* (1972), p. 8; Berwyn Howells SWML interview.
[42]   Interview with Howard Jones, 10 February 2004.
[43]   Interview with Dan Canniff, 17 February 2004.

CAWU members at the NCB offices at Cardiff, Ystrad Mynach, Tondu and Pontarddulais, until instructed by the EC to desist on 26 January. Some clerks were still being turned away the following week, however. Similarly, at Penrhiwceiber pit, tensions culminated in a confrontation between 300 pickets and police on 4 February over the prevention of NACODS work. This led to the officials' union deciding that its members should not work for the duration of the strike.[44]

Safety work was a key area where rank-and-file activism overrode NEC instructions. Initially, the union advised its members to continue safety work and to allow NACODS to do likewise. A few days into the strike, however, men at Garw, Ffaldau, Caerau, St John's and Cwmgwili defied this advice. By the end of January, ten south Wales pits were completely without cover. On 16 February, an Area conference called for a complete removal of safety cover in the coalfield and for a national conference to discuss taking similar steps. Despite this, the Area officials pressed for the maintenance of safety operations. However, cover was not always as essential as was claimed; Lawrence Daly said that he thought the NCB was 'grossly exaggerating' the problem.[45] At Penrhiwceiber, for instance, safety men were withdrawn and the Board subsequently told Glyn Williams that the pit would flood. He informed Mike Griffin (the lodge secretary) that he intended to ask the men to resume safety work to save the pit, only to be informed that the colliery was not at risk and that the whole 'scare' was an NCB ruse.[46]

Extensive support from the general public, particularly in south Wales, was a significant bonus for the miners during the 1972 strike. The Area leadership was keen to build on this: around half a million leaflets were printed and distributed as far afield as Swindon, while NUM delegations addressed factory meetings to publicise their case. In the valleys, some shopkeepers offered food to miners to help them through the strike period. In early February, Gelligaer Urban District Council was the first Welsh local authority to launch its own miners' relief fund and to send a message of support to the Area head-quarters.[47] This was partly because they were seen to be leading the fight against restrictive government policies and also due to the

[44] *WM*, 13 January–5 February 1972 passim.
[45] *WM*, 10, 27, 28 January 1972.
[46] SWML interview with Glyn Williams (AUD/113).
[47] *WM*, 9 February 1972; *The Miner*, 7 February 1972.

miners' willingness to ensure the continued distribution of coal where it was urgently needed. A further example of the strong links between the Area and local communities was in Glynneath, where miners spent their mornings during the strike chopping firewood to give it free to pensioners and families without coal.[48] Building on this level of public backing, the south Wales miners took part in several highly successful rallies during the strike. On 27 January, over 15,000 miners and their families marched through Cardiff and attended a rally addressed by Lawrence Daly. The Area was also well represented at a demonstration in London in early February and at a lobby of parliament later that month.

Across Britain, the strike's defining moment was the 'battle of Saltley Gates'. Picketing of the Saltley Marsh coke depot, located on the outskirts of Birmingham, to prevent movement of its coke supplies had begun on 5 February. Events reached a climax on 10 February, when 10,000 workers from Birmingham joined the 2,000 miners – including a contingent of 200 south Wales men – picketing and closing the Saltley gates.[49] This was an important victory: when it was announced at an NEC meeting, all the left-wingers present stood up and cheered. Despite this, Glyn Williams felt that the event's powerful symbolism was not matched by its actual strategic significance.[50]

Following the success at Saltley, it was apparent that the miners had gained the upper hand. An even more telling indicator was the onset of an electricity shortage, with the government announcing a state of emergency on 9 February. Two days later, a three-day week for industry was introduced, while power cuts began throughout Britain. The NEC, backed by a decision at an Area conference on 16 February, felt sufficiently confident to reject an improved wage offer from the Board. With the Heath government on the defensive, a Court of Inquiry, led by Lord Wilberforce, was set up to examine the miners' case. This heard evidence on 15 and 16 February and its report, published several days later, stated that: 'The British coal mining industry is in some ways unique . . . [A] serious fall has occurred in the relative pay position . . . [and] it is unreasonable to expect miners' wages to be held down.'[51] The Wilberforce Report

[48]   Interview with Harry Samuel, 20 January 2004; *WM*, 3 February 1972.

[49]   *The Times*, 10, 11 February 1972; Francis and Smith, *The Fed*, p. 474; Ralph Darlington and Dave Lyddon, *Glorious Summer: Class Struggle in Britain, 1972* (London, 2001), pp. 56–62.

[50]   Dai Francis and Glyn Williams (AUD/258) SWML interviews.

[51]   Quoted in *The Times*, 19 February 1972.

recommended substantial wage increases for mineworkers: an extra £5 a week for surfacemen, £6 for underground daywagemen and £4.50 for NPLA workers. The initial reaction to the proposals in south Wales was mixed. After negotiation on the details, however, the NEC agreed to the deal, which was seen as being a favourable one. A South Wales conference on 21 February supported this recommendation. On 23 February a national ballot voted over-whelmingly for a return to work, after a strike of seven weeks. Although a minority of miners argued that the settlement was inadequate, South Wales as a whole voted strongly for acceptance of the proposals.[52]

The miners' victorious struggle in 1972 sent shock waves through British political and economic life.[53] Cliff True (Fernhill lodge) told Area delegates: 'We have just written some glorious pages in the history of the miners. Greater perhaps than anything that has happened in the last 50 years . . . This is not only the biggest victory in respect of wages, but it is for all the working class.'[54] Speaking at the Area annual conference in May 1972, Glyn Williams called for Heath to be 'driven from office' and replaced by a Labour government committed to nationalising other important industries. Furthermore, the strike demolished one of the biggest myths of contemporary economics by proving that Britain still depended on coal for its electricity. Within the NUM itself, the strike's success consolidated the rising influence of the Left. Less apparent, though no less significant, was the fact that union leaders schooled in the lessons of the defeats of the 1920s and 1930s – men such as Glyn Williams, Dai Francis and Ben Morris (the Area chief administrative officer) – came to realise that a clash with the government did not lead inevitably to defeat.[55] A younger generation drew more militant conclusions. For Arthur Scargill, the Yorkshire Area president, 'We took the view that we were in a class war . . . We were out to defeat Heath.'[56]

[52] *WM*, 19, 26 February 1972.

[53] For a variety of appraisals of the significance of the 1972 strike, see Eric Wigham, *Strikes and the Government, 1893–1974* (London: 1976), Darlington and Lyddon, *Glorious Summer*, and Stuart Ball and Anthony Seldon (eds), *The Heath Government, 1970–74: A Reappraisal* (London: 1996).

[54] ASC, 21 February 1972.

[55] Glyn Williams (AUD/258), Ben Morris (AUD/22) and Haydn Matthews SWML interviews.

[56] Arthur Scargill, 'The New Unionism', *New Left Review*, 92 (1975), 13.

In the coal industry, the strike ironically opened up the prospect of enhanced stability and brighter prospects. The key factor was the raising of miners' morale: the strike showed the continuing centrality of coal and brought about wage increases which made it an industry worth working in. The combined effect of these changes reversed the manpower drift which had afflicted the industry since the late 1950s. Heightened workforce morale had other, more unexpected side-effects – such as increased output and improved attendance levels.[57]

TRADE UNION DEVELOPMENTS IN THE EARLY 1970s

Localised disputes remained an intermittent feature of working life for south Wales mineworkers in the early 1970s. Nevertheless, these disturbances became markedly less disruptive in the coalfield in this period: total annual tonnage lost in south Wales owing to disputes fell from 209,000 tons in 1969–70 to 94,000 tons in 1972–3.[58] This reduction did not reflect a decline in the willingness of the South Wales NUM to struggle but rather a trend towards concentration of industrial action in national disputes which had the potential to effect significant improvements in miners' wages and conditions.

The formation of the Wales Trade Union Council in 1973 was a further example of this greater unity. The Area had made sporadic calls for the establishment of a Wales-level TUC structure since 1966 but the project had always foundered on the lack of enthusiasm from other unions. However, the 1972 strike had illustrated the necessity of a WTUC, since solidarity in Wales during the dispute was hampered by the TUC's archaic regional structure. In October 1972, the TGWU Wales Region agreed to the principle of a Welsh TUC and invited the EC to begin discussions on this subject.[59] These unions were the driving forces in establishing the WTUC. After some initial problems, the WTUC was formed in 1973–4. Dai Francis was elected chairman at the inaugural conference in April 1974, a reflection of the continuing importance of the miners in the Welsh labour movement.

---

[57] *WM: Growth Of A Nation, Pt.2*, 20 June 1972.

[58] David Ingli Gidwell, 'Philosophy and Geology in Conflict: The Evolution of a Wages Structure in the South Wales Coalfield, 1926–1974', *Llafur*, 1/4 (1975), 204.

[59] EC, 10 October 1972.

Inter-union solidarity was once again to the fore with the Area's participation in the TUC's one-day May Day strike against the government's pay policy in 1973. This strike was official TUC policy; consequently, Gormley caused uproar by suggesting that the NUM would not take part, owing to the recent ballot acceptance of a modest pay rise. Glyn Williams said he was 'amazed' at the idea that the miners would not follow TUC policy, whilst the Area office was inundated with telegrams and phone calls from lodges protesting at non-participation.[60] At an Area conference in April 1973, the call for a May Day strike was backed overwhelmingly. As it turned out, the Area was the most enthusiastic participant in the one-day strike in Wales, with all fifty of the coalfield's pits shut and all 34,000 mine-workers out on strike. Across Britain, about 1.6 million workers struck – including 125,000 from Wales, or one in seven of the working population. In south Wales, the biggest demonstration was a march of 6,000 workers (mainly miners) through Cardiff.[61]

MINERS AND COMMUNITY IN THE SOUTH WALES COALFIELD

The struggle by the south Wales miners against the policies of the Heath government reflected a recurrent theme in their history, namely, their ready involvement in the life of valleys communities and their willingness to lead broad campaigns on their behalf. The historical contribution of the south Wales miners to their communities was undeniably immense, both in terms of physical infrastructure (welfare halls, libraries, sporting facilities) and traditions of culture and self-education. This participation in community life remained a feature of the miners in the later twentieth century. Brynlliw lodge, for instance, organised an annual pantomime outing for miners' children to Swansea's Grand Theatre, delivered Christmas hampers to all retired members and arranged an annual day-trip to Tenby, in addition to paying regular contributions to local charities and organisations – and it was by no means unique.[62] In the Beddau area, the local lodge organised jazz and brass bands, pigeon clubs, darts teams, rugby and football clubs in the community,

---

[60]   EC, 10 April 1973.
[61]   *WM*, 2 May 1973.
[62]   Interviews with Eric Davies (30 January 2004) and Terry Thomas (16 February 2004).

amongst other social activities. As a Cwm lodge official later observed, 'In every community where there was a pit there was an active lodge. And . . . every part of community life involved the NUM lodge . . . The NUM lodge *was* the community.'[63]

This affinity of lodge and community often manifested itself in the Area assuming a central campaigning role on local issues not directly connected to the coal industry. The early 1970s saw the miners participate in numerous struggles: for example, Merthyr Borough Council's opposition to school milk cuts, Bedwas and Machen UDC's opposition to the Housing Finance Act, protests against the Hirwaun gas storage tanks, and the campaign against the closure of DHSS buildings in the Garw valley. Less dramatic – but no less indicative of this symbiotic relationship – was the Area's criticism of the inadequacies of arrangements to enable miners to buy their NCB-owned homes, and the call at its 1973 conference for a major house-building programme to alleviate the shortage of affordable accommodation.[64]

EDUCATION

The year 1973 saw South Wales celebrate the seventy-fifth anniversary of the formation of the SWMF. One of the main ways in which the Area leadership sought to consolidate some of the cultural gains made by the miners was through the opening of the South Wales Miners' Library, in October 1973. Established as a part of University College, Swansea, and continuing to operate to the present day, the Library was a miners' forum for adult education and an archive for a wealth of lodge records and books from institute libraries that would otherwise have been destroyed once their respective pits closed. As *The Miner* reported the following month, 'The library is intended to help forge closer links between the University and the South Wales community as well as being a testimony to a generation of miners fervently committed to improving the standards of working class education.'[65]

Another important landmark in the educational work of the South Wales NUM was the re-establishment of its education courses,

---

63   Interview with Billy Liddon, 1 April 2004.
64   EC and Area minutes, 1970–4 passim.
65   'South Wales Miners' Library opens', in *The Miner*, November 1973.

to coincide with the opening of the Library. These courses operated on an extra-mural basis, with the Board giving men paid leave to attend them. Miners who took part later recalled that they provided useful information on industrial relations, economics, mining law, safety issues and the Area's history, as well as enabling men to become more effective union representatives. Not surprisingly, the courses had a strong political slant. Hywel Francis, then a lecturer at the University College of Swansea, was a central figure in establishing and running them; one lodge official later remarked that '[w]e used to call it, facetiously, they were "Hywel's Marxist courses". Hywel didn't like it [being called that], mind! . . . But they were very good courses.' In the view of another miner, 'it did galvanise a lot of young people in terms of education . . . [and] trade union activities . . . [T]his radical tendency was *always* there . . . [but the education scheme] helped to sharpen that strong radical tendency in the Welsh miners.'[66] One indicator of the scheme's success was that the vast majority of those who attended went on to become leading figures in either the Area or their own lodges.

THE CHANGING OF THE GUARD

The vigorous struggle by the NUM in the early 1970s was reflected in a significant degree of change in lodge committee personnel across the south Wales coalfield. Eric Davies, a Brynlliw lodge official, later commented:

> In the Seventies, a lot of young people came back into the industry. And so, there was . . . a lot of *young officials*, in lodges . . . [T]here was that radicalism there. It was a tradition that young people had now taken up . . . [I]f you look at some of the lodges around about 1970-ish, who were the leading lights – they were all fairly young people . . . [T]here was a lot of younger people coming through. Tyrone O'Sullivan, for example. There was people like Dane Hartwell, people like myself, Terry Thomas, Des Dutfield . . . [T]here was people like Ivor England in Maerdy, Arfon Evans. You can go across the coalfield and you can see the young element that was . . . *revitalising* the Union in terms of pushing forward.[67]

---

[66]   Quotations taken from (respectively) interviews with Dane Hartwell (10 December 2003) and Eric Davies.

[67]   Eric Davies interview.

Abernant colliery: one of the NCB's 'super pits' of the 1960s

Pit closures in the 1960s: protest against the closure of Rhigos colliery

NUM (South Wales Area) Executive Council and Officials, 1972: (back row) E. Cooper, G. Mann, E. John, A. Haywood, G. Pritchard, D. C. Davies (middle row) D. Hayward, T. Walker, V. Court, I. Matthews, E. Jenkins, G. Rees, H. Matthews, E. Hughes (front row) B. Jenkins, E. Williams (Vice-President), D. Francis (General Secretary), G. Williams (President), B. Morris, W. H. Thomas, L. Rogers

General view of Penallta colliery from the baths, with the afternoon shift waiting to descend

Picketing outside Port Talbot steelworks, 3 April 1984

'The Battle of Orgreave', 18 June 1984

Early morning picket, Celynen South colliery, 6 November 1984

Distributing food packages, Maerdy Miners' Institute, February 1985

Abernant colliery: one of the NCB's 'super pits' of the 1960s

Pit closures in the 1960s: protest against the closure of Rhigos colliery

NUM (South Wales Area) Executive Council and Officials, 1972: (back row) E. Cooper, G. Mann, E. John, A. Haywood, G. Pritchard, D. C. Davies (middle row) D. Hayward, T. Walker, V. Court, I. Matthews, E. Jenkins, G. Rees, H. Matthews, E. Hughes (front row) B. Jenkins, E. Williams (Vice-President), D. Francis (General Secretary), G. Williams (President), B. Morris, W. H. Thomas, L. Rogers

General view of Penallta colliery from the baths, with the afternoon shift waiting to descend

Picketing outside Port Talbot steelworks, 3 April 1984

'The Battle of Orgreave', 18 June 1984

Early morning picket, Celynen South colliery, 6 November 1984

Distributing food packages, Maerdy Miners' Institute, February 1985

Among the Area's leadership, the clearest manifestation of this revitalised radicalism was the coalescence of the official hierarchy and the unofficial movement, with militants being elected to most of the senior positions in the South Wales NUM. One of the four new members voted onto the executive in late 1971 was Haydn Matthews, a prominent activist from Maerdy. Leading members of the unofficial movement who were already EC members extended their influence, with Don Hayward becoming Area chief administrative officer in November 1972 and Emlyn Jenkins miners' agent for the Rhondda, Aberdare and Merthyr district in October 1974. Emlyn Williams was elected unopposed as president of the south Wales miners in October 1973 – there had not been a walkover since William Abraham (Mabon) became SWMF president in 1898. Ron Saint, one of the leaders of the unofficial strikes of 1969 and 1970, stood successfully for a seat on the council in January 1973, which he explained on the grounds that the Area leadership was now advocating militant policies.[68] The election of George Rees as general secretary in January 1976 completed the process. By then, three out of the four Area officials, together with a sizeable minority on the EC, had been active members of the unofficial movement. Their success was a clear indication of the rising left-wing influence among the union's grassroots. The most significant effect of this was that the South Wales leadership showed an increased assertiveness on behalf of their members' rights. At the same time, however, it began the process of absorption of the unofficial movement in the official structure of the union, thereby limiting its room for manoeuvre in certain respects.

At the same time as this process of radicalisation was unfolding across the coalfield, the industry's increased mechanisation was exerting a different kind of influence on the balance of power in the Area. In 1957, technical craftsmen (primarily electricians and fitters) had comprised 6 per cent of the total workforce; by 1981 this figure had increased to 20 per cent.[69] Consequently, craftsmen came to assume a more central NUM role. Before the onset of mechanisation, it was practically unprecedented for them to be lodge secretaries or chairmen, offices traditionally dominated by faceworkers. By the

[68] AAC, 1973.
[69] Roy Church, 'Employers, trade unions and the state, 1889–1987: the origins and decline of tripartism in the British Coal Industry', in Gerald D. Feldman and Klaus Tenfelde (eds), *Workers, Owners and Politics in Coal Mining* (Oxford: 1990), p. 64.

early 1970s, however, craftsmen were leaders in many lodge committees. The career of George Rees is an example: in 1958, he was the first craftsman to be become a lodge secretary in south Wales and subsequently was the first craftsman to become Area general secretary.

THE COUNTDOWN TO 1974

The period 1972–3 was an unsettling one for miners. The gains won at the Wilberforce inquiry proved to be transitory, while the government continued to struggle with Britain's economic problems. Even union moderates felt aggrieved at the inadequacy of miners' incomes. By April 1973, the average miner earned only 88 per cent of the average manufacturing wage, compared with 93 per cent when the Wilberforce Report was published, in February 1972.[70] As NUM leaders were well aware, high wages were necessary to boost recruitment in order to fulfil the expanded tasks set for the industry. At the 1972 Area conference, delegates called unanimously for wage increases of £7 a week for underground and surface daywagemen and men on Grades B and C of the Third Wages Structure, and £5 per week for NPLA workers and men on Grade A of the Third Wages Structure. Emlyn Williams warned that if this demand were not met, the south Wales miners would expect the NEC to call for strike action in 1973. This resolution was subsequently adopted at the National Conference that year, making the official NUM position a call for weekly minima of £40 NPLA, £32 underground and £30 for surface.[71]

During 1973, South Wales was at the forefront of attempts to ensure that the miners' hard-won gains were not lost. In January and February 1973, many lodges wrote to the EC demanding the full implementation of the NUM's wage proposals. An Area conference on 20 February called for national strike action and in the following month the Area leadership organised a lobby of the TUC in support of the wage claim. In March, the NEC's decision to ballot the membership on industrial action was followed in south Wales by a series of meetings across the coalfield in support of the NUM's

---

[70]   Michael P. Jackson, *The Price of Coal* (London: 1974), p. 157.
[71]   ASC, 20 December 1972.

official wage policy. Despite this campaigning, the national ballot rejected the strike call. Nevertheless, the 1973 Area conference called for weekly rates of £50 NPLA, £43 underground and £34 for surface, backed by the threat of industrial action. Speaking in support of this, Emlyn Williams pointed out the inherent politicisation of negotiations as a result of Heath's incomes policy: 'basically this claim is a reasonable one, but in order to obtain this figure we have to enter conflict with this Government'. Although in June 1973 several lodges wanted to campaign on the £50 NPLA claim, the Area endorsed the national decision to call for wages of £45 NPLA, £40 underground and £35 for surface.[72] In October, frustration at the lack of progress in negotiations led the south Wales miners to call for an overtime ban.[73] The NEC rejected unanimously the NCB's wage offer of a 7 per cent increase, and on 26 October 1973, a National Conference decided on an overtime ban from 12 November.

The overtime ban soon made itself felt; the day after its introduction, coal rationing was introduced for hundreds of households in south Wales. In the run-up to the ban, Glyn Williams stated that '[i]t may well be that we could lose public sympathy this time, but . . . we have an energy crisis on our hands and to get more coal the coal board must pay wages which attract men back to the pits'. This was a pertinent point, since recruitment to the industry was still not keeping pace with the gradual decline in manpower levels.[74] In January 1974, Dai Francis told the EC that the overtime ban had cut the coalfield's output by 49 per cent, an indication of the vital role played by overtime in the production process. Despite this, the introduction of a three-day working week and concentration by the government on maintaining maximum output from oil-fired power stations lessened the effectiveness of the ban. Consequently, the Area leadership called for an intensification of the overtime ban and arranged a conference to discuss the calls from some of the more radical lodges for strike action.[75]

During the overtime ban, the South Wales leadership strove to obtain the maximum rank-and-file support for the struggle against the NCB and the government. Rallies throughout the coalfield in November 1973 were strongly in favour of lobbying the NEC in

[72] EC, 19 June 1973; ASC, 8 August 1973.
[73] ASC, 18 October 1973.
[74] WM, 2 November 1973.
[75] EC, 22 January 1974; WM, 10, 23 January 1974.

support of the wage claim, while a mass meeting of trade unionists in Cardiff expressed solidarity with the miners' struggle. Building on this, by early January 1974 250,000 leaflets explaining the NUM's case had been issued to the general public by the Area. The miners also enlisted the aid of the south Wales Labour MPs, who agreed to speak out in support of the wage claim.[76] In January 1974, mass meetings were held in every district in the coalfield, while the NCB's modest pay offer of an extra 40p–70p a week for mineworkers was dismissed by Emlyn Williams as 'not even worth commenting on'.[77] Despite inevitable NCB warnings that any strike would threaten some collieries with flooding, the south Wales miners reacted enthusiastically to the NEC's decision in late January to hold a national ballot. As in 1972, the overtime ban concentrated miners' attention on the inadequacy of their basic wage, and in the ballot there was an 81 per cent vote for a strike. South Wales was the most enthusiastic for industrial action, with 93.15 per cent in favour.[78]

The run-up to the strike saw the government raising the stakes, with Heath calling a general election in early February 1974, to be held three weeks later, under the slogan 'Who governs?' The NUM was under some pressure not to strike during an election but the NEC decided to persist, a viewpoint with which an Area conference on 7 February concurred. The same conference discussed picketing arrangements, and plans were also drawn up to ensure that the CEGB did not stockpile coal before the stoppage. The days immediately preceding the strike saw an intensification of unofficial action, as miners grew impatient at the delay. In early February, the coalfield was only operating on 30 per cent of total output due to the numerous unofficial walk-outs.[79] Predictably enough, there were attempts by the conservative media and business organisations to discredit the South Wales NUM: for example, there were unfounded allegations of ballot-rigging in the Swansea district and a 'Red scare' by right-wing business organisations which branded the Area's leaders as dangerous extremists. Leaders from other unions rallied to the Area officials' defence, while Lance Rogers (the Rhymney Valley district miners' agent) said:

---

[76] EC, 20 November 1973, 2, 7 January 1974.
[77] WM, 3 January 1974.
[78] The Times, 5 February 1974.
[79] WM, 29 January, 9 February 1974.

I speak for all South Wales miners in defending the integrity and motives of both Dai Francis and Emlyn Williams in the face of the attempt . . . to bring them into disrepute. Thank God the miners have leaders, Marxist by training and understanding, who have led our cause and who are committed to restoring the miners to their proper place in society.[80]

The 1974 strike

The second national NUM strike in two years began on 9 February 1974 and lasted four weeks. Having refused to compromise its pay restraint policy, the government announced a state of emergency and a three-day week for industry, which some miners saw as unnecessarily provocative. For Allen, Heath's actions were the key factor in politicising this strike:

> The Government [in 1974] was in an untenable position. It intervened in the running of the economy on a large scale and in such a way as to touch the subsistence interests of workers at every important point so that trade unions could not take up even marginal matters concerning wages, hours of work and working conditions without offending Government policy. Yet whenever this happened the Government cried "constitutional crisis".[81]

The whole exercise was a calculated political risk for Heath; it backfired because he misread the mood of the population.

The miners' strike during a general election campaign inevitably meant that it would be somewhat different from its predecessor in 1972. The most obvious effect was the campaigning by the South Wales NUM in support of Labour candidates; in return, Labour MPs addressed miners' meetings across the coalfield. Men from the Rhymney district also canvassed on behalf of Tony Benn in his Bristol constituency. For all the solid support given to Labour by the south Wales miners, this election provides insight into the complex relationship between the two, as reflected in the experience of Charlie Blewett, the Labour candidate in Cardiff North West.[82] He would be the last in a long line of 'miners' candidates' to stand in a parliamentary election in south Wales. His lack of success in 1974 was not due to a lack of campaigning by fellow miners but rather

---

[80] *WM*, 31 January, 2, 5 February 1974.
[81] Allen, *Militancy of British Miners*, p. 244.
[82] *The Miner*, 22 February, 15 March 1974.

because the NUM no longer wielded sufficient influence in local Labour branches to be able to have their candidate accepted in any of the 'traditional mining seats' in the valleys.

The continuing oil crisis was a significant factor in the 1974 strike. In autumn 1973, OPEC had reduced production and quadrupled oil prices, making the government less able to rely on the main alternative energy source to coal. As one miner later observed, 'I think we won '72 and '74 because of the shortage of oil . . . I know it's not as *simple* as that, right. But there was a shortage of oil at the time – and full advantage was taken of it . . . [O]il played a *major* factor, I think, at the time.'[83] The continuing centrality of coal to Britain's energy requirements meant that voltage reductions and power cuts soon became necessary once the strike was underway.

Although the strike was similar in some respects to the 1972 dispute, Dai Francis believed that in comparison '1974 was a picnic'.[84] There were none of the large-scale confrontations which had been a feature of the 1972 strike, and certainly no repeat of the Saltley Gates episode. Picketing was relatively low-key but the solidarity shown by other trade unions in 1974 meant that there was even less need for more than token NUM picket lines. The NUR, ASLEF and other unions took their own initiative in preventing the movement of coal stocks, while the steelworkers co-operated in reducing their output level to almost a standstill. South Wales miners also monitored docks further afield, in Bristol, Bournemouth and elsewhere, in order to prevent unloading of coal.[85] The completeness of the stoppage prompted a Garw valley lodge secretary to reflect that '[t]he 1974 strike was meek and mild. We had so much public support, I doubt if we picketed *anywhere*', and he commented that this situation was close to becoming a general strike.[86]

In south Wales, as in the other coalfields, miners established their own services in response to social welfare problems caused by the strike. The Area leadership and the lodges provided coal for schools, hospitals and OAP homes and refused to collect payment for coal delivered to needy families. Miners volunteered for hours of unpaid work in moving this coal to ensure that it was done properly. Similarly, the Area took steps to ensure that safety work was

83   Dane Hartwell interview.
84   Quoted in Francis and Smith, *The Fed*, p. 477.
85   *The Miner*, 22 February 1974; EC, 13 February–7 March 1974 passim.
86   Berwyn Howells SWML interview.

undertaken where it was necessary to prevent the flooding of a particular pit; over the course of the strike, this was carried out at Ogilvie, Blaenant, Morlais and Clydach Merthyr.[87]

In 1974, the actions of the Heath government transformed the dispute from an industrial issue into one of central significance in British politics. In this respect, circumstances acted to reinforce the NUM's historical 'vanguard' role by placing them in the forefront of the confrontation. In south Wales, the miners' awareness of the wider needs of the community, along with the active support of the trade union movement, ensured that they received the overwhelming backing of the public. The Area leadership nevertheless remained keen to publicise their case; at the Wales versus France international rugby match, for instance, miners handed out thousands of leaflets to fans. On 26 February, over 5,000 people attended a miners' rally in Cardiff, and with such a strong belief in the certainty of imminent victory that the *Western Mail* said that '[t]he rally could have been a celebration'.

Developments in policing methods in the 1974 strike prefigured the measures that would be used against the miners ten years later. Surveillance and intelligence-gathering were the clearest examples, with South Wales Police Headquarters establishing a special communications room to collate information on miners' pickets.[88] In the run-up to the dispute, Emlyn Williams told the executive that 'there is no doubt that the Police will take a harder line than in the 1972 Strike and will start to arrest some of our members'.[89] The fact that this did not happen in 1974 underlines the importance of trade union solidarity in ensuring the completeness of the miners' victory.

As the strike rumbled on, the NUM's case was submitted to a Pay Board inquiry for consideration. The miners' contention was that faceworkers needed an extra £8.90 a week (a 24.2 per cent increase) merely to restore the position won by the 1972 strike.[90] The investigation of the Pay Board confirmed that miners' wage levels were 8 per cent behind the average manufacturing wage and that they would require at least an extra £5 a week to bring them into line.[91]

[87] *WM*, 16, 19 February 1974; *The Miner*, 22 February 1974.
[88] *WM*, 12 February 1974.
[89] EC, 6 February 1974.
[90] *The Times*, 19 February 1974.
[91] *WM*, 22, 23 February 1974.

The formation of a minority Labour government in early March 1974 led to a speedy resolution of the dispute, with a promise to repeal the Industrial Relations Act and return to free collective bargaining. The NEC accepted the new proposals: £32 per week for surfacemen, £36 for underground workers and £45 for NPLA, with an extra 50p per shift for craftsmen Grade IA elsewhere below ground and on non-mechanised faces, and a number of benefits regarding holidays and shift allowances. A South Wales conference on 8 March agreed with the NEC's decision, despite some minor complaints. A ballot of the Area's membership voted overwhelmingly for acceptance, by 27,075 votes to 1,466.[92] In the immediate aftermath of the strike, Emlyn Williams called it 'a wonderful victory. It has brought down the Tory Government, and has been the means of introducing free collective bargaining.' Speaking at the same conference, Dai Coity Davies (head of the Area's social insurance department) reiterated this point and made a prescient observation:

> This was a brilliant victory both industrially and politically. I want to hold . . . the Government to the promise that has been made – 'The Miners made it possible to elect a Labour Government and the Labour Government will never forget the Miners for this' . . . I would like to sound a note of warning. Coal is important, and we are, at the moment, riding on the crest of a wave, but in less than ten years there will be oil made available and, I say to this Conference – take advantage while the sun shines.

CONSEQUENCES OF THE STRIKES

The strikes of 1972 and 1974 had important consequences for both the NUM and British politics more broadly. Within the union, success increased both left-wing optimism and right-wing caution. Gormley's opinion was that 'success led to an attitude of mind . . . where people, the moment they don't get what they want, think and talk of strike action immediately'; for Scargill, '[h]ere was the living proof that the working class had only to flex its muscles and it could bring governments, employers, society to a total standstill'.[93] As Ashworth notes, the strikes made the miners more radical, for several

---

[92] EC, 12 March 1974; *WM*, 4 March 1974.
[93] Joe Gormley, *Battered Cherub: The Autobiography of Joe Gormley* (London: 1982), p. 118; Scargill, 'The New Unionism', 19.

reasons.[94] First, they were successful when everyone else believed they would fail, with dire results for the industry. This gave strikes a new prestige. Systematic use of mobile mass pickets increased the ability of miners to achieve dramatic results, as at Saltley in 1972. Additionally, the government took the key step of politicising the strikes, particularly by calling an election on the issue in 1974, whereas the main catalysts for action had originally been miners' concerns about wage levels. Henceforth, the idea arose that the miners could now not only win a strike but also topple a government. Within Labour, the miners' victories gave an impetus to increased Leftist demands for more radical policies. However, the Conservatives did not forget their defeats in 1972 and 1974. After their fall from office, the perceived need for an aggressive solution to 'the trade union problem' became an important undercurrent in Tory thinking. As one collier reflected, 'I think the damage was done for later years by certain parties who *directly* believed that we had pulled the government down. It was not our intention to pull the government down – our intention was to increase our wages.'[95]

CONCLUSION

In many respects, the years 1970 to 1974 were one of the most successful periods of the post-1947 history of the coal industry as far as the miners of south Wales were concerned. During the Heath government, coal was reasserted as the most important fuel source for the British economy, as a result both of global increases in oil prices and the practical example of the 1972 and 1974 strikes. The era of mass pit closures of the 1960s gave way to a cautious optimism about the future prospects for coal. Within the NUM, these years saw the realisation of developments that originated in the previous period: a change in personnel and policies in the union as a result of the radicalism caused by discontent at low wages and colliery closures. In south Wales, the 1970 strike was an example of this increasing rank-and-file ferment, which was sufficient to prompt the EC to give official support for unofficial strike action. In the early 1970s, reform of the wage structure in the industry had the effect of

[94] William Ashworth, *The History of the British Coal Industry, Vol. 5: 1946–1982, The Nationalised Industry* (Oxford: 1986), pp. 607–8.

[95] Interview with Glyn Roberts, 19 March 2004.

drawing the Areas closer together, providing the miners with an identifiable focus for their aims. The combined effect of these developments, increased militancy and greater unity, was to open up the prospect of the NUM taking decisive national action in support of clearly-defined goals – something which had never seemed likely in the 1960s. These factors were amplified by the confrontational industrial relations policy of the Heath government, which politicised the miners' dispute and pushed them into reasserting their traditional historical role as the vanguard of the labour movement. In this context, it is not surprising that the history of the south Wales miners in this period should be characterised by struggle and radicalisation.

IV

INTERLUDE: 1974–1979

For the south Wales miners, the years 1974 to 1979 were an interlude between their epic clashes with the Conservative governments of Heath and Thatcher. Continuing trends in the energy industry and the influence of the NUM combined to ensure that this period saw coal consolidate its central position in the British economy. In this context, the union was able to win several reforms, improving conditions in what was still an arduous and dangerous industry. For the miners, this was undoubtedly one of the most favourable periods in the post-war era. Despite this seeming optimism, the period of Labour government in the 1970s saw several paradoxes. After the victorious strike of 1974, rank-and-file radicalism was at its most widespread, yet there was no major clash with either the government or the National Coal Board. In the later 1970s, this militancy saw left-wingers exploit their prominence in the South Wales Area and the NUM as a whole, while at the same time 'moderates' were able to augment their dominance of the upper echelons of the union's structure. Most significantly, this period opened with the miners fresh from having demonstrated their solidarity; yet it also saw developments which had serious implications for the unity of the NUM.

A 'NEW DAWN' FOR COAL?

The south Wales miners were in an optimistic but determined mood in the spring of 1974. Addressing their annual conference, Area president Emlyn Williams spelt out the lessons which the union had learned over the past few years and made several observations about the key issues that were to face them in the later 1970s:

> [I]n this form of society survival depends on the use of strength when you have it. We have been fools for too long. Indeed, we were fools between 1946 and 1956 when we had the strength in the economy but did not use it. We were fools after 1956 when we believed the [NCB] . . . and successive Governments that nothing could be done about it.

He condemned productivity deals as 'a tactic of the Board to destroy
the newly won militancy of the British miners' and reiterated the
need for good wages to attract new recruits to the industry. He
concluded:

> The months that lie ahead will be testing, but as long as we maintain the
> solidarity . . . that we have over the past five years, we will find that our
> demands for a better industry will be met . . . We are entering an era of the
> new miner, and whilst we emphasise our loyalty to a Labour Government,
> we also remind them that our greatest loyalty is to the men we represent.

The election of the new Wilson administration in March 1974
seemed to contemporaries to represent 'a new dawn' for coal.
In 1974, approval was granted for the NCB's *Plan for Coal*: this aimed
to increase annual production from 130 million tons in 1973 to 135–
150 million tons by 1985, together with a £600 million programme
of investment in the industry's infrastructure.[1] The Department of
Energy also inaugurated a Tripartite group, comprising government,
NCB and NUM, to examine the future of coal. In 1977, this
recommended increasing annual production to 170 million tons by
2000, with the prospect of up to thirty new mines being opened.[2] At
that time, the government stated that Britain was on course to
achieve energy self-sufficiency by 1980.[3] The 1974 strike had
established the miners as one of the best-paid sections of the labour
force and the later 1970s saw a decline in absenteeism and increased
recruitment, both factors reflecting the transformation of coal into a
'high-wage high-productivity industry'.[4] Furthermore, Secretary of
State for Energy Tony Benn pressed for greater research into
advanced uses for coal (such as liquefaction and other conversion
technologies) and sought to find out why British coal received almost
no EEC subsidies compared with French and Belgian coal.[5]

In south Wales, the mid-1970s brought a relative calm to the
mining industry. George Rees (Area vice-president, 1974–6, and
thereafter Area general secretary) later commented: 'I think in
the Seventies we thought that there was a future for the industry.

[1]   Hywel Francis and David Smith, *The Fed: A History of the South Wales Miners in the Twentieth Century* (London: 1980), p. 480.
[2]   Gerald Manners, *Coal In Britain: An Uncertain Future* (London: 1981), p. 15.
[3]   *The Times*, 24 January 1977.
[4]   Peter James, *The Future of Coal* (London: 1982), pp. 184–5.
[5]   *WM*, 21 March 1978.

Everybody thought there was a future for it.'[6] The six-fold increase in oil prices between 1970 and 1974 had led to a reappraisal of the importance of coal. Commenting on the discovery of a vast coal bed near Margam in 1977, *The Times* observed that '[m]ining in Wales no longer has the dog-eared and depressed look it had between 1955 and the early 1970s . . . The pendulum is swinging back . . . Now a lot of money is being spent on the search for reserves of coal that will be part of Britain's energy bank in the next century.'[7] Another factor in the renaissance in south Wales was the appointment of Philip Weekes as NCB Area director in 1973, since he took seriously the need for development.

Increased NCB capital expenditure was a defining feature of the mid- to late 1970s, with over £90 million invested in the coalfield.[8] The most important development was the new drift mine opened in March 1978 at Betws, near Ammanford. Similarly, Blaenant, Taff Merthyr, Cynheidre and Aberpergwm all underwent extensive redevelopment in this period. Further indicators of increased investment in south Wales were the opening of the first £500,000 coalface at Merthyr Vale in January 1976, together with the allocation of £6 million for new equipment for 1976 alone.[9] Optimism about the coalfield's future was given an additional boost by NCB decisions in 1977 to consider sinking new collieries at Margam and Ystradgynlais.[10]

During the 1960s, the decline of coal in south Wales had been driven by a 'vicious circle' of shutting what were regarded as uneconomic collieries and the consequent exodus of manpower in search of more secure work. In the years immediately after the 1974 strike, the opposite occurred: men returned to the coal industry in the belief that it would provide a decently-paid, long-term job. As the 1975 Area conference noted, improved wages and conditions were the key to solving the manpower shortage, a point which the NUM had argued throughout the 1960s. This could be seen clearly in the increased Area membership, up from 27,380 in 1974 to 28,879 in 1976.[11]

[6] Interview with George Rees, 8 December 2003.
[7] *The Times*, 11 July 1977.
[8] *WM*, 29 January 1979.
[9] *WM: Economic Review*, 21 January 1976.
[10] *The Times*, 11 July 1977; EC, 11 October 1977.
[11] EC, 13 April 1976, 15 April 1977.

The willingness of the NCB to consider industrial expansion in south Wales in the mid-1970s meant that its aims were more in line with those of the NUM than they had been in the 1960s. At the 1974 Area conference, Emlyn Williams called for greater flexibility for local management and more investment in the industry, in addition to improved wages, conditions and job security for miners. In his annual presidential address in 1977, he highlighted the major projects at Betws and Blaenant as the first steps towards the kind of investment that the union wanted. The traditional industrial relations antagonism was not completely absent, however. Addressing miners' delegates in May 1975, he accused the management of expensive miscalculations regarding technical equipment and materials, costs and said: 'It is time that the method of scrutinising the operations of nationalised industries was improved so that the . . . cover by which managers hide their inefficiency and place it unjustly on the shoulders of working miners can be removed'.[12]

THE MINERS AND INDUSTRIAL DEMOCRACY

Industrial democracy, or workers' control, was an important feature of NUM discourse in the later 1970s, the product of a powerful union thinking optimistically about an industry which seemed assured of a bright future. In interviews conducted with contemporary and recently-retired Area officials about 1980, a recurrent aspiration was for workers to have a greater voice in the running of their industry. As Emlyn Williams pithily expressed it, 'I would rather have seen socialisation than nationalisation'.[13] In many ways, coal-mining was a good candidate for workers' control: the dispersed nature of working underground (with coalfaces in one colliery sometimes several miles apart) was not suited to centralised managerial control structures; the union regularly carried out safety checks, through its own system of inspectors; and lodges took an active role, in conjunction with the management, in assigning tasks to the appropriate personnel. In 1975, the EC called for elected union representation on the NCB's board of directors and also sent representatives to a conference in Chesterfield on industrial democracy in the mines.[14]

[12]   *WM*, 6 May 1975.
[13]   SWML interviews with Emlyn Williams (AUD/33), Glyn Williams (AUD/113) and Dai Francis (AUD/131).
[14]   EC, 1 April, 19 August 1975.

Area conferences in 1975, 1976 and 1980 called for the introduction of democratic structures in the coal industry, while Professor Vic Allen of Leeds University spoke to the 1978 annual conference about industrial democracy. In April 1977, the EC agreed to organise a weekend school on workers' control, while in December of that year Area representatives participated in an NEC-organised forum on the subject, addressed by Tony Benn and Cliff Shepherd (the NCB industrial relations director).

Both the government and the NCB were receptive to the idea of industrial democracy in this period. Ultimately, however, the NUM decided against accepting any such proposals as the Board was prepared to concede.[15] Mike Griffin, a South Wales representative at the forum, expressed this view clearly:

> [The NCB] have always wanted a production committee to set targets. Is that to be the role of the NUM – to sit down with management to increase production? . . . [T]he NCB has failed to fulfil its promise to increase production [and so] we are here discussing how to increase production. If they want production committees, let them say so – don't dress it up in fancy clothes and call it industrial democracy. We have never had power and we have never had anything out of consultation. All we have is all we have fought for.

Des Dutfield (another South Wales delegate) concurred: 'There are no halfway measures. You either have control or you do not have it, and unless and until we have it, the responsibility for running the industry must remain where it is now, and not on the shoulders of the workmen.'[16]

THE PRODUCTIVITY DRIVE

Despite the eventual failure of the movement towards industrial democracy, the mid-1970s saw the NUM willing to co-operate in making the industry a success. George Rees later recalled: '*We* partook in the production drive, something which we'd never, ever done before . . . And we lifted the production levels in south

[15] For more details on this viewpoint, see Arthur Scargill and Peggy Kahn, *The Myth of Workers' Control* (Nottingham: 1980).

[16] *The Miner*, December 1977/January 1978.

Wales in a number of pits to better than they'd *ever* been before.'[17]
As from July 1974, lodges took part in productivity committees
with the management, while in March 1975 the Area agreed to
'teach-ins' aimed at creating '1,000 ton faces' at selected pits.
Further participatory ventures included accepting the Board's new
National Scheme for Training for Work and joint NUM-NCB
initiatives to persuade local councils to choose coal central heating.[18]
Co-operation did not mean unquestioning compliance, however. In
a meeting with the Board in October 1975, the EC expressed
concern that NACODS was not treating the productivity drive with
the same seriousness as the NUM. It also reaffirmed its willingness to
help make the coalfield viable – but saw little point in boosting
output while there were large coal stockpiles throughout the region.[19]

Participation by the south Wales miners in the productivity drive
remained tinged with scepticism. In October 1975, Coedely lodge
complained to the EC that it was not the job of the NUM to get the
men to produce more coal for the same wages. For all the talk of co-
operation, the potential for friction remained. A clear example of
this occurred at Graig Merthyr colliery, where the management
insisted on significant increases in output right up to the day the pit
closed, in June 1978. Not surprisingly, miners' dissatisfaction
eventually filtered through the Area's structure. Speaking at the 1977
conference, Emlyn Williams criticised any attempt to tie unions
to managerial structures by means of 'workers' participation'
schemes, pointing to the Area's disastrous post-war experiences
of co-operation with the NCB. In February 1978, South Wales
temporarily suspended all consultation with the Board in protest at
its interference in their ballot on the incentive bonus scheme.

INDUSTRIAL RELATIONS TRENDS

Despite a residual level of localised friction, the overall trend
in industrial relations in this period was one of relative harmony.
The main reason for this was the existence of national-level wage
agreements and colliery-level consultative committees, both of

---

[17] George Rees interview.
[18] EC, 9 July 1974, 4 March 1975, 24 August 1976; interview with Mike Banwell,
9 March 2004.
[19] EC, 18 November 1975.

which reduced the incidence of disputes. A Blaengwrach miner later recalled:

> I was a lodge official at that time in the Seventies . . . [A]s soon as you saw things not being done correctly, you'd make it *known* to the manager . . . [Y]ou also had, and I think you got to give the Coal Board credit where it's due, they set up these production meetings and safety meetings . . . [S]o there was a much better *dialogue* in the pit, there was a much better system of dealing with disputes. All the years I was lodge secretary, I don't think we had one dispute in my own pit . . . And, I mean, that wasn't *unique*, during that period. Because . . . the structures were set up to deal with the situations . . . I'm not saying it always worked like that . . . [but] you didn't have the pit disputes in the 1970s that you had in the early Sixties.[20]

COLLIERY CLOSURES IN THE 1970s

The contrasting rates of colliery closures was another important indicator that the south Wales coalfield in the later 1970s was not faced with anything like the problems of a decade before. Between 1974 and 1979 there were seven colliery closures; the equivalent figure for 1964–9 was forty-eight. Unlike in the 1960s, in the 1970s the government wished to retain the coal industry at its current size; pits were generally only closed if they had irreparable problems. Consequently, such closures as did occur in the later 1970s were relatively uncontroversial. Beynon, for instance, never re-opened after a major fire in April 1975. Glyntillery, Bargoed and Caerau collieries were closed due to geological difficulties (in December 1975, June 1977 and August 1977, respectively), with their lodges offering little more than token protestations.

The only closure in south Wales which was contested seriously in this period was that of Ogilvie colliery, near Deri. Despite being a high-output colliery with an excellent industrial relations record, Ogilvie was threatened with closure because the Board deemed that too high a proportion of its coal was unsaleable. Following the news in April 1974 that the NCB intended to close the pit, an action committee – comprising the lodge, miners' wives and local residents – was formed to keep it open. The following month, the Area annual conference called on the NEC to support the appeal to save Ogilvie.

[20] Interview with Dane Hartwell, 10 December 2003.

Meanwhile, the action committee organised a 300-strong lobby of parliament and a meeting with Energy Minister Eric Varley. This initiative took the Area leadership by surprise but it nevertheless joined the campaign.[21] Emlyn Williams warned that '[i]f the closure of Ogilvie becomes a reality it will bring dismay and resurrect in the minds of the miners and their families the spectre of pit closures that was a byword when the Labour Government were in office from 1964 to 1970'.[22] In January 1975, the NCB announced that Ogilvie would shut. While the lodge wanted to fight on, the EC accepted the closure reluctantly. The Area president observed that every option to save Ogilvie had been tried apart from strike action, 'and on the basis of past closures we would never get the support of the membership'.[23] Ogilvie shut in April 1975, without the threatened sit-ins and demonstrations. Evan Jones, the lodge secretary, said: 'I saw men of 50 or 55 leaving the pit with tears running down their cheeks . . . [T]o lose a pit . . . is like having a death in the family. It's difficult for outsiders to understand how emotionally involved a man can become.'[24] Ogilvie showed that, even in a relatively stable period, the threat of an uncertain future was never completely absent for the south Wales miners.

THE MINERS AND POPULAR CULTURE IN SOUTH WALES

Throughout the 1970s, the South Wales NUM retained its traditional cultural services to its members. The Miners' Gala and Eisteddfod remained showpiece events. In May 1975, Dai Francis called the Eisteddfod 'the most important cultural event in the country'. The film star Richard Burton thought it sufficiently significant to donate £100 to the Eisteddfod fund and express the wish to attend the 1970 Eisteddfod. The Eisteddfod remained in touch with other developments in Welsh cultural and sporting life: the Welsh contingent of the victorious British Lions rugby team were awarded souvenir miners' lamps at the 1971 Eisteddfod.[25]

The Area Gala also remained popular, with the Galas of 1975 and 1976 being amongst the largest ever organised. The 1976 Gala

[21] *WM*, 8, 9, 14 May 1974; EC, 21 May, 4 June 1974.
[22] *WM: Challenge To A Nation*, 28 June 1974.
[23] EC, 21 January 1975.
[24] *WM*, 11 April 1975.
[25] EC, 24 August 1970, 24 August 1971; AAC, 1975.

commemorated the fiftieth anniversary of the General Strike and featured Tony Benn as guest speaker, in addition to presentations being made to Mervyn Davies and Terry Yorath (captains of the Welsh rugby and football teams) – an example of the synthesis of culture and politics in south Wales mining communities. These occasions were a ready-made forum of political ideas and an array of left-leaning groups was allowed to have stalls there in the later 1970s: from Militant and the CP to the Spanish Solidarity Committee and the Anti-Nazi League.[26]

COMPENSATION, PENSIONS AND EARLY RETIREMENT

The years 1974 to 1979 were a period of progress in many respects for the south Wales miners. Several reforms were introduced to provide more equitable treatment for mineworkers, ranging from compensating those whose health had been affected by working in the industry to redressing inequities in working conditions. One of the most important reforms was the Pneumoconiosis Compensation Scheme, introduced in 1975. This scheme provided a loss of earnings allowance for men forced out of work by pneumoconiosis. Also, even a 1 per cent diagnosis was eligible for a decent lump sum payment, whereas men formerly received only disablement benefit from the DHSS. The Pneumoconiosis Compensation Scheme was not perfect, however. Its biggest anomaly was that miners who had commuted their pensions into (relatively small) lump sums prior to nationalisation were ineligible for it.[27] The 1975 Area conference accepted the Pneumoconiosis Compensation Scheme as a definite step forward, although this did not preclude annual conferences from calling for further improvements to it for the rest of the decade.

The Mineworkers' Pension Scheme was another legislative innovation welcomed by the miners, a superannuation-based scheme introduced in April 1975. In addition to this legislation, the south Wales miners took a broader interest in pensions. Resolutions passed at their 1975 annual conference called for mineworkers' widows to be included within the terms of the Mineworkers' Pension Scheme, as well as for a 'threshold agreement' for all British pensioners, to ensure that their incomes kept up with the cost of living.

[26] EC, 10 June 1975, 25 May 1977, 23 May 1978; AAC, 1976.
[27] *The Miner*, April/May 1975; interview with Viv Williams, 25 February 2004.

The introduction of the Voluntary Early Retirement Scheme (VERS) in 1977 represented the attainment of a long-held aim of the miners. Under this scheme, mineworkers aged between 60 and 65 received a tax-free £500 lump sum and could retire early on an income only marginally less than their previous year's earnings. Despite its popularity amongst those eligible for it, the VERS had ambiguous consequences for the union. On the one hand, the retirement of many senior men facilitated the emergence of a new generation of lodge leaders: men such as Phil Bowen at Blaenant and Ian Isaac at St John's (who were only 30 and 24 when they became lodge chairman and secretary respectively).[28] On the other hand, it was not guaranteed that those who retired would be replaced, so that the VERS created manpower shortage problems that might not otherwise have existed.

The struggle for the VERS was a key NUM priority in the mid-1970s. Demands for it had featured recurrently at Area conferences between 1971 and 1976, before becoming union policy in July 1976. After negotiations with the NEC, the NCB's final offer was for early retirement for those aged 64. An Area conference in November 1976 agreed with the NEC's rejection of this, Emlyn Williams commenting that the fight for early retirement 'is not a campaign, it is more of a crusade'. A ballot in December backed the call for industrial action, with South Wales (where 92 per cent voted for action) in the vanguard. Following this show of defiance, the NCB quickly offered a compromise. The deal which emerged was for early retirement for men aged 62 years as from August 1977, reducing to 60 years as from August 1979; this was accepted by the NUM in January 1977.[29] Despite this agreement, several other matters still concerned the south Wales miners. The key failing of the VERS was its stipulation of twenty years' underground service, which barred around 20 per cent of surfacemen who might otherwise benefit from it. Spurred on by grassroots pressure, in April 1978 the NEC persuaded the NCB to modify the scheme so as to include surface workers.[30] The attainment of the VERS, on essentially the terms of its own choosing, was undoubtedly one of the most significant reforms won by the NUM during this period.

---

[28]   Interviews with Phil Bowen (26 March 2004) and Ian Isaac (2 and 8 April 2004).
[29]   ASC 29 November 1976, 18 January 1977; *The Miner*, January 1977, February/March 1977; EC, 22 December 1976, 1 February 1977; *WM*, 16 December 1976.
[30]   *The Miner*, May/June 1978.

RADICALISM AND SOLIDARITY

The strikes of 1972 and 1974 had re-established the miners in the vanguard of the labour movement, popularising a buoyant radicalism. At the 1974 Area conference, Charlie Blewett (Penallta lodge) observed: 'although [Conference] . . . is quiet this arises because of our confidence . . . The last three years have shown us that power is there when we need it.' A further indication of this was discernible at the following year's annual conference. Here, moderate lodges such as Bargoed and Oakdale moved resolutions on topics ranging from the introduction of industrial democracy to a call for the immediate end to internment without trial in Northern Ireland, while the Penallta delegate urged the desirability of establishing a socialist state in Britain.

This radicalism was mirrored to a certain degree at national level, most notably on the subject of colliery closures. The new outlook was exemplified by the NEC's decision in February 1976 to implement a national overtime ban against the proposed closure of Langwith colliery in Derbyshire. Although the ban soon ended, it was unprecedented for the NEC to consider action to defend one particular colliery. South Wales miners were among the main advocates of the overtime ban.[31] The 1976 National Conference supported unanimously the Area's demand for opposition to pit closures. Moving the resolution, EC member Des Dutfield stated: '[i]n the Fifties and Sixties, when a pit was put on the jeopardy list, it was no use looking to other pits for support – the men were too afraid that they might end up with their pit on the list . . . We must not allow that position to return.' Proof that the NUM national leadership seemed willing to contemplate a more combative policy came in October 1978, when the NEC decided to ballot the membership on industrial action against pit closures.[32]

Trade union solidarity remained a defining feature of the south Wales miners during the later 1970s. The clearest example of this was the strike at the Grunwick film processing factory in London in 1977, over wages and the right to union representation; it was a dispute whose clashes between pickets and police provided a foretaste of events during the miners' strike of 1984–5. In June 1977,

---

[31]   ASC, 13, 26 February 1976; *The Miner*, March/April 1976.
[32]   *The Miner*, July/August 1976, October/November 1978.

the EC and a busload of South Wales pickets (in addition to representatives from other militant Areas) went to London to bolster the picket line. The EC members were 'astounded at the brutality of the police' who 'were acting like fascists', and they agreed to participate in a national day of protest in July 1977 about this.[33] At the request of the Grunwick strike committee, south Wales miners also joined the mass picket in October 1977 and participated in a trade union conference held in November in Pontypridd, which a speaker from the committee attended. There were many other instances of this kind of solidarity. South Wales miners opposed the imprisonment of two building workers, Des Warren and Ricky Tomlinson, and attended several demonstrations in London in 1974 and 1975 to call for their release. Support for the nurses' wage claim in mid-1974 was widespread amongst the miners: the Area leadership urged the NEC and the WTUC to back them and made public statements approving NUPE's stance, while miners at Brynlliw, Morlais and Graig Merthyr staged token strikes in response to an appeal by flying pickets from Morriston Hospital. The Area also gave official backing to NUPE demonstrations against public sector cuts in February 1976 and February 1977. Similarly, in December 1977, an Area conference reaffirmed support for the strike by the FBU and stated that it would ensure that no miners crossed picket lines. The miners also remained deeply concerned about rising unemployment levels: annual conferences in 1975 and 1976 called for employment for all, while south Wales miners also lobbied the Welsh Office in May 1976 and parliament in April 1977.[34]

In keeping with its traditional radicalism, the South Wales NUM retained a keen interest in politics. Its 1975 annual conference carried a resolution to cut arms expenditure by £1 billion, the 1977 conference called for increased investment and public spending, and in 1978 Emlyn Williams proposed the nationalisation of Britain's major financial institutions. Condemnation of cuts in social services and health expenditure imposed by the government and the IMF was a recurrent feature of Area conferences in the later 1970s. The miners supported the creation of a Welsh Assembly and the Area leadership were very active in the ultimately unsuccessful devolution

[33]   EC, 28 June 1977.
[34]   EC and Area minutes, 1974–8 passim; *The Miner*, January/February 1975; *WM*, 24, 25 July 1974, 6 May 1976; *The Times*, 24 July 1974.

campaign in late 1978 and early 1979. In another referendum held in the 1970s, annual conferences in 1974 and 1975 called for a 'no' vote on continuing membership of the EEC. The NUM, with its democratic ethos, was understandably appalled by the rise of the National Front during this period. The EC called for a lobby of an NF rally in Cardiff in June 1976 and the following month the NUM National Conference demanded action against the neo-Nazis. In 1978, the Area affiliated to the Anti-Nazi League and agreed to support the ANL's national carnival. Annual conferences between 1975 and 1977 carried resolutions opposing the government's military 'solution' in Northern Ireland. The South Wales NUM also remained an inveterate supporter of many other left-wing and progressive causes.

EMLYN WILLIAMS

The Area leadership fully reflected this sense of left-wing radicalism among the south Wales miners. This could be seen clearly in the case of Emlyn Williams, who was installed as president in early 1974. His speech to the 1976 annual conference was arguably his finest hour, a syndicalist clarion call with strong echoes of Noah Ablett and A. J. Cook. Defending his demand for £100 per week wages for faceworkers (with appropriate differentials for other grades), he said:

> At some point of time some workers have got to challenge the grossly unequal distribution of wages in British society . . . [and] insist that we are all paid according to what we contribute to the community . . . Why should men who risk their lives through injuries and disease, who work physically hard, who produce a commodity which is essential for British industry, not be paid accordingly? And if the answer is that society cannot afford it, then my reply is that society must be changed so it can afford it.

This uncompromising statement panicked stockbrokers and caused a fall in the exchange rate and the value of the stock exchange, propelling Williams into national prominence with such rapidity that the *Daily Mail*'s report on the conference inadvertently featured a picture of the playwright and actor Emlyn Williams instead.[35]

---

[35] *WM*, 4, 6, 7 May 1976.

During the 1970s and beyond, Emlyn Williams's style was one of 'leading from the front and relying on the dying art of platform oratory'.[36] At the 1978 annual conference, he emphasised that 'we have got to . . . create a new resolve amongst South Wales miners . . . We must campaign until every miner is involved . . . We want an articulate, intelligent, politically-conscious labour force, for that is our only safeguard against being prostituted in the future by money and false promises.'[37]

In addition to his NUM work, Emlyn Williams was also involved in the campaign for the democratisation of the structure of the Labour Party. As the NUM's elected representative on Labour's NEC between 1974 and 1978, he was arguably the most significant Marxist within the party. As a member of the League for Democracy, he advocated the right to elect the Labour Party leader democratically, the right to have re-selection of MPs and the assertion of the authority of conferences as the ultimate decision-making body in the party. One of the key themes of his address to the 1978 annual conference was the need for a democratic overhaul of the Labour Party's internal machinery. In 1980, Emlyn Williams predicted 'the inevitability of true democracy' within Labour.[38]

DECLINING COMMUNIST INFLUENCE AND THE MINERS' FORUM

After Labour, the other main political party in the South Wales NUM was the Communists. However, the post-war decades had seen a waning of CP influence: Will Whitehead, who had resigned in 1966, was the last party member to be Area president. The fortunes of the CP declined further following the retirement of Dai Francis as Area general secretary in 1976. Although his successor, George Rees, was also a Communist, Dai Francis had been a major figure among the south Wales miners. One indication of his personal prestige was his election to the Gorsedd of Bards in August 1974, in recognition of his contribution to Welsh culture through the Miners' Eisteddfod, and his nomination for the post of chancellor of the University of Wales in July 1976.[39] This type of respectability was

---

[36] Hywel Francis, 'Emlyn Williams (1921–1995)', *Llafur*, 7/1 (1996), 5.
[37] AAC, 1978.
[38] Emlyn Williams SWML interview.
[39] EC, 14 August 1974, 13 July 1976.

not without its paradoxes for a party built ostensibly on grassroots militancy. As Gwyn Alf Williams observed, the 'residual prestige [of the CP] . . . was such that, pariahs elsewhere except in Scotland, Communists in south Wales found themselves in the disconcerting predicament of having become almost as respectable as an eisteddfod'.[40] In October 1977, for example, an Area conference discussed the NCB's sacking of four Taff Merthyr men for leading several walkouts, and their links with such 'subversive organisations' as the South Wales New Miners' Charter Movement. Long-standing Labour member Mike Griffin (Penrhiwceiber) observed: 'We have spoken about subversive elements in the past, but these men argue in accordance with their beliefs. Not so long ago the Communist Party members were called subversives, but now the boot is on the other foot.'

At national level, a similar mixture of progress and setback was experienced by the Miners' Forum movement, in which South Wales played a key role. In some respects, the emergence of Yorkshire as a left-wing Area in the early 1970s shifted the political centre of gravity in the NUM. This meant that the Forum's usage of conferences to bring about change in union policy met with a reasonable degree of success. It also provoked much resentment from the right-wing forces which had traditionally dominated the NUM. Consequently, left-right factionalism became prevalent; for example, during the 1978 National Conference, Yorkshire delegates called repeatedly for Gormley's resignation.

A noteworthy failure for union militants was their attempt to enable the leading figure in the Forum – Mick McGahey, the Scottish miners' president – to stand for the NUM national presidency. Gormley was due to retire but hung on until the 1980s, in order to prevent a Communist becoming president; by then (under NUM rules) McGahey was too old to be eligible. All attempts to alter this rule proved unsuccessful. With McGahey thus barred, the NUM Left turned to Arthur Scargill. This development had consequences for the subsequent direction of left-wing strategy in the union. One lodge secretary later recalled:

> When I first went [to Broad Left meetings, in around 1973] . . . I thought it was good. But . . . in the end . . . it became . . . a *listening* place rather than

[40] Gwyn A. Williams, *When Was Wales?* (London: 1985), pp. 271–2.

a talking place . . . [W]hen Arthur came to prominence, it changed it slightly
. . . and then we used to go up and listen to *Arthur* . . . We didn't have that
part to play, then, as it was before.[41]

In the aftermath of the miners' defeat in 1985, Emlyn Williams
reflected bitterly that, with the leftwards shift in the NUM 'balance
of power' in the 1970s, the Broad Left failed to maintain the same
level of strategic thinking which it had employed in the 1960s: 'We
built this Union on strategy – and then when we became the power
in the NUM, we just threw it overboard'.[42]

NEC STRUCTURE AND NUM POLITICS

Any assessment of the strategy of the NUM Left in the 1970s has to
recognise that its actions followed from an approach which sought to
radicalise the union structure and use it as a vehicle for the pursuit
of militant objectives. The intra-NEC factionalism of the later 1970s
was exacerbated by left-wing frustration at the stymieing of the
wishes of the democratic majority of NUM members by the right-
wing's procedural manipulation and dominance of the union upper
echelons. The three interrelated phenomena were: the democratic
deficit in the NEC structure, the power of Gormley, and the role of
patronage and careerism. In this respect, the machinery and
operation of the NEC structure was a significant factor in the
mitigation of NUM militancy at the moment of its greatest potential
influence.

For the south Wales miners, the biggest problem with the NEC
was its unrepresentative structure, owing to the retention of much of
the old MFGB federalism in the NUM's constitution. Their Area,
with a membership of approximately 28,000, had two seats on
the NEC – the same number as Cumberland and North Wales
combined, each of which had only 1,000 members at most.
Consequently, the smaller Areas wielded disproportionate influence
in the NEC, a situation which some thought analogous to the 'rotten
boroughs' in eighteenth-century parliamentary politics. Many of
these Areas were decidedly moderate and uncritical supporters of

---

[41]   Dane Hartwell interview.
[42]   SWML interview with Emlyn Williams (AUD/574).

the Labour leadership.[43] Rule 7 of the union's constitution stated that the NEC should review the situation occasionally with a view to integrating the smaller Areas and to ensure a representative make-up of the NEC; however, its built-in right-wing majority meant that the status quo remained.[44] Even compromise solutions, such as the call for NEC voting to use a card vote system weighted to reflect the actual sizes of the Areas, were rejected on the grounds that they would democratically undermine the power of the moderates.

The key factor in the NEC's conservatism was the national president, Joe Gormley. Ever since the formation of the NUM, the presidency had been held by right-wingers, who kept a tight grip on the union's rules. What was new about Gormley's tenure was that he wielded more power than his predecessors, owing to the centralisation of decision-making processes as a result of the many national-level agreements in place by the 1970s. Another reason was that Lawrence Daly, whom the Miners' Forum had hoped would oppose NEC conservatism, had capitulated, handing over use of his powers to Gormley.[45] Thus armed, Gormley could get the NEC to reject policies decided by National Conferences, supposedly the highest authority within the union, for example, by overturning the decision to oppose the Social Contract in 1974. As Emlyn Williams told the 1976 Area conference, 'There are people in this union who are more concerned with preserving the right-wing control of the NEC than they are with practising democracy.' Gormley was a master of procedural chicanery and also not averse to using his presidential authority to suit his own ends. George Rees, one of the Area's two representatives on the NEC, later commented that 'Joe was a clever man, mind. Cleverer than a cart-full of monkeys.' He gave a vivid example of Gormley's style of chairing meetings:

> Arthur [Scargill], now, was challenging him on procedure. And Arthur was good. You got to hand it to Arthur, I had the greatest admiration for him. And he was challenging Joe on procedure, and me and Emlyn were sitting there, and Emlyn said to me, 'we got Joe this bloody time'. And he started quoting Walter Citrine and he started quoting Wal Hannington [authorities on chairing trade union meetings] . . . You could have heard a pin drop . . .

---

[43] The most obvious exception to this general point was Kent, one of the most left-wing coalfields in Britain.

[44] *The Miner*, May/June 1978; Emlyn Williams (AUD/33) and Dai Francis SWML interviews.

[45] Dai Francis SWML interview; Emlyn Williams SWML interview (AUD/33).

[Gormley] said, 'Arthur, you're right. You're dead right in your interpretation, right as far as Citrine is concerned, and right as far as Wal Hannington. But', he said, 'there's only one difference.' And Arthur said, 'What's that, Joe?' 'I'm the bloody chairman here, not Walter Citrine! Put it to the vote.' And they put it to the vote and we lost![46]

Patronage and careerism were the cement which held together the right-wing dominance of the NUM national leadership. The numerous small Areas, together with larger moderate Areas such as Nottinghamshire, constituted a majority on the NEC, with most of them holding the same political viewpoint as Gormley; the small, moderate Areas depended completely on the president, without whose support they might find themselves absorbed into an arguably more rational and democratic structure. While such a shake-up would not have affected the miners in the smaller Areas significantly, it would have had serious implications for their salaried full-time representatives. The value of these posts to their incumbents was increased further by the NEC decisions in 1974 and 1978 to introduce significant pay rises for Area officials. In September 1978, the South Wales leadership questioned the NEC's award of two wage increases to National and Area officials that year (which Emlyn Williams and George Rees had voted against), stating that the membership would react very badly to it.[47] By the end of the 1970s, the salary of a miners' agent was almost double the wages of an ordinary mineworker – a factor which inevitably created a degree of distance between senior full-time officials and the rank and file. In May 1978, the south Wales miners criticised full-time NUM leaders who took up directorships of private companies in addition to their union work. In the view of one lodge secretary, some national leaders were very 'careerist' and 'looked to their lifestyle rather than looked to championing the needs of their members'.[48]

THE SOCIAL CONTRACT

One of the fiercest controversies in the labour movement between 1974 and 1979 was over the Social Contract, the government's wage

[46] George Rees interview.
[47] EC, 9 July 1974, 12 September 1978.
[48] Ian Isaac interview.

control policy. This issue was posed in a much sharper form than it had been under the Heath administration, since miners were now forced to choose between maintaining the wage levels earned by the 1974 strike and their loyalty to the Labour government. Although the position was never uncontested, South Wales annual conferences voted consistently against the Social Contract. At the 1975 conference, Emlyn Williams was one of the first union leaders to reject the contract. This stance brought the south Wales miners into open conflict with official NEC policy.[49] Towards the end of the decade, this defiance spread within the NUM, with the 1977 and 1978 National Conferences opposing the Social Contract.

In the context of the Social Contract, inflation and the successful strikes of 1972 and 1974, the struggle over wages was a central topic for the south Wales miners in the later 1970s. In 1974, they called for weekly wages of £65 for NPLA, £50 for underground work and £40 for surfacemen. A national ballot in March 1975 accepted the NCB's offer, although the escalation of the cost of living led to a hardening of the miners' stance: the 1975 Area conference demanded rates of £100 NPLA, £85 underground and £80 surface. Although this resolution was carried at the National Conference, Gormley allowed the NEC to overturn it on the basis of adhering to TUC policy, prompting Cliff True (Fernhill) to exclaim: 'How the hell Joe Gormley gets away with this, really amazes me'.[50]

In accordance with its policy, the Area leadership organised meetings throughout the coalfield against the NEC's acceptance of wage controls. Although the south Wales miners rejected the Board's £6 pay offer in August 1975 by 12,161 votes to 10,253, they were outvoted nationally by 60.5 per cent to 39.5 per cent.[51] The following year, the Area conference reaffirmed the call for £100 NPLA rate, with the EC deciding to publish a leaflet in support of it. In the national ballot in June 1976, growing discontent led to a fall in the majority in favour of acceptance to 53.4 per cent, with South Wales one of five Areas to return an overall 'no' vote. At the National Conference the following month, Gormley caused uproar by prohibiting any discussion of wages, on the basis of the recent ballot decision.[52] The frustration felt by many miners was expressed at the

[49]   ASC, 14 August 1975, 17 May 1976.
[50]   ASC, 18 July 1975.
[51]   *The Miner*, September/October 1975.
[52]   EC, 11 May 1976; *The Miner*, June/July 1976, July/August 1976.

1977 National Conference by Area representative Terry Thomas, who reminded delegates that in 1972 Daly had proclaimed that miners would never again accept an incomes policy: 'Well, we are on our knees again. What we won in 1972 and 1974 we have given back with wage restraint.'[53] By 1978, the question had become complicated by the incentive bonus scheme, but the National Conference still called for a basic wage of £110 NPLA (with appropriate rates for other grades), the amount needed to regain the purchasing power levels of March 1975. Although take-home pay had increased between November 1971 and March 1978 for surfacemen from £20.67 to £43.54, for underground workers from £22.06 to £47.54, and for NPLA from £28.27 to £57.01, the increase in the retail price index of 134.5 per cent meant that the real value of wages had declined by 10 per cent, 8 per cent and 14 per cent respectively.[54] Despite this, a national ballot accepted the NCB's modest £6.50 pay offer in 1979.[55]

Although the south Wales miners began this period in full support of the Labour government, increasing bitterness at its policies – particularly the Social Contract – forced them to reassess their attitude. It must be remembered that the first post-war British administration to adopt monetarism was the Callaghan government. The NUM Left objected to Labour implementing policies which would have been opposed fiercely by the unions had they been proposed by a Conservative government. One of the most dramatic expressions of the Area's resentment was the annual presidential address by Emlyn Williams. In May 1976, he called the Social Contract 'a sop' to the IMF and stated that 'if the Government wishes to survive it must pursue Socialist policies. If it has the death wish, it is not the miners' responsibility.' At the 1977 conference, he warned the government to ignore the CBI and instead implement its 1974 election manifesto. The following year, the Area president launched a scathing assault on the Labour government, criticising it for blaming workers for the economic crisis while leaving profits untouched, for being 'a lackey' to the IMF, and for attacking civil liberties and pandering to the Tory Right and the National Front over immigration. Even so, the Area's broad political strategy remained unaltered. Albeit reluctantly, the South Wales NUM

[53]   *The Miner*, July/August 1977.
[54]   NUM Wages Pay Claim 1979 (Appendix B).
[55]   *The Miner*, April/May 1979.

was prepared to work towards the re-election of the Callaghan government.

CLOUDS ON THE HORIZON

The late 1970s were an unsettling time for the south Wales miners. In addition to their disillusionment with the Labour government, these years saw the resurfacing of issues which had plagued their industry in the recent past and also the first signs of serious problems for the future. Although these issues did not amount to a crisis for the miners on the same scale as that of the 1960s, collectively they indicated that the 'new dawn' for coal which had seemed so tangible in 1974 might prove to be merely an interlude in the broader pattern of struggle and confrontation.

While pit closures remained uncommon in the 1970s, an increasingly frequent occurrence was integration, the underground link-up of previously autonomous collieries. Cynheidre and Pentremawr were merged in March 1974; a year later, the integration of Lady Windsor (in Ynysybwl) and Abercynon, Garw and Ffaldau (in the Garw valley), and Windsor (in Abertridwr) and Nantgarw took place. Morlais joined with Brynlliw in 1977. In January 1975, plans were announced for the link-up of Deep Navigation, Taff Merthyr and Merthyr Vale. Later that year, the NCB's ten-year plan for south Wales admitted that mergers and closures would continue. Consequently, at the 1975 Area conference, miners' agent Emlyn Jenkins complained that 'the Board . . . are deliberately destroying good pits by these amalgamations', while other delegates saw link-ups as part of a programme of preparing the coalfield for another round of closures.

Fears for the south Wales coalfield were given another dimension by the emergence of EEC plans for the long-term restructuring of coal and steel production in the European Common Market. At the 1975 Area conference, Emlyn Williams drew ominous parallels between this and the NCB's policy of colliery integration, stating: 'To me it has all the signs of a contraction policy in line with the energy report recently issued by the European Coal and Steel Community which projects that the peripheral areas, such as South Wales, will be cut by 50 per cent over the next 10 years'. In October 1980, he expressed the view that the roots of the crisis surrounding the coal industry were to be found in policy decisions taken by the Callaghan government and in the ECSC's 1975 Consultative Document on Energy Policy.[56]

Coal imports and stockpiling in south Wales had become a concern for the Area by the end of the 1970s. The Area's proposed solution was an expansion of NCB coal consumption at Aberthaw, Uskmouth, Carmarthen Bay and Didcot power stations, together with support for the attempts by the Secretary of State for Energy to establish a co-ordinated fuel policy.[57] Tony Benn was keen to see a reduction in stockpiles, intervening in mid-1976 to ask both the CEGB and British Steel to increase coal consumption in south Wales.[58] The decline in the steel industry in the late 1970s posed a threat to the Area's coking coal collieries, since BSC reduced its order significantly. On investigation, however, it transpired that Llanwern steelworks was still importing coal, even though this was £10–12 per ton more expensive. The continuation of BSC imports led to increasing stockpiles of coking coal. The most pressing situations were at Maesteg and Nantgarw, where 700,000 tonnes and 480,000 tonnes respectively were being stored by May 1978. In September 1978, the EC arranged to discuss again the question of coal imports with the unions at the BSC plants.[59] By June 1978, even this problem had been overshadowed by the surplus of power station coal – with stockpiles in Wales reaching 2.6 million tonnes, mainly due to the failure of the giant Aberthaw B station to operate at full capacity. With each tonne of stockpiled coal costing the NCB £3.50 to handle and store, it was clear that this was becoming a serious drain on the already stretched resources of the South Wales Board.[60]

In 1974, increased investment and brighter prospects in their industry had given the south Wales miners the impression that they were assured of a secure future. By April 1975, eighteen of the coalfield's forty-three collieries were profitable, and the number was increasing as productivity improved.[61] However, with the onset of the steel recession and the gradual evaporation of the optimism of 1974, the Area began to face up to the likelihood of hard times ahead. In March 1977, Coedely lodge complained that the NCB was

[56]   Emlyn Williams SWML interview (AUD/33).
[57]   ASC, 15 December 1975, 4 February 1976.
[58]   *The Miner*, July/August 1976; EC, 18 June 1976.
[59]   *The Miner*, April/May 1978; EC, 12 September 1978; AAC, 1978.
[60]   *WM*, 30 June 1978.
[61]   *WM: Quarterly Economic Review*, 23 April 1975.

conditioning some pits for closure by withholding investment and allowing problems with morale to develop. In November 1977, the Area leadership met the NCB to discuss the coalfield's declining output. The Area's preferred solution was to increase miners' morale through pithead meetings with top management and Area officials, an attendance bonus payment to combat absenteeism and pit-level industrial democracy. It also pointed out that insufficient investment outbye[62] often caused bottlenecks in clearing the coal, nullifying the effect of improved coalface mechanisation. The following month, miners' delegates rejected NCB allegations of a 'malaise' amongst the men, instead pointing to the inadequacies of the management, for example, a failure to procure sufficient supplies to ensure continuous production, inability to organise operations effectively, and the low quality of work done by colliery overmen. Regardless of the actual reasons for the problems, the situation was scarcely helped by comments by Philip Weekes in the *Daily Express* about 'lazy' south Wales miners, to which the Area responded with amazement and indignation.[63]

By the late 1970s the future of the south Wales miners no longer seemed as bright as it had been only a few years previously. In 1975–6, the coalfield was in a reasonably viable position: ten pits made a total profit of £9.6 million, although this was outweighed by losses in the other twenty-five collieries. By 1977–8, nine collieries were still profitable but total losses had climbed to £32 million. Another cause for concern was the return of a gradual manpower drift from the industry. Whereas the mid-1970s had seen an increasing number of mineworkers, in 1977 the Area's membership fell from 28,879 to 27,600. In May 1978, the NCB announced that plans for the new coking coal colliery at Margam would be shelved, due to the steel recession and the coalfield's shaky financial position – a 'Catch 22' scenario with which the south Wales miners were only too familiar. Several other pits faced uncertainty at this time: in 1978, the NCB briefly considered closing Abernant and Maerdy, both heavy loss-makers employing over 2,000 men each. The seriousness of this situation prompted meetings between Tony Benn, the South Wales Board and the Area officials in June and September 1978. In the latter meeting, Benn told Weekes that employment levels must be

---

[62] The underground area of the colliery away from the coalfaces.
[63] EC, 29 November, 13 December 1977; ASC, 14 December 1977.

maintained, announced the formation of a tripartite committee to investigate the subject, and expressed optimism that £250 million would be invested during the next decade to develop the south Wales coalfield and put it back on a viable financial footing.[64]

THE INCENTIVE BONUS SCHEME

All of the main problems facing the south Wales miners in the later 1970s – stagnant output levels, the wages struggle, and the 'moderate' dominance of the NEC – were brought to a head by a single issue, the introduction of the incentive bonus scheme. Alongside the strikes of 1972 and 1974, this was the most important development in the history of the NUM in that decade. The scheme represented the antithesis of the factors which had brought about the miners' victories of the early 1970s. As such, it played a crucial role in undermining NUM unity, which was to prove decisive in 1984. Consequently, the incentive bonus scheme has been a focus of historiographical attention. For Ashworth, it was an ambiguous development that boosted miners' average earnings but lessened inter-Area solidarity. Francis and Smith observe that the problem of improving basic wages was aggravated by the scheme because it weakened the NPLA. For Allen, the episode showed that the NUM Right was happy to ignore its much-vaunted 'constitutionalism' in order to push through the incentive system.[65]

The introduction of the NPLA in 1966 had been one of the biggest gains made by the NUM in the post-war period and represented the realisation of a long-held objective. Establishment of a daywage system across the whole industry had had several far-reaching repercussions, for example, the dramatically reduced incidence of localised strikes which had previously characterised coal-mining industrial relations. In 1956, the industry accounted for 78.4 per cent of all strikes in Britain; by 1970, this figure was only 4.1 per cent.[66] Payment of the same wage for the same work was seen

[64]   EC, 28 April, 6, 27 June, 27 September 1978; minutes, Eighteenth Colliery General Review Meeting, Llanishen, 21 June 1978; WM, 27 May 1978.
[65]   William Ashworth, The History of the British Coal Industry, Vol. 5: 1946–1982, The Nationalised Industry (Oxford: 1986), p. 372; Francis and Smith, The Fed, pp. 480–1; V. L. Allen, The Militancy of British Miners (Shipley: 1981), pp. 272–5.
[66]   The Miner, May/June 1978.

by the south Wales miners to embody an important principle. Furthermore, a universal daywage system shifted the onus for production away from the workers, since they were now paid a guaranteed rate. Consequently, productivity levels began to stagnate from around 1974, as the management proved unable to increase output. The NCB's proposed solution was a system whereby miners would earn more if they produced more – in other words, a return to piecework.

Hostility to the bonus scheme was particularly widespread in south Wales, partly because of safety factors, partly because of difficult geological conditions and partly because it created competition and tension in the workplace as miners strove to maximise their own output; it was the antithesis of co-operative trade union principles. As Emlyn Williams commented in 1978: 'It's the law of the jungle and we haven't even got spears'.[67]

As a result of these concerns, in the mid-1970s the Area discussed several solutions which addressed the output question without forcing miners into competition with one another. Following the first ballot defeat of the incentive bonus scheme in late 1974, the NUM adopted Dai Francis's plan for a national-level productivity system. Under this plan, output bonuses would be tied to a national target, without individual collieries being labelled as either 'successes' or 'failures'. The NCB seemed prepared initially to consider this option, before events swung back in its favour. As late as May 1977, however, South Wales was still reaffirming its support for a National Bonus Scheme. The other main suggestion which the Area discussed in 1975 was for an increase in faceworkers' wages relative to those of other grades, so as to increase the numbers of the men most directly responsible for extracting coal. This was not ideal – but it was deemed better to retain a daywage system rather than succumb to a piecework 'free-for-all'.[68] Neither of these plans became a reality.

Although the proposals for an incentive bonus scheme were couched in terms of increasing pits' productivity, the broader political implications of the reintroduction of piecework were never far from the surface. The NCB supported it as a way of increasing profitability and compromising NUM unity. The secret Miron Report, produced for NCB chairman Derek Ezra in December 1973, argued

---

[67]   Quoted in Francis and Smith, *The Fed*, p. 481.
[68]   ASC, 2 November 1974, 18 February 1975; AAC, 1977; EC, 15 February 1975; *WM*, 8 January 1975.

that incentive schemes, in addition to the promotion of non-NUM unions in the industry, would be an important part of breaking left-wing influence in the NUM.[69] While they were unaware of this report, many miners nevertheless saw the bonus scheme as a politically motivated attempt to curtail the power of their union. As one lodge secretary later reflected: 'The productivity scheme . . . [started] to create fissures and splits in the Union. And *I* think . . . that the Labour government . . . *weren't* sorry to see that come in . . . I mean, there was at that time an element in the Labour Party that saw the unions as an impediment.' In the view of Terry Thomas, then an EC member, 'Callaghan's government decided that they could not afford to have the miners united. *That* is why that incentive scheme was introduced.'[70]

The NCB's incentive scheme proposals first emerged in its 1974 *Plan for Coal*. Although the NEC was willing to discuss it, the Area leadership was completely against the idea. In September 1974, a South Wales delegation lobbied a National Conference to reiterate their opposition to piecework. In the run-up to a ballot on the subject, the miners were subjected to a massive campaign in favour of the scheme by the media and colliery management, in which Gormley participated actively. Despite this, the NUM membership rejected the bonus scheme comprehensively, by 62.7 per cent to 37.3 per cent. The south Wales miners responded even more emphatically: 83.1 per cent 'against' and only 16.9 per cent 'for'.[71]

Following this unambiguous ballot result in November 1974, plans for an incentive bonus scheme faded into the background for a few years as the NUM and the NCB discussed other means of boosting productivity. However, by April 1977 rumours were circulating in south Wales that other Areas were defying union policy and allowing their members to work under piecework systems.[72] At the 1977 Area conference, miners' delegates underlined their opposition to the incentive bonus scheme. Emlyn Thomas (Maerdy) stated that 'piecework schemes [are] . . . another feature of the capitalist system designed to exploit and coerce workmen . . . [W]e will not support a

[69]   Jonathan Winterton and Ruth Winterton, *Coal, Crisis and Conflict: The 1984–85 Miners' Strike in Yorkshire* (Manchester: 1989), pp. 9–11; Seumas Milne, *The Enemy Within: The Secret War Against The Miners* (London: 1995), p. 9.

[70]   Interviews with Dane Hartwell and Terry Thomas (16 February 2004) (respectively).

[71]   EC, 14, 28 August, 9, 19 November 1974, 21 January 1975; ASC, 2 November 1974; *The Miner*, January/February 1975.

[72]   EC, 15 April 1977.

return to a piecework system . . . [A]nyone who has the temerity to suggest such a change has not got the wellbeing of his members at heart.' Nevertheless, in August 1977 Gormley allowed various Areas to arrange their own incentive bonus schemes – a complete abrogation of NUM policy. In October 1977, the south Wales miners restated their position at an Area conference and lobbied the NEC, protesting against the plans to foist incentive schemes on the union. Later that month, the NUM held its second national ballot on incentive bonuses – and once again voted against them (by 55.7 per cent versus 44.3 per cent). South Wales was the most resolutely opposed, with 83 per cent rejecting piecework.[73]

Even a second national ballot victory was unable to prevent the introduction of the incentive bonus. Shortly after the result was announced, it emerged that Nottinghamshire, Leicestershire, South Derbyshire, North Western, and Midlands Areas were intent on establishing their own incentive schemes. South Wales miners condemned this development, lobbying the NEC in protest. In December 1977 Gormley ruled, with the support of a majority on the NEC, that any Areas which had voted in favour of incentives could introduce them. A South Wales conference voted for industrial action in protest at the NEC's stance and called unanimously for Gormley's removal from office. Terry Thomas told delegates: 'What we are facing now is far more important than production and wages put together, we are fighting for the preservation of this Union'. The South Wales leadership also joined the Yorkshire and Kent Areas in taking the NEC to court to stop the maverick coalfields. Unfortunately for them, the High Court ruled that the ballot result was not binding on the NEC and decided in favour of the 'rogue' Areas.[74] Gormley's role infuriated South Wales activists; a quarter of a century later, some of them still stated that '[t]he biggest traitor, to my mind, was Joe Gormley' and '[w]e hated Gormley – he had sold us out'.[75] A letter from a Brynlliw worker in *The Miner* following the High Court's ruling expressed the Area's bitterness on the subject:

RIP – On 21 December, 1977, the [NUM] . . . died in the High Court, London.

[73] EC, 9 August 1977; *WM*, 2 November 1977; ASC, 19 October 1977.
[74] *The Miner*, November/December 1977; EC, 29 November 1977; ASC, 14 December 1977; *WM*, 22 December 1977.
[75] Interviews with Billy Liddon (1 April 2004) and Tyrone O'Sullivan (22 March 2004) respectively.

Pallbearers were the South Wales, Scotland, Yorkshire and Kent Areas which tried in vain to uphold the result of a democratic secret ballot against any kind of productivity deal with the NCB. Executioners were Jim Callaghan, ably supported by Joe Gormley and Lawrence Daly who will go down in history as the men who dissected a once great Union into small, fragmented, greedy collieries.

Although this flouting of democracy by the Right was controversial enough in its own terms, it created a powerful precedent and was to have even more significant consequences in 1984. At that time, when 'moderates' claimed that the Left had ignored the union's democratic decision-making processes, striking miners could respond by recalling the way in which incentives had been foisted on the NUM.

Once the incentive bonus scheme was a reality in the 'moderate' coalfields which were keen to see it implemented, it became increasingly difficult to avoid it elsewhere. Opposition crumbled quickly and by January 1978 only South Wales and Yorkshire were still holding out. Amidst the growing realisation that South Wales was fighting a losing battle, it was decided to ballot the Area's membership – although even this was not controversy-free, since the Board issued pro-incentive leaflets to miners prior to the vote. The result of the ballot, announced in late January, was for the south Wales miners to accept a pit-by-pit bonus scheme, the last Area to do so.[76]

Acceptance of the incentive bonus scheme by no means resolved the problems. On the contrary, by May 1978, the Area conference noted that the return of piecework had led to risks being taken and safety standards being compromised. Increasingly, men were asked to speed up production, tempted by bonus payments. Some were also paid for working through meal breaks, which produced tensions between faceworkers and outbye workers. Within a short time, a myriad of technical complications and anomalies caused by the scheme had emerged.

Once the incentive bonus scheme was in place, the south Wales miners realised that it was there to stay and so took steps to mitigate its worst effects. Wherever possible, lodge officials ensured that the expected production levels were not too high to exclude the

[76] ASC, 11, 19, 21 January 1978; *The Miner*, January/February 1978, February/March 1978; *WM*, 21, 27 January 1978.

possibility of earning bonuses; also, some lodges organised pooling schemes which ensured that every worker on a given grade received the same bonus rate. Additionally, the Area leadership was keen to introduce a more equitable bonus system. In August 1978, an Area conference agreed that there should be an equal rate for surface and outbye workers in collieries that were part of integrated units. Following discussion with the Board, the EC pressed for a uniform Area bonus for all surface and outbye grades throughout the coalfield. Miners' delegates agreed to this in December 1978, though it was subsequently overturned on a mandated card vote from the lodges in February 1979.[77]

Although ultimately the Area had little choice but to accept the incentive bonus scheme, this did not mean that it was happy about it. At the 1978 annual conference, Emlyn Williams criticised the damage which had been inflicted on the NUM: 'The acceptance of piece rates was . . . a rejection of principles that lie at the core of our union . . . Those of us who believe in the unity and dignity of miners have suffered a severe blow far greater than the rejection of any wage claim. Unity is easy to damage, but it is difficult to repair.' Speaking after him, Charlie Blewett (Penallta) made a telling assessment of the introduction of the incentive bonus scheme and the Area's struggle against it:

> We know in South Wales that radical thoughts and actions are of vital importance. Moderate thoughts lead to stagnation and could lead to a retreat from objects which we have already obtained.
>
> Emlyn . . . has correctly diagnosed the defects and the retreat of the moderates who have sacrificed National Unity for thirty pieces of silver. This is shown quite clearly by the introduction of the Incentive Scheme and those who have accepted the thirty pieces of silver to my mind are traitors . . . If history will show this treason it will also show that the South Wales Miners fought hard . . . against the Incentive Scheme.

The establishment of the incentive bonus scheme signalled the end of wage equality in the coal-mining industry. Although 'equal pay for equal work' had been a long-held aspiration of the miners, it was only a reality for a few years – between 1971 (the first year of full NPLA parity and the introduction of the Third Wages

[77] ASC, 10 August, 6 December 1978, 22 February 1979; EC, 24 October, 7 November 1978.

Structure) and 1978, when piecework was reintroduced. The NCB was also able to manipulate the bonus scheme to persuade men to accept transferral to other collieries. Furthermore, most significantly, it reinforced the conservatism of 'moderate' coalfields such as Nottinghamshire which were soon receiving substantial bonus payments.[78] These Areas subsequently became determined opponents of any disruption that might upset the money they were earning. All these factors, together with the bitterness caused by the way that piecework was imposed on the membership, ensured that the NUM was never again to be as united as it had been before the introduction of the incentive bonus scheme.

CONCLUSION

For the miners of south Wales, the years 1974 to 1979 were a mixture of respite, misplaced optimism and disappointment. In some respects, it was one of the best phases of the post-war era for them: investment in the coalfield, and reforms which improved the situation of many current and former mineworkers. These developments reflected the continuing importance of coal in world energy markets and the favourable bargaining position established by the NUM through its strikes in 1972 and 1974. This relative stability was emphasised by the absence of any significant programme of colliery closures and a short-term increase in the numbers of miners employed in the coalfield.

Despite this progress, other developments during this period ensured that a more pessimistic scenario came to confront the Area. The 'new dawn' heralded by the Labour victory in 1974 proved to be an illusion, particularly following the onset of IMF-imposed austerity measures from 1976 onwards. Although the government's Social Contract was opposed consistently by the south Wales miners, it was accepted by the majority of the other Areas, resulting in an erosion of the favourable wage levels established earlier in the 1970s.

An important consideration in this period was the role played by the NEC and the national officials. Although National Conferences

---

[78] It should be noted, however, that it was not just moderate coalfields that benefited from incentives. Parts of Yorkshire enjoyed payments on a comparable level to Nottinghamshire in the 1980s. Moreover, some moderate coalfields such as north Wales and Lancashire gained little from the scheme.

were theoretically the highest authority in the NUM, in reality any of their decisions with which the leadership disagreed were either reversed outright or ignored quietly. Right-wing dominance of the union's hierarchy was perpetuated by the archaic NEC structure, alongside the increased powers which had accrued to the national president. These developments to a large extent nullified the previously successful strategy of the left-wing forces in the union (including the South Wales Area) of using conferences to promote a more militant stance by the NUM.

A de facto monopoly of NUM executive power enabled Gormley and the leaders of the 'moderate' Areas to circumvent the aspirations of the left-wing Areas and began the process of undermining the grassroots solidarity that had brought about the union's victories in 1972 and 1974. The introduction of the incentive bonus scheme, despite being rejected twice by the national membership, was extremely controversial and was a bitter pill for South Wales to swallow. While men in some Areas may have earned more as a result of the return of piecework, this was bought at the expense of the unity which had been the key to re-establishing the prestige and strength of the NUM in the early 1970s. Ultimately, despite the optimism felt in 1974, the south Wales miners ended the decade in the disconcerting knowledge that they were in a weaker strategic position to resist the policies of the new Thatcher administration than they had been when they had confronted the previous Conservative government.

V

CONFRONTATION: 1979–1983

The years 1979 to 1983 were a period of crisis and confrontation for the south Wales miners. The optimistic future which had seemed certain during the 1970s was replaced in the early 1980s by a pit closure programme on a scale unseen since the first Wilson governments. Unlike the passive resentment which had characterised the British miners for much of the 1960s, this development provoked NUM anger, with no-one offering more determined resistance than South Wales. In the early years of the Thatcher administration, the growing tension was punctuated by a succession of stand-offs, in which the south Wales miners sought to ensure that their jobs and their way of life were not consigned to 'the dustbin of history'.

Despite the recurrent confrontations during the first term of the Thatcher government, there was no decisive showdown between the miners and their opponents – instead, the pressure built up until it exploded in the 1984–5 strike. The massive significance of this epic clash was self-evident, with the result that the historiography of mineworkers in Britain in the 1980s has understandably focused heavily on it. Nevertheless, developments between 1979 and 1983 provide a variety of insights and explanatory contexts for the events of 1984–5. The eventual defeat of the miners in 1985 was all too real; however, subsequent political myth-making about 'the Iron Lady' has overemphasised the inevitability of the outcome. In every year of the first Thatcher administration, the south Wales miners were in the vanguard of attempts to instigate NUM action aimed at saving their industry – and for a brief while, they even seemed to succeed.

THATCHER AND THE MINERS

The south Wales miners viewed the election of the Thatcher administration in May 1979 with dismay. As one collier later reflected, 'we *hated* Thatcher . . . [W]e hated the Conservative Party and all they stood for.' The Cwmtillery lodge secretary stated that '[w]e knew what sort of government Thatcher was – it was right of a Conservative government and just left of a fascist government'.[1] This visceral opposition was expressed in frequent demonstrations by Area members outside high-profile Conservative events throughout this period. Despite this resentment, the Thatcher administration was generally expected to be a transient phenomenon in a broader pattern of Labour governments, much as Heath had been between 1970 and 1974, particularly since it presided over a deep recession and was very unpopular for most of its first term.

The recession of the early 1980s was the worst that Britain had seen since the 1930s. Unemployment increased from one million in 1979 to 3.1 million by late 1982, staying at over three million until 1987.[2] Area president Emlyn Williams articulated the feelings of the south Wales miners when he stated that '[t]his level of unemployment . . . is a crime against humanity'.[3] The Area campaigned actively against unemployment, for example, supporting the National Union of Unemployed and Workers and participating in the People's March For Jobs to London in mid-1981 and September 1982.

In addition to the unemployment situation, the miners were also concerned at the Thatcher government's public expenditure cuts. In November 1979, 900 south Wales miners participated in a mass lobby of parliament.[4] The 1981 Area conference opposed the education and social security cuts and also criticised Labour-run local authorities that were willing to implement them. In May 1982, miners' delegates called for strike action against a reduction in social security benefits. The Area also campaigned against the closure of local hospitals, one of its main successes being to keep Rhydlafar Hospital open.[5] On a broader level, a perennial feature of annual conferences at this time was the calls for the improvement and defence of the NHS. The 1980 conference, for instance, asked the NUM National Conference for industrial action against government health service cuts.

[1]   Interviews with Colin Thomas (14 January 2004) and Graham Bartlett (20 February 2004) (respectively).
[2]   Joe England, *The Wales TUC, 1974–2004: Devolution and Industrial Politics* (Cardiff: 2004), p. 59.
[3]   *The Miner*, May/June 1981.
[4]   *WM*, 22 November 1979; *The Miner*, December 1979/January 1980.
[5]   EC, 1979–1982 passim.

As Heath had done, Thatcher came to power determined to take on the unions. Consequently, the 1980 and 1982 Employment Acts curtailed unions' collective bargaining powers and restricted their legal ability to take strike action. At their 1979 conference, south Wales miners condemned plans to outlaw secondary picketing and restrict 'closed shop' agreements. Similarly, the 1980 NUM National Conference called for non-cooperation with the Employment Bill, while the Area lobbied the 1980 annual conferences of both the TUC and Conservatives on this topic. The South Wales annual conferences in 1981 and 1982 expressed hostility towards the new legislation and called on the TUC to defy it. At the 1981 conference, Emlyn Williams declared: 'As real democrats we have a responsibility to stop an oppressive Government just as in the early 1930s the German trade unions had a responsibility to prevent the spread of Nazism . . . We have a social responsibility to take extra-Parliamentary action against Mrs Thatcher's Government.'

In facing up to the Conservative threat, the Area was well aware of the need for solidarity with other unions engaged in the struggle. The clearest example of this was the industrial action by NHS NUPE members in 1982: the south Wales miners held one-day strikes in support of the health workers in June and September 1982, with the EC also asking members to join nurses' picket lines in July 1982. A march through Cardiff in June 1982 was attended by around 15,000 demonstrators, with the miners comprising a major contingent. In January and July 1982, the Area assisted ASLEF in its struggle against the government; similarly, during the NUS's strike in November 1980 the EC sent a bus-load of miners to help picket Southampton docks. Furthermore, the Area was a stalwart defender of trade unionism in other prominent cases, asking the TUC in November 1979 to call a strike in support of Derek Robinson, the TGWU convenor sacked from the Longbridge car plant, and backing the campaign by GCHQ workers for union rights.

The south Wales miners' industrial militancy was augmented by a wider awareness of contemporary political developments. In the heightened Cold War tensions of the early 1980s, nuclear power was once again a pressing concern. Area policy was clear, calling for a ban on nuclear weapons and attacking the government's apparent fixation with atomic power. South Wales miners took part in CND demonstrations in London in October 1980 and October 1983, while Emlyn Williams spoke at a conference in Llandrindod Wells in

March 1980 against government plans to dump nuclear waste in Wales. At the 1981 and 1983 annual conferences, he argued for unilateral nuclear disarmament as a step towards world peace. At the same time, South Wales was an active supporter of the Greenham Common protesters. Speaking at the 1983 National Conference, Area vice-president Terry Thomas opposed the American military presence in the country, arguing that Britain should not be allowed to become Reagan's 'unsinkable aircraft carrier'.

Government policy towards the NUM in the 1980s was shaped by the events of the 1970s. Following the downfall of the Heath administration, many Tories became convinced of the need for a showdown with the miners. The Ridley Report, leaked in 1978, explicitly stated Conservative intentions to defeat the unions as part of the broader political objective of a monetarist reconfiguration of the economy.[6] Thatcher's election in 1979 made it inevitable that there would be a major period of coal 'rationalisation', as the government sought to break the NUM and rapidly shrink the industry as a prelude to its privatisation. As George Rees (Area general secretary from 1976 to 1997) later commented: 'Many of us saw the introduction of Margaret Thatcher at that time as the beginning of the end. And she wasn't long in establishing what she wanted in the coal industry – she wanted it closed!'[7]

THE RETURN OF MASS PIT CLOSURES

The year 1979 was a turning point for coal. In the 1970s, the main trends in the industry had been increased production and investment. After 1979, the coalfield was hit by several adverse developments: the election of a much less sympathetic government; a world recession in steel; a decline in output; and the BSC decision to use coal imports.[8] These meant that, once again, the south Wales miners faced a major pit closure programme.

The Area leadership did not react to this new threat with the reluctant compliance which had characterised its approach in

---

[6]   *The Economist*, 27 May 1978. See also John Saville, 'An open conspiracy: Conservative politics and the miners' strike of 1984–5', *Socialist Register*, 22 (1985), 295–301.

[7]   Interview with George Rees, 8 December 2003.

[8]   Minutes, Special Meeting Between NCB and EC, NCB Offices, Llanishen, 2 June 1980.

the 1960s, adopting instead a combative strategy against closures. The campaign in 1978–9 to save Deep Duffryn colliery, near Mountain Ash, was a key development, drawing explicit links between the fate of the mine and its dependent community. Mobilisation of local action groups and nearby pits also pointed to this 'community socialism', which was to become a feature of the 1984–5 dispute. The Deep Duffryn struggle was the initial skirmish in the broader war over pit closures.

When the Board announced in late 1978 that Deep Duffryn was to shut, the south Wales miners agreed to resist the closure. Although the Area leadership supported the fight, a key factor was the readiness of local lodges to carry out their own campaigning.[9] In July 1979 the Deep Duffryn Action Committee travelled to Jersey to persuade the NUM National Conference to assist them. There, Area after Area pledged their support: Scottish Area president Mick McGahey declared that 'Deep Duffryn is not a South Wales issue. It's an issue for every coalfield in Britain.'[10] As the momentum for a strike began to gather, the NCB backed down, agreeing to reprieve Deep Duffryn. At an Area conference on 10 July called to discuss this news, Emlyn Williams said that '[i]t now seems clear that this Union will not take closures as lightly in the future as in the past'.[11]

The epilogue to the Deep Duffryn campaign proved disappointing for the south Wales miners. The Area had pinned its hopes on a new coalface but by early September 1979 bad geological conditions meant that there was no alternative but to accept the colliery's closure.[12] Nevertheless, the episode was to have significant consequences for the NUM. As a result of the appeals to save Deep Duffryn, the 1979 National Conference endorsed a South Wales motion calling for strike action if the NCB proposed a closure to which the NUM objected. It was this resolution which was used in March 1984 to get the NEC to call for a strike against the closure of Cortonwood colliery in Yorkshire.

As Deep Duffryn showed, the early 1980s saw the re-emergence of the spectre of mass colliery closures. One Maerdy miner later

[9] EC, 6 March, 10 April, 22 May, 9 July 1979; *The Miner*, April/May 1979, July/August 1979.
[10] *WM*, 6 July 1979.
[11] ASC, 10 July 1979.
[12] See pp. 162–3 for a more detailed discussion of some of the potential adverse geological conditions that could threaten the viability of a coalface.

recalled: 'coming up into the Eighties – *pit closures* . . . were then starting to bite. And men could see there wasn't going to be no end to it . . . And south Wales was taking the *brunt* of it, at that time.'[13] In early 1979, the Board stated its intention to shut ten south Wales collieries by 1984. Addressing the 1979 conference, Emlyn Williams warned: 'Our Coalfield is under threat . . . [W]e are facing a massive programme of contraction.' Area conferences in 1979 and 1980 called for strike action against any closure not caused by geological exhaustion. This point was emphasised at the 1980 conference by Mike Griffin (Penrhiwceiber), who said that '[t]he only policy the NCB knows . . . to make the Industry viable is to close uneconomic collieries. This policy can easily be exposed by what took place in the 1960s when pits were closed but still the industry was not made viable.'

Within the Area, there was an awareness that this new wave of pit closures was the result of a systematic policy of reducing productive capacity in the 'peripheral' coalfields. Between 1980 and 1984 the pace of closures increased dramatically, with the total British mining workforce declining by an average of 13,300 a year. To make matters worse, in June 1983, a Monopolies and Mergers Commission report called for the closure of 27 out of the 33 south Wales collieries.[14]

The prospect of sweeping closures went hand-in-hand with a rapid deterioration in the financial performance of the south Wales coalfield. In 1979–80, it made an operating loss of £61 million; this climbed to £72.5 million in 1980–1 (despite a 4.5 per cent increase in productivity, a 200,000 tonne increase in output and a fall in real operating costs), due to low global coal prices. By 1981–2, only Deep Navigation and Betws made a profit, while only Blaenant, Taff Merthyr, Penallta, Marine and Cwm/Coedely came close to breaking even.[15]

INVESTMENT AND 'ENFORCED UNVIABILITY'

A key cause of the decline of the south Wales coalfield in the early 1980s was the cessation of NCB investment. Research carried out by

[13]   Interview with Mike Richards, 27 January 2004.
[14]   *The Miner*, November 1982; *WM*, 24 June 1983.
[15]   Minutes, Review Meeting, NCB Offices, 25 April 1980; EC, 21 July 1981; *WM*, 24 June 1983.

the Area discovered that (with the exception of three years) NCB capital investment between 1970 and 1983 was less per capita for south Wales than anywhere else, with most of the coalfield's operations carried out on current revenue and then charged to the individual collieries at high interest payments. The Area's opinion was that there was 'an anti-South Wales bias existing within the National Board'.[16] In 1981–2, only £30 million in capital had been allocated to south Wales, compared with £1.6 billion for Yorkshire, £400 million for Nottinghamshire and even £140 million for Scotland (which was a much smaller coalfield).[17] NCB expenditure per capita on major projects in south Wales was under 3 per cent of the Doncaster figure and less than 1 per cent of the figure for north Yorkshire in 1983–4. The new MINOS computer technology primarily was deployed in the Midlands and Yorkshire; although south Wales, Kent, Scotland and Durham represented 35 per cent of the total number of pits, only 12 per cent of MINOS applications were situated there.[18]

NCB investment in south Wales did not cease completely in the early 1980s but the situation remained deeply unsatisfactory from the miners' point of view; they were only too aware that pits could not operate efficiently without sufficient capital expenditure. One miner later pointed out: 'it's *quite easy* to make a pit lose money. Management could do it . . . [by] not getting the right stuff into the pit . . . Buying old [machinery and] . . . things that are not suited to the conditions . . . *Lack of investment*, it'll close pits, look. They can *condition* a pit for closure – on *any pit* . . . And that's what we faced in the Eighties.'[19] At an Area conference in January 1983, the EC outlined its proposals: commencement of the Margam and Glyncastle projects; new drifts at Nantgarw and Aberpergwm; Phurnacite plant investment; further development at Betws; reconstruction of washery facilities at Maerdy, Lewis Merthyr/ Tymawr, Merthyr Vale, Abertillery and Marine; increased surveying of coal reserves; recruitment to the industry; and the replacement of powered roof supports and pit machinery where necessary.

By the early 1980s, the south Wales miners were concerned that NCB unwillingness to invest in their coalfield was jeopardising its

[16]   ASC, 12 January 1983.
[17]   EC, 24 November 1982.
[18]   Huw Beynon (ed.), *Digging Deeper: Issues in the Miners' Strike* (London: 1985), p. 238.
[19]   Mike Richards interview.

viability. In February 1981, strike action had prompted the Board to promise a major capital expenditure programme, with the EC calling for investment in the seven closure-threatened pits. However, as the *Western Mail* commented in July 1981, '[t]he blank cheque envisaged by miners when the Government backed down . . . earlier this year appears to have turned into small change for South Wales mines'.[20] At an Area conference the following month, miners were unhappy that NCB plans did not mention improvements for the collieries which had been facing closure. By December 1982, the Area leadership had concluded that this was a deliberate tactic to shut particular pits, since the failure to develop new reserves would lead inevitably to the cessation of mining there.[21]

A good example of this 'enforced unviability' was provided by Britannia colliery, in the Rhymney valley. In November 1980, a shortage of available reserves led the lodge to accept NCB proposals for a reduction of the workforce (by transferrals to other pits) in order to extend the life of the colliery; however, the following month it was reported that Britannia needed a second coalface to remain viable. This was a 'Catch 22' situation, since the transferrals made it unlikely that there would be sufficient manpower to work another face. This relative under-investment is exemplified by the recollections of one miner who transferred to Taff Merthyr and was surprised at the high-technology equipment there, the like of which he had never seen at Britannia. He commented: '[if] Britannia had the machinery that we had in Taff Merthyr . . . Britannia would have been *open today* . . . [W]hat they were doing, they'd *starve* a colliery of investment and then they'd say, "oh, the pit is not profitable", and then it was earmarked for closure.'[22] In November 1981, Britannia miners held a one-day strike in opposition to the run-down of their pit. In an attempt to reflect these viewpoints, in May 1982 the EC demanded extra drivages at Britannia.[23] By July, the struggle had become sufficiently high-profile for Arthur Scargill (recently elected NUM national president) to ask the EC for information about the situation. In November 1982, the Board denied that it intended to

[20]   *WM: Economic Review*, 27 July 1981.
[21]   ASC, 24 August 1981; EC, 1 December 1982.
[22]   Colin Thomas interview.
[23]   A drivage is a tunnel branching off from existing underground colliery workings dug in order to access new reserves.

shut Britannia; however, in April 1983 it announced that one of its two coalfaces would shut, a scenario which guaranteed closure.[24]

The Britannia case highlights a complication faced by the NUM in the struggle against closures: the role played by adverse geology in a decision to shut a pit. Superficially, the issue appears simple: if a pit is exhausted, unworkable or excessively dangerous, then it should be closed. But in reality the constant pressure exerted on colliery workings underground by the weight of earth above and around them meant that the situation was never a static one. Adequate working conditions had to be maintained constantly by miners, or they would quickly deteriorate. The extensive faulting in the geological strata of the south Wales coalfield compounded this problem. In practice, these factors meant that a closure decision could become a 'grey area', subject to individual assessments. As a Maerdy miner pointed out:

> Mining is not like working in the factory. You knock your machine off in the factory, and when you come back tomorrow . . . the machine is there and you just start it up . . . *Mining can change overnight*. You could have a perfect place, a face – perfect. You leave it today, you come back tomorrow and there's . . . geological problems . . . And that's how a pit then becomes non-viable . . . Well, in a *fortnight* [of work by the miners], that face becomes viable and *the pit becomes viable*. But if [the management] wanted to *close it*, they could use the times that it was non-viable.[25]

Technological advances were a further factor, since it was possible for these to overcome geological difficulties which would otherwise have caused closure, for example, dust suppression technologies. Consequently, investment levels have a bearing on specific considerations, as the south Wales miners were aware. Their 1980 annual conference criticised the NCB's lack of progress in developing equipment suited to conditions in the coalfield and also called for further research into reducing dust levels.

The struggle at the coalface to keep a troubled colliery working was a dynamic interaction between the miners' efforts, technical and investment considerations, and geological vicissitudes. Lodges which had been determined to oppose closure through strike action could

---

[24] EC, 26 November 1981, 6 May, 13 July 1982, 19 April 1983; *WM*, 1 November 1982.
[25] Mike Richards interview.

sometimes be forced to concede defeat owing to poor geology, as happened at both Coegnant and Blaengwrach. These factors could interact in other ways. In the case of Cwmtillery, the Area persuaded the management that a drivage into a new seam could make the pit viable, but when conditions there became unsafe the men were willing to see the pit close, in 1982. At Fernhill, the lodge agreed to focus production efforts on one particular face; when, in February 1980, the working environment proved dangerously dusty, there was little choice but for the pit to shut. With Morlais, excessive water in the coalface meant that by April 1981 its miners became the leading advocates of its closure. Exhaustion of reserves was the reason for closure at Blaenafon, although the absence of other geological problems meant that it has been able to continue in its later incarnation as the Big Pit Mining Museum.

THE RECRUITMENT EMBARGO

Alongside its investment policy, the NCB contributed directly to the decline of the south Wales coalfield through its recruitment embargo. This policy was a direct consequence of its overall strategy of making the industry smaller but more profitable. Across Britain, NCB annual recruitment declined precipitously, from 28,824 in 1980 to 5,730 by 1983. This inevitably sapped the vitality of the industry. In 1982, only 62 apprentices started work in south Wales, even though there were 1,400 applicants. As one miner recalled: '[T]hey stopped youngsters coming *into* the pits . . .'81 it started. I remember Mike Griffin from Penrhiwceiber lodge bringing it up in the conferences. Your future of your pit is . . . your young people. If you don't train your young people, *you've had it.*'[26]

The recruitment embargo did not escape the attention of the south Wales miners. In July 1980 several lodges reported manpower shortages; by late 1980, suspicions were being roused that the Board was attempting to condition pits for closure. In the immediate aftermath of the Area's short-lived strike in February 1981, the Board agreed to a slight increase in the number of apprentices, though this did little to alter the downward trend in manpower

---

[26]   Mike Richards interview; EC, 30 March 1982, 21 June 1983.

levels.[27] By October 1981, the lack of recruitment had become a serious issue. In January 1982, the Area leadership told Philip Weekes (the South Wales NCB director) that twenty-three lodges were asking for extra recruitment. The problem remained a point of contention. In March 1983, the Board proposed to reduce manpower at Abertillery; in contrast, the lodge felt that only increased recruitment could make the pit viable and subsequently resisted attempts to transfer men elsewhere.[28]

Transferring men between collieries was an important part of the process of reducing manpower levels. One lodge secretary later commented that the NCB had an 'insidious campaigning method' to close a pit: it would generate low morale, create petty conflicts and then persuade the men they would be better off in another mine. 'The Coal Board were well practised [in] . . . how to close a coal mine. And they knew how to [demoralise] . . . the men, so that they think, "oh, I've had enough of this. I'll go to the next mine, then".'[29] Transferrals occurred frequently in this period: for example, the Cwmgwili workforce was dispersed to other collieries in November 1980 and some men went from Tymawr to neighbouring Lewis Merthyr in March 1981. Transfers were not always unproblematic: controversy erupted in January 1981 when Taff Merthyr lodge refused to accept Britannia transferees, arguing that the Britannia men should fight to retain their pit and that transfers could lead to overmanning which would jeopardise Taff Merthyr. Furthermore, as the industry shrank, the prospects that a transferred miner would retain his job-type and pay-grade were reduced. Following the Brynlliw closure announcement in September 1983, the EC discussed the problem in the light of the fact that 520 Brynlliw men required jobs but only 180 vacancies were available elsewhere, and it noted with concern that soon there would be compulsory redundancies when pits shut.[30]

The Board's manpower reduction policy led to an increasing sense of frustration for the south Wales miners. At an Area conference July 1980, Dan Canniff (Oakdale) stated that '[w]e accepted

[27]   EC, 15 July, 21 October 1980, 28 April 1981.
[28]   Minutes of meeting with Area director, Pontypridd, 15 October 1981; Minutes of meeting at NCB Offices, Llanishen, 29 January 1982; EC, 22 March, 12 April, 7 June 1983.
[29]   Interview with Ian Isaac, 2 and 8 April 2004.
[30]   EC, 12 September 1983.

this position in the 1960s of non-recruitment and we allowed countless pits to close. We should not fall into the same trap now.' In September 1981, Penrhiwceiber demanded an Area-wide strike against the recruitment ban, a call which was reiterated by other lodges. Under this pressure the Board backtracked, agreeing to some selective recruitment and handing over discretionary control of substitute redundancies to the miners' agents.[31] Although this seemed a step forward, the 1982 Area conference was concerned that men who left the industry were still not being replaced on a one-for-one basis. Some miners were convinced that decisive action was needed. At Celynen South, there was an overtime ban between March and May 1982 against the NCB's withholding of manpower and investment. Although this was successful in its own terms (in that another fifty men were recruited to the pit), the lodge felt that a chance had been lost for the Area to make a general stand on the question.[32] A more dramatic protest occurred at Bedwas in October 1982, when nineteen men staged a brief 'stay-down' strike.[33] Against this backdrop of escalating confrontation, an Area conference in December 1982 agreed to hold a strike ballot. There, Emlyn Williams stated: 'Since the [national] Ballot [the previous month, which rejected strike action] we have seen the . . . [NCB] at its worst – the Area Director giving public assurances on the future of the South Wales coalfield but in informal meetings indicating quite clearly that the strategy of the Board . . . is that of slow strangulation.'[34]

THE STEELWORKERS' STRIKE

Although the south Wales miners had enough difficulties with internally-generated crises in the coal industry, from the late 1970s onward they also had to face several external threats. The most significant of these was the decline of the south Wales steel industry.[35] In December 1979, British Steel announced plans to halve output in Llanwern and Port Talbot and make 11,300 men

[31] EC, 18 September, 17, 26 November, 15 December 1981; Minutes of meeting with Area director, Pontypridd, 15 October 1981.
[32] Interview with Ray Lawrence, 11 March 2004; EC, 2 March 1982; *SWM*, July 1983.
[33] ASC, 6 October 1982.
[34] ASC, 8 December 1982.
[35] For a discussion of this whole episode from a WTUC perspective, see England, *The Wales TUC*, pp. 46–57.

redundant – a development which threatened the jobs of 6,000 south Wales miners. By February 1980, the Area leadership feared that BSC plans to import Port Talbot's entire coal requirement meant that twenty-one pits and 15,000 mining jobs could go. Consequently, it is not surprising that the Area was keen to support the steelworkers' struggle against job cuts. An Area conference on 11 December 1979 pledged strike action if necessary, while some lodges wanted the WTUC to call a general strike.[36]

The steelworkers' strike, which began on 2 January 1980, was a significant opportunity for the south Wales miners to fight for trade union solidarity and indirectly to defend their own jobs. Throughout the ISTC strike, the south Wales miners maintained an embargo on steel supplies entering the collieries; any steel which was required had to be salvaged from old workings in the pits. This refusal of supplies caused major problems in some places, since there could be no underground roadway advances without steel ring supports; several pits ran the risk of closure through an insistence on sticking to their principles in this respect.[37]

In addition to the steel embargo, the south Wales miners seemed intent on more proactive steps, joining the ISTC in pressing the WTUC for further action. An Area conference on 11 January (later backed by an overwhelming lodge mandate) called unanimously for a strike from 21 January. This plan met with opposition from the TUC and the NUM NEC and only with lukewarm support from other unions so that, in spite of the Area's protests, the WTUC decided on a 'day of action' instead, rearranging the proposed strike for 10 March.[38] At an Area conference on 21 January, the militant tone was reflected by Jim O'Flynn (Llynfi Sundries lodge): 'I have been a moderate in this Union but I fear that if we do not fight on this occasion then anarchy will arise.' The 'day of action' on 28 January 1980 was one of the biggest one-day strikes in Welsh post-war history. Around 100,000 workers took part, paralysing ports, railways, collieries and public transport throughout Wales, while 15,000 trade unionists marched through Cardiff. In the aftermath of this stoppage, the WTUC threatened to call a general strike in Wales.

[36] EC, 20 December 1979; *WM*, 3, 8 December 1979, 21 February 1980; *The Times*, 30 January 1980.
[37] Interviews with numerous south Wales miners; EC, 25 January 1980.
[38] EC, 16 January 1980; ASC, 21 January 1980.

Following the 'day of action', it seemed likely that the south Wales miners would strike in support of the steelworkers. In early February 1980, the EC strove to ensure a sizeable contingent of miners at an ISTC rally in Port Talbot, while Maerdy and Penrhiwceiber demanded that the Area begin the strike before the agreed date. In response to pressure from the steelworks strike committees and also from some sections of the Area rank and file, the EC decided to press for strike action as from 25 February.[39] An Area conference on 20 February agreed overwhelmingly to this, subject to ratification by lodge meetings, despite the WTUC decision to cancel its planned stoppage. It seemed that the government had stumbled into a confrontation with a powerful trade union alliance for which it was ill-prepared. In an article entitled 'Has Mrs Thatcher's strategy been upset?', *The Times* commented that 'Mrs Thatcher is turning out to be a weak Prime Minister'.[40]

Events did not turn out as expected. Across the coalfield, lodge meetings rejected the strike call. This surprised the Area officials, given the miners' traditional militancy and the reports of a pro-strike mood at grassroots level. The result was due to a combination of factors: scepticism about the readiness of the ISTC leadership to fight against job cuts and the subsequent shift in the emphasis of its strike from jobs to wages; WTUC vacillation during February 1980; unwillingness to take action in isolation from other unions; NCB interference in the ballot process; and anti-strike pressure from the media. In March 1980, Emlyn Williams conceded that the Area leadership had 'marched the troops up and down the hill so many times they were confused, and when we wanted an army they were not available'.[41] After the ballot, there was the brief possibility of the steelworkers picketing them out, although they decided against it, even though it was probable that miners would have respected ISTC picket lines.[42]

Regardless of the reasons for it, the south Wales miners' decision not to strike in February 1980 was a serious setback for a campaign against the government's 'downsizing' of the public sector industries.

---

[39] EC, 5, 8, 15 February 1980.

[40] *The Times*, 23 February 1980.

[41] *The Miner*, March, April 1980; EC, 21, 24 February 1980; *WM*, 22, 23, 25 February 1980.

[42] EC, 24 February 1980; *The Guardian*, 23 February 1980; *The Times*, 23 February 1980.

One lodge chairman later remarked that '[m]iners didn't quite understand the full implication of not supporting the steelworkers for future attacks to come', especially since many pits relied on the coking coal market.[43] The ballot result was also a personal blow for Emlyn Williams: speaking at the 1980 Area conference, he called it 'possibly the most humiliating defeat ever inflicted on a [union] leadership by its members'. It is also likely that united action at that time would have placed the Thatcher government in as difficult an industrial relations situation as that faced by Heath in the 1970s. One lodge secretary later stated: '*That* should have been where we made a stand'.[44]

Following the collapse of the steel strike in April 1980, the ensuing cutback in BSC's productive capacity had inevitable repercussions for the coalfield. In November 1980, Weekes told the Area officials that the British Steel cuts would probably lead to closures but that he hoped to mitigate this by arranging for some coking coal to go to Didcot power station instead. Nevertheless, the loss of much of the coking coal market had serious implications, since the shift to power station usage led to a fall in proceeds of £19 a tonne. This 30 per cent drop in revenue meant that many south Wales collieries became heavy loss-makers overnight. The other main consequence was increased stockpiles: in September 1980, seven million tonnes of coal were being stored in the coalfield, with this figure rising at a rate of 50,000 tonnes per week.[45]

The steel strike episode taught the NUM a significant lesson about relying on the TUC. In March 1980, a National Conference discussed coal imports in the light of recent events in south Wales. Emlyn Williams called the TUC and the WTUC 'talking shops' and criticised their policy of sporadic 'day of action' token strikes, commenting that 'if they think that's the way to defeat this Government they're living in cloud cuckoo land'.[46] Consequently, it became more likely that the miners would minimise TUC involvement in any future conflict in which they found themselves. In late February 1980, some EC members told WTUC general secretary George Wright that they had no confidence in either the WTUC or the TUC, while in September 1980 Emlyn Williams

[43]   Interview with Arfon Evans, 1 April 2004.
[44]   Ray Lawrence interview.
[45]   EC, 15 April, 18 November 1980; ASC, 17 September 1980, 9 February 1981.
[46]   *The Miner*, April 1980.

stated: 'Our destiny . . . obviously does not lie within the constitution of the Wales TUC'.[47] Despite these disagreements, the south Wales miners took part in the TUC national 'day of action' on 14 May 1980. In Wales, the miners were the largest group of participants, with Emlyn Williams joining George Wright in addressing a rally in Newport.

A 'HISTORICAL MISSION TO LEAD IN CLASS STRUGGLES'

A prominent trend in the historiography of the British labour movement in recent years has been a post-modernist-driven scepticism of the centrality of institutions such as unions to the lives of ordinary working-class people. However, as Taylor observes, these viewpoints downplay the extent to which miners identified with their union as the best vehicle for advancement of their interests and saw themselves as the most politically-conscious section of the working class.[48] The south Wales miners exemplified this vanguard role. As their president pointed out in May 1981, 'we are associated in people's minds with resistance and struggles . . . There is no doubt in my mind that miners have an historical mission to lead in class struggles.'[49] Speaking at the 1980 Area conference, Emlyn Williams also spelt out in stark terms the crisis facing south Wales and the need for the miners to lead the resistance:

> We are talking about not just the destruction of miners' jobs but about the lives of communities . . . The social fabric of our valley communities will disintegrate . . . We are . . . suffering from . . . a policy of de-industrialisation which is changing the whole character of British industrial life.
>
> It is not a problem that can be resolved by a Labour Government in four years' time. How can a future Labour Government revive something which does not exist?
>
> Ours is a terminal disease unless we take emergency action . . . Not to strike is to capitulate. We know that with sufficient determination Government policies can be altered.

[47]   EC, 29 February 1980; ASC, 17 September 1980.
[48]   Andrew Taylor, *The NUM and British Politics, Vol. 1: 1944–1968* (Aldershot: 2003), pp. vii–viii.
[49]   *The Miner*, May/June 1981.

The spur for the miners to galvanise themselves for an impending confrontation was the NCB closure programme unveiled in May 1980; this stated that six of the biggest loss-making collieries in south Wales should close during the coming year. Even more ominously for the Area, the Board intended to shut Lewis Merthyr/Tymawr without going through the usual review procedure. This incensed the NUM, with even the national president, Joe Gormley, insisting that the NCB follow the statutory processes. In response, the south Wales miners initiated a coalfield-wide campaign for national industrial action if the threat of closures was not lifted. At an Area conference in June 1980, Llynfi Sundries delegate Jim O'Flynn observed: 'I know there were sharp criticisms made earlier this year of the Area Officials . . . but . . . everyone now realises that if we had gone into the fight in February we would not be in the state we are in today'. Following this conference, the Area's lodges agreed unanimously to support the struggle.[50]

The South Wales campaign against pit closures gathered momentum in the second half of 1980, owing to pressure from the Lewis Merthyr men and also the strategy of the Area leadership. During the summer, several lodges called for an overtime ban as a prelude to possible strike action, while Lewis Merthyr and Tymawr men also lobbied the 1980 National Conference. Between September and November 1980, pithead meetings were held to galvanise the membership for the struggle against closures. The NEC supported this stance, deciding to organise a national withdrawal from the colliery review procedure unless the threat to Lewis Merthyr/Tymawr was lifted.[51] On 20 November, an Area conference underlined the readiness of the miners to strike in order to defend their industry. Emlyn Williams welcomed the NEC offer of aid but (in a contribution which highlighted the key elements of the strategic thinking of the NUM Left in the early 1980s) he stressed the need for the south Wales miners to fulfil a vanguard role in the forthcoming confrontation:

> [W]hen the crunch comes the National President will insist on an Individual Ballot . . . before strike action. We all know . . . that Areas unaffected by closures . . . will not succumb to an appeal for industrial action that will be worded against the more progressive Areas. The answer is that somewhere

50   ASC, 16 July 1980; *WM*, 22 May, 3, 4 June 1980; EC, 4, 10, 24 June, 1 July 1980.
51   EC, 18 November 1980.

in the British Coalfield one Area has got to make the initial sacrifice and immediately extend their appeal . . . for support to the grass roots of the British Coalfield . . .

Our experience with the British TUC [is] . . . one of being constitution-alised out of action, and if anyone thinks that . . . the TUC would agree to this action . . . they are living in a fool's paradise . . .

We have effectively now, for a twelve month, blocked the Coal Board's aspirations on Tymawr/Lewis Merthyr and it is, I hope, possible that discussions will drag out until January of 1981. This has been, and always will be, the right time for miners to show positive resistance to closures. I would plead with the leadership here that the task is to prepare our men for the inevitability of a clash with the Coal Board and this Government . . .

I want immediate backing for Strike Action if the Board decide to close Tymawr/ Lewis Merthyr. We already have the mandate but do we have to kindle the fire?

THE 1981 STRIKE: A DEFEAT FOR THE PIT CLOSURE PROGRAMME?

The Area leadership's certainty of a clash over colliery closures in early 1981 was driven partly by its own strategy and partly because the Board was scheduled to announce in February 1981 how it would implement the cutbacks proposed by the Coal Industry Act (1980). The south Wales miners braced themselves for a con-frontation: both they and the Yorkshire Area had strike mandates and rumours were circulating that the NCB planned to shed 25,000 jobs and cut annual output by nine million tonnes. Faced with the probability that the blow would fall heavily on south Wales, on 9 February 1981 an Area conference decided that strike action would commence on 23 February. Emlyn Williams declared: 'I won't call it a strike. I would call it a demonstration for existence. The miners in south Wales are saying "we are not going to accept the dereliction of our mining valleys, we are not allowing our children to go immediately from school to the dole queue. It is time we fought".'[52]

Although the NUM had been expecting it, the NCB's announcement still came as a harsh blow: twenty-three pits were to close, five of which were in south Wales.[53] While it is not surprising that Welsh miners were at the centre of resistance, what was unusual

---

[52] ASC, 16 January 1981; EC, 3 February 1981; Hywel Francis, 'Emlyn Williams (1921–1995)', *Llafur*, 7/1 (1996), 7.

[53] Report of Meeting held at NCB Offices, Llanishen, 13 February 1981.

was that opposition was led by the politically-moderate Coegnant lodge. When placed 'in jeopardy' in 1980, the men there had complied with the management's plans to reduce the workforce, accepted lower earnings and even set up a new £1.5 million coalface a fortnight ahead of schedule. Coegnant passed its 'fitness test' and on 12 February had been congratulated by NCB officials who visited the colliery. The next day, the men were devastated and infuriated to learn that their pit had nevertheless been listed for closure. As Coegnant lodge secretary Verdun Price pointed out, '[t]he only answer for us was to become militant – we were left with no alternative'.[54] The Coegnant men struck immediately and set about picketing other south Wales pits. Price later recalled that he received a telephone call from Emlyn Williams at the time, in which the Area president stated his tacit approval for this unofficial action.[55] On 16 February, a hastily-convened Area conference carried unanimously the EC's recommendation of an all-out stoppage, to begin the following day.[56] The strike for which the south Wales miners had been preparing was now underway.

With the south Wales coalfield solidly on strike, the Area sought to spread its campaign further afield. Arrangements were made to picket the steelworks, power stations and coking plants, as well as various NCB ancillary sites. Other unions agreed to halt coal movement throughout the region, while the strike also received WTUC approval. The EC asked the other Areas for support: Kent, Scotland and Durham joined the strike promptly, while Yorkshire had a mandate to begin action the following week – all of which defied the national officials' requests to wait until a ballot could be held. South Wales pickets also entered the north Wales coalfield, much to the dismay of the leadership there: Ted McKay, the North Wales general secretary, denounced them as 'yobbos'.[57] In south Wales, '[m]en talked seriously of holding out [on strike] until

[54]   WM, 14, 16 February 1981; The Guardian, 17 February 1981; The Times, 18 February 1981; EC, 3 February 1981.

[55]   Interview with Verdun Price, 15 March 2004.

[56]   For a first-hand account of this conference, see Kim Howells and Merfyn Jones, 'Oral history and contemporary history', Oral History, 11/2 (1983), 15–20.

[57]   Keith Gildart, North Wales Miners: A Fragile Unity, 1945–1996 (Cardiff: 2001), p. 145. For more on the internal factionalism of Welsh mining trade unionism in the late 1970s and early 1980s and how the divisions between North Wales and South Wales were a harbinger for the fragmentation of national unity in 1984, see Gildart, North Wales Miners, 137–53.

September'.[58] Events were gathering momentum and appeared close to becoming a full-blown national strike, developing along the Area-by-Area basis supported by the NUM Left.

Faced with this prospect, the Thatcher administration back-tracked. As John Biffen, a cabinet minister, noted at the time, 'the spectre that frightened the government was the very clear evidence that there would be massive industrial action'.[59] Realising that coal stocks were low, on 18 February it agreed to withdraw the closure programme and promised to double the NCB grant.[60] Conservative opinion was outraged at this 'U-turn'. Backbench Tory MPs criticised Thatcher and demanded the resignation of NCB chairman Derek Ezra. The director-general of the Institute of Directors slammed the government's 'scandalous surrender', commenting sarcastically that '[w]e might as well ask the miners' union when it wants to call the next general election'. James Prior, the Secretary of State for Employment, denied press allegations that he had been plotting against the prime minister in secret meetings with Gormley.[61] It was all a far cry from Thatcher's later image as 'the Iron Lady'.

Although the government had apparently conceded defeat, the NUM still had to decide whether to continue the strike. In the NEC, Emlyn Williams and George Rees argued against ending it until the government had given written guarantees but they were outvoted by 15 to 8. Despite this, the strike continued in south Wales until an Area conference had met on 20 February. This was not simply a formality: since the south Wales miners had begun the strike, they were in an influential position to determine the next step. After a long discussion, the EC agreed to accept the NEC recommendation, albeit with a mandate for an immediate return to action if government promises were not fulfilled. At the conference, Emlyn Williams conceded that he was somewhat suspicious that 'what has been offered is far more than we came out for' but pointed out that the NUM needed to be seen to be accepting the victory it had won. Although most delegates concurred, a few still had reservations. Ivor

---

[58] Howells and Jones, 'Oral History', 17.

[59] Quoted in John McIlroy, *Trade Unions in Britain Today* (2nd edn, Manchester: 1995), p. 196.

[60] M. J. Parker, *Thatcherism and the Fall of Coal* (Oxford: 2000), pp. 14–15; *The Guardian*, 19 February 1981.

[61] *The Times*, 20 February 1981.

England (Maerdy), for example, warned that '[w]e have nothing in writing and I am concerned if we return to work pit closures will continue'.[62]

In view of the events which were to occur in subsequent years, the decision of the Area conference on 20 February 1981 not to continue the strike has assumed a counterfactual significance. For instance, Tyrone O'Sullivan contends:

> As I saw it, Thatcher was offering us a basket of goods but there was a hole in the bottom of the basket and everything . . . was rapidly falling out . . . [W]e were bought off and I blame the Union in South Wales.
>
> The miners in Yorkshire and Kent were waiting . . . [and i]f we had voted for a full strike, they would have supported us – they argued that . . . the government was simply playing for time. Unfortunately only seven local lodge votes supported the continuation of the strike and the rest supported the South Wales union leadership. We would live to regret that decision for many years and I believe it was that vote that allowed the Thatcher Government to go on and not only destroy the NUM but also the whole trade union movement.[63]

Even within the Area leadership, the issue had been contentious. Mike Banwell, an EC member, later argued that 'we let them off the hook . . . I think it was a missed opportunity. I think we should have . . . said . . . "let's get our demands . . . met before we return to work".' By contrast, a fellow EC representative Dane Hartwell pointed out that 'once they had done a U-turn . . . it's very difficult to then to say to your men, "right the threat's been taken away . . . but you should remain on strike" . . . *I* don't think the men would have worn it . . . [and] we could have been accused of just *wanting* to prolong the strike.'[64]

Regardless of later arguments, in February 1981 most south Wales miners felt that they had won some kind of victory against the closure programme – even though '[t]he triumph seemed curiously intangible'.[65] Assessing the strike at the 1981 Area conference, Emlyn Williams called it 'a success, but not an unmitigated one' and pointed

    [62] ASC, 20 February 1981.
    [63] Tyrone O'Sullivan, with John Eve and Ann Edworthy, *Tower Of Strength: The Story of Tyrone O'Sullivan and Tower Colliery* (Edinburgh: 2001), p. 93.
    [64] Interviews with Mike Banwell (9 March 2004) and Dane Hartwell (10 December 2003).
    [65] Howells and Jones, 'Oral History', 18.

out that the key lesson was the necessity of confronting the government over pit closures: 'It is . . . a universal truth that in class struggles, if you fight you stand to win or lose, but if you do not fight, you stand only to lose.'[66]

The February 1981 confrontation was a defeat for the government, although not ultimately a significant one. As NUM national vice-president Mick McGahey remarked at the time, it was 'not so much a U-turn, more a body swerve'; Terry Thomas, Area vice-president from 1983 to 1989, later commented that 'in rugby terms, we were fed a dummy'.[67] The 'U-turn' was a tactical concession because the government realised that it was insufficiently prepared for a NUM strike. Its main long-term result was to strengthen Thatcher's resolve to tackle the union when the time was ripe. The 'generous settlement' of 1981 proved to be a mirage. Retrospectively, it could be argued that it was a mistake not to get the concessions in writing; on the other hand, it is possible that the government would eventually have evaded any written agreement in the same way that it reneged on its verbal promises. Within a few months, doubts had begun to emerge. In April 1981, Emlyn Williams told an Area conference: 'we have not yet attained the victory that we so earnestly desired . . . and indeed a feeling is creeping in that possibly on taking the word of the National Executive and the President that we returned to normal working too quickly'. In December 1982, he stated pessimistically that '[w]e should have, looking back in hindsight, returned only when we had copper-bottomed guarantees. Nothing in the March 1981 Coal Industry Financial Bill has been given to the South Wales coalfield.'[68]

LOCALISED DISPUTES AND THE INCENTIVES EFFECT

Colliery-level disputes remained commonplace in south Wales in the early 1980s – indeed, their frequency had increased following the reintroduction of piecework in the industry several years earlier. One example was the strike at Aberpergwm in August 1983 over bonus payments. Many other factors could cause stoppages. At Trelewis

---

[66] AAC, 1981.

[67] Quoted in Seumas Milne, *The Enemy Within: The Secret War Against The Miners* (London: 1995), p. 9; interview with Terry Thomas, 16 February 2004.

[68] ASC, 8 December 1982.

Drift, for instance, there were strikes in July 1981 and February 1982 against the management's refusal to allow dispensations for men working in atrocious water conditions. Given the Board's recruitment embargo, an additional source of conflict was disagreement over the most effective use of manpower: there was a dispute at Marine in April 1981 over shift-working patterns and a three-day strike at St John's in May 1983 over coalface manning levels. While few of these stoppages related directly to the major problems facing the south Wales miners, they nevertheless reflected the tension in the industry at that time.

On a more general level, the incentive bonus scheme placed several obstacles to NUM unity. Reporting to an Area conference in February 1979 on the effect of the scheme, George Rees conceded that south Wales output was up by 9.3 per cent but that this in itself did little to safeguard the coalfield: 'If we do not produce [enough] the Board want to close pits, if we overproduce the markets are not available – [leading to] further pit closures.' In this context, bonuses for certain collieries and coalfields were a major problem for the NUM if they hastened the process of closure elsewhere. Further evidence of the impact of piecework was the acceptance at the 1979 Area conference of the EC resolution calling for £71 a week for surface workers (with appropriate differentials) – a modest demand compared to those of the 1970s. Delegates accepted this reduced aspiration partly to minimise the crisis facing the industry but also because they thought that a call for action would never be supported by men at collieries whose bonuses were more than the basic rates that the NUM would be demanding. As the Area had predicted, incentive bonuses increased disparities between coalfields, collieries and job-grades, and also masked a relative decline in basic wages. In the pits themselves, the scheme undermined the relatively harmonious industrial relations of the 1970s, as men and management disagreed frequently over the incentive rate and the output 'norm' required to trigger bonus payments. This soon became the most common cause of local grievances.[69]

Once the incentive bonus scheme had been established, south Wales miners accepted that its abolition would prove impracticable: their 1979 conference rejected calls for it to be abandoned, while the St John's proposal at the 1983 conference for the replacement of

---

[69]   EC, 1979–83 passim.

pit-level bonuses by a National Productivity Scheme (the Area's preferred policy in the mid-1970s) did not even receive the support of a second lodge to allow it to be debated. Notwithstanding this, the general response was to work towards mitigating the most divisive aspects of the incentive scheme. Throughout the early 1980s, the Area leadership pressed for a uniform bonus rate in integrated collieries for all EBG[70] and surface grades. Also, every Area annual conference between 1979 and 1983 called for improvements in the incentive bonus scheme. Some of the main grievances were discrepancies between different grades; 'inbye' craftsmen not receiving the same bonuses as faceworkers; insufficient allowance for adverse geological conditions; and the fact that calculation of bonuses on a weekly basis meant that a whole week's worth of payments could be undone by poor results on any one day. By May 1983, the south Wales miners had concluded that the fairest solution would be an Area-wide bonus scheme, which would pay a uniform rate to the various grades across the whole coalfield.[71]

GOVERNMENT ENERGY POLICY POST-1981

In February 1981, the plan for a widespread closure programme was met head-on by the miners and rebutted comprehensively. Subsequently, the government changed tactics, introducing piecemeal cutbacks which did not provoke a direct NUM challenge. In south Wales, this meant the withholding of investment and recruitment so that collieries would eventually be forced to close. By 1983 most of the closures announced in February 1981 had been carried out, reducing total industry manpower by 22,000. *The Miner* newspaper warned that the NCB planned to cut a further 70,000 jobs by 1990, together with the closure of 95 pits (out of a British total of 207) by 1987. In an Area conference in May 1983, EC member Des Dutfield described the NCB's 'divide and conquer' policy as 'the oldest Tory trick in the book' and warned that 'if we don't change our tactics we are going to lose the fight'.[72]

---

[70] Elsewhere Below Ground: underground mineworkers who worked 'outbye', that is, not actually at the coalface (which was termed 'inbye').

[71] AAC, 1983.

[72] ASC, 24 August 1981, 8 December 1982, 23 May 1983; *The Miner*, November 1982; Parker, *Thatcherism and the Fall of Coal*, p. 35.

If one half of the Thatcher government's post-1981 policy towards the coal industry was to weaken the NUM without pushing it into a confrontation, the second part was to prepare to be able to withstand a strike once it was ready for a showdown.[73] As part of this strategy, coal stocks were built up from 37 million to 57 million tonnes between 1981 and 1984. By early 1983, 750,000 tonnes a year of non-NCB coal was being used at Aberthaw power station, one of the main markets for the south Wales coalfield; at the same time, it was costing the South Wales Board £200 million a year to store unwanted coal. Reporting on these stockpiles, the *South Wales Miner* stated sardonically that '[t]hanks to the genius of the Coal Board's salesmen, [the coal] . . . is moving so slowly that spontaneous combustion will claim it before any customer does'.[74]

In addition to this stockpiling policy, a central part of the Thatcher government's plan was diversification of the energy sources used by the CEGB, with the emphasis on oil, gas and nuclear power. In the early 1980s, nuclear power seemed the main threat to coal. The development of the new Sizewell reactor in Suffolk, coupled with the fact that several south Wales coal-fired plants (Uskmouth, Rogerstone, and Carmarthen Bay) were nearing the end of their working lives, led to fears that the CEGB would replace them with nuclear installations, thereby removing one of the coalfield's most important markets; even Aberthaw faced possible replacement. The prospect of up to twelve new nuclear reactors in south-west England led the Area's newspaper to comment grimly that '[t]he whole Bristol Channel area is rapidly becoming Europe's most nuclear-intensive region . . . If this nightmare becomes a reality, the people of South Wales won't *need* lights in the 21st century [original emphasis]. The glow from their own radioactivity will be illumination enough to guide them to and from the dole office.'[75]

REDUNDANCY SCHEMES

In south Wales, NCB policy between 1981 and 1983 was implemented partly by the 'slow strangulation' of selected collieries and also by

[73]   For more on this, see John Saville, 'An open conspiracy: Conservative politics and the miners' strike of 1984–5', *Socialist Register*, 22 (1985), 301–3.
[74]   *SWM*, February 1983; EC, 9 August 1983; Ben Fine, *The Coal Question: Political Economy and Industrial Change from the Nineteenth Century to the Present Day* (London: 1990), p. 161.
[75]   *WM*, 20 December 1982; *SWM*, November 1982, February 1983.

measures to shrink the overall size of the industry. The prime example of this was the Redundancy Agreement, introduced in March 1981. The South Wales opinion of this was spelt out by Emlyn Williams at an Area conference the following month; he called it 'an instrument to destroy the unity of the miners . . . [I]t is fool's gold and no-one has the right to prostitute his job when we have such high unemployment figures.' One miner later recalled the effect of this scheme:

> [The government] done a U-turn and in no time they were up to their tricks again . . . [T]hey brought in . . . redundancy payments . . . [t]o split the workers. They *actually* got men to sell their jobs . . . [T]hese men were offered this money, something they'd never seen in their lives before . . . They were coming up to retirement, some of them . . . And *most* men finished with ill health anyway. Or incapacity – which was a small amount [of money compared to the redundancy scheme]. So, *that's why* we got into difficulties.[76]

The apparent similarity of the Redundancy Agreement and the VERS might have made the Area's strong opposition to the former policy and its support for the latter seem confusing. The reason for this approach hinges on the different aims of the two policies: the VERS enabled men to retire early, whereas the redundancy scheme aimed to reduce the size of the industry. The fundamental distinction between them was that the Board was theoretically obliged to replace men who retired under the VERS, while it was not with the Redundancy Agreement. Furthermore, redundancy payouts were far more than under the VERS, in order to induce men to opt for it. The absence of any formalised NUM input into deciding who was eligible for redundancy also meant that the Board could easily use it to undermine the Area leadership. In mid-1981, for example, redundancy was offered to Betws and Cynheidre men without consultation with either the lodge leaderships or the Area NUM – even though there were over a hundred vacancies at Cynheidre. Altogether, 734 men took redundancy in south Wales in 1982–3, at a time when the coalfield required 5,000 new recruits to ensure adequate manning levels.[77] Mike Griffin appraised the situation at an Area conference in November 1981: 'The Board are

---

[76] Mike Richards interview.
[77] EC, 30 June, 14 July 1981, 12 April 1983.

offering Redundancy because they know that Redundancies cannot continue without collieries closing.'[78]

A similar process was at work in the Board's programme of colliery amalgamations. While these were portrayed as 'modernisation', in practice they made it probable that coal-winding would be centralised on one of the sites in question, leading to the closure of the other surface workings. Evidence of this was provided in September 1982 and 1983 by NCB proposals to close the colliery surfaces at Blaenserchan (which would join with Six Bells and Marine) and Coedely (which was linked with Cwm).[79] This scenario ensured that the south Wales miners were deeply unenthusiastic about the Board's plans, which emerged in August 1982, to integrate Maerdy and Tower and also to link Deep Navigation, Penrhiwceiber and Taff Merthyr. However, if the issue was presented starkly in terms of either integration or closure then eventually miners felt they had little choice. By January 1984, for example, both Tower and Maerdy lodges had agreed to an amalgamation of their collieries. However, no progress had been made on this before March 1984.[80]

NUM POLITICS AND THE RISE OF ARTHUR SCARGILL

Despite their active campaigning against pit closures, the south Wales miners remained keenly interested in NUM internal affairs. One of their perennial grievances was the composition of the union's NEC, which gave disproportionate influence to the smallest Areas. This was of particular concern to South Wales in the early 1980s, since if its membership fell below 22,000 (as seemed likely within the next few years) it would be reduced to one NEC seat, giving it the same influence as Cumberland, which had only 650 members. Consequently, Area conferences in 1981 and 1983 called for a democratisation of NEC decision-making. This reform was seen as important because these decisions had a central bearing at critical junctures in the union's history. As Mike Griffin pointed out at the 1981 conference, the strike in February 1981 was called off because of the 15–8 vote in the NEC, even though the eight votes

---

[78]   ASC, 27 November 1981.
[79]   *SWM*, June 1983; EC, 2 September 1982, 26 October 1983; *WM*, 22 October 1983.
[80]   EC, 24 August, 2 September 1982, 11 October 1983, 4 January 1984.

represented 129,000 members, whereas the fifteen vote 'majority' represented only 125,000.[81]

Joe Gormley retired as NUM president at the end of 1981. Gormley had been the bulwark of NUM conservatism for a decade and represented the antithesis of the radicalism of the south Wales miners. In April 1981, for instance, he provoked outrage in the Area when he reportedly commented that he was happier dealing with Conservative ministers than he had been with Tony Benn while the latter was Secretary of State for Energy.[82] Once he had retired, the Area was free to express its opinion – and it did so in characteristically robust language. Its 1982 annual conference deplored Gormley's 'cavalier' attitude towards National Conference decisions and stated that any future NUM officials who similarly disregarded the will of the membership should be expelled. Emlyn Williams made an equally damning assessment: 'Here was a man whose capacity for intrigue knew no bounds . . . He ignored any decisions he disliked . . . [and it] was indicative of his attitude that he was prepared to help out this hated Tory Government . . . [O]ur President retired with members demanding his dismissal.'

Gormley's departure provided the chance to elect a president willing to play a more proactive role in the crisis facing the coal industry. With McGahey ineligible for consideration (he was too old), the candidate for the NUM Left was Arthur Scargill, the Yorkshire Area president. Scargill addressed South Wales annual conferences in 1980 and 1981, and received their formal backing. He also benefited from the support of the CP and the various other left-wing groups that were emerging in the early 1980s, all of which wanted to see the union adopting a more militant stance. In the run-up to the election, he spoke at several meetings in south Wales. In the NUM presidential election in December 1981 Scargill scored a resounding victory with over 70 per cent of the vote, a result which appeared to represent a clear mandate for action against pit closures.[83] Describing Scargill's election as 'a tremendous victory for progressive reforms in the Union', Emlyn Williams said: 'For the first time in the history of the NUM we have a progressive leadership . . . There are no limits this Union cannot reach with an active, democratic,

[81] AAC, 1981.
[82] EC, 14 April 1981.
[83] EC, 20 October 1981; *The Miner*, February 1982.

campaigning leadership.'[84] Scargill's success, followed by the election
of Peter Heathfield (the North Derbyshire Area secretary) as NUM
general secretary in January 1984, meant that all three national
officials were now left-wingers.[85]

PREPARING FOR A SHOWDOWN, 1980–3

In the unsettled atmosphere of the early 1980s, the Area leadership
was determined to resist pit closures through strike action. In this
respect, it is possible to trace a direct 'line of descent' from the
unofficial movement's strategy in the 1960s to the official Area policy
by the 1980s – a point made by veteran EC member and 1960s
activist Ben Davies in his final speech to the EC before retiring in
April 1982.[86] In many ways this is not surprising, given that three of
the Area's four most senior posts were filled by men who had led the
unofficial movement (Emlyn Williams, George Rees and Don
Hayward), while many other EC members and lodge leaders had
risen to prominence during the 1969–74 upsurge of radicalism. The
south Wales miners' historical 'vanguard' role was prominent in the
thinking of the Area president. In October 1980, he stated that
'[t]here is an understanding now that South Wales have got to make
the first sacrifice and I believe that we have got to avoid . . . being
constitutionalised out of action by . . . the National Executive and
Joe Gormley'.[87]

By March 1983, however, the British miners had rejected strike
action three times in less than eighteen months. Consequently,
Emlyn Williams told the 1983 Area conference:

> We have . . . to ask ourselves serious questions about the consciousness
> of our members . . . [A]lthough I would like to think that miners were
> politically different and better than other groups of workers, in reality
> they often behave like others. All trade unionists in Britain are operating
> under vicious Government pressures from legislation and criminal levels
> of unemployment. To put it bluntly, unemployment takes the guts out of
> people.

[84]   AAC, 1982.
[85]   For details, see Andrew Taylor, *The NUM and British Politics, Vol. 2: 1969–1995*
(Aldershot: 2005), pp. 182–3.
[86]   EC, 20 April 1982.
[87]   SWML interview with Emlyn Williams (AUD/33).

The South Wales president was not the only person to make this point. In the early 1980s, for example, the Garw Valley and Abernant lodge secretaries, together with Glyn Williams (the former Area leader), all said that there had been a decline in political consciousness among the miners in recent years.[88] Partly this was due to reluctance to jeopardise bonus payments through industrial action; however, the issue was more complicated than that. In 1980, former Area general secretary Dai Francis claimed that Labour right-wingers had fomented apathy so as to retain control of their localities. Retrospectively the Blaenant chairman made a similar comment, highlighting the role of an 'anti-struggle movement' within Labour to lessen resistance to closures and persuade the miners not to support the steelworkers' strike in 1980. This point was underlined by Emlyn Williams in February 1981, when he attacked 'the Labour Councillors for Moderation in the South Wales Coalfield' who 'in February of 1980 deliberately carried out a character assassination of myself'.[89]

Faced with this challenge, the Area leadership strove to prepare for a final confrontation with the NCB and the government. At the 1983 Area conference, Emlyn Williams called for a heightened political consciousness among the south Wales miners:

> [I]t needs more than good intentions by the leadership to persuade the NCB to meet our demands. It needs an alert, politicised membership, not simply at branch officer level but at the level of the ordinary rank and file. This level has been our Achilles heel. The evidence of the past year has shown that in many ways the leadership has been ahead of the rank and file and this is not a healthy situation. I am generalising, of course, because there have been situations, over Lewis Merthyr/Tymawr, for example, when this has not been the case. *You must also remember that the standards expected of the South Wales miners is high* [my emphasis]. In my view it is not a victory when 55 per cent of our membership supports an official call for strike action because I expect an 85 per cent response. I was disappointed last November when only 59 per cent of the South Wales miners supported the NEC call for industrial action over pay and pit closures. *Our reputations as political leaders in the British coalfields, built by Arthur Horner, Bill Paynter and Dai Francis, is at stake* [my emphasis].

[88]   SWML interviews with Glyn Williams (AUD/113), Berwyn Howells (AUD/21) and Ron Williams (AUD/115).
[89]   SWML interview with Dai Francis (AUD/131); interview with Phil Bowen, 26 March 2004; ASC, 9 February 1981.

Rather than simply calling for greater radicalism, however, in the early 1980s the Area leadership took seriously the task of building up rank-and-file activism, encouraging the formation of local action committees and emphasising to the membership the need to oppose closures.[90] The Area's education scheme played a useful role here, partly through its day-release courses, partly in conjunction with Llafur, the Welsh labour history society. In April 1980, for example, the fifth annual Llafur weekend school focused on the crisis facing the coalfield, with the main speakers including McGahey, Will Paynter and Philip Weekes. It was as part of this approach that Kim Howells was appointed as research officer in May 1982 to provide information to assist the struggle. The leadership also organised mass meetings on the subject (including an eight-week campaign in autumn 1980), while the 1983 Area conference called for 'teach-ins' to counteract 'the constant barrage of propaganda from the Capitalist Press'. One indication of the success of these measures was that the percentage of south Wales miners voting for strike action in national ballots rose from 54 per cent in January 1982, to 59 per cent in November 1982 and 68 per cent in March 1983.[91]

One of the Area's most important campaigning innovations in this period was the launch of a monthly newspaper, *South Wales Miner*, as a means of boosting rank-and-file awareness of political circumstances, both generally and within the industry. South Wales already received the NUM's national paper, *The Miner*, but it was felt that this did not provide sufficient detail on south Wales developments to counter the NCB's paper *Coal News*. The first issue appeared in October 1982 and its front page made it clear that its key objective was to galvanise the membership for the struggle:

> The 'South Wales Miner' will give NUM members . . . information about their industry . . . normally denied them by the Coal Board, television and newspapers.
>
> Our paper will campaign to reverse the scandalous run-down of this coalfield . . .
>
> Most important[ly] . . . it will provide a voice for the ordinary rank and filer and show that we suffer similar problems right across this coalfield.
>
> Our aim will be to inform and unite our membership so we can abolish the insecurity and doubt which have bedevilled our industry.

[90] Haydn Matthews and Emlyn Williams SWML interviews.
[91] EC, 22 January, 2 November 1982, 11 March 1983.

Although the Area worked consistently in the early 1980s to prepare for a showdown with the NCB, an important strategic question was the choice of the best issue on which to make a stand. Clearly, colliery closures was the main threat. However, as Emlyn Williams told the 1983 conference, '[t]he most difficult thing in the mining industry is to get coalfield solidarity for action over a single pit . . . We have a long history of disappointment and frustration on this issue. Some of you will remember the Afan [*sic*] Ocean Colliery closure in 1969.' In June 1986, he commented that it was far easier to have successful national strike action over wages than over pit closures.[92] Furthermore, closures were a defensive issue conditional on reacting to an NCB announcement, whereas with wages it was possible for miners to take the initiative. Bearing this in mind, although they were prepared to fight colliery closures wherever necessary, the left-wing Areas (and, after Scargill's election as NUM president, the national leadership) also looked to utilise wages as the 'spearhead' for the broader struggle against government plans to run down the coal industry.

Following Scargill's election in December 1981, three attempts were made to initiate strike action via a national ballot.[93] In each case, the leadership tried to choose the issue which seemed most likely to produce a positive result. In late 1981 and early 1982, the focus was on wages. In December 1981, South Wales lobbied the NEC against the NCB's offer. An Area conference on 5 January 1982 endorsed the NEC call for strike action. When the national ballot was held later that month, however, the result was a defeat for the NEC, by 113,144 votes (55 per cent) to 91,477 (45 per cent) – although South Wales voted for a strike by 10,687 (54 per cent) to 8,939 (46 per cent). The most controversial aspect of this result was Gormley's last-minute exhortation to miners to reject the NEC recommendation. Union left-wingers were incensed and although a vote of censure against Gormley on the NEC was defeated by 13 votes to 12, many south Wales lodges called for his instant dismissal.[94] The EC meeting on 22 January 'made [it] crystal clear that in the opinion of the South Wales Executive Council Joe Gormley had turned into a traitor'.[95]

---

[92] *SWM*, June 1983; SWML interview with Emlyn Williams (AUD/574).
[93] For details, see Taylor, *The NUM and British Politics, Vol. 2*, pp. 174–80.
[94] EC, 15 December 1981; *The Miner*, February 1982; *WM*, 19 January 1982.
[95] EC, 22 January 1982.

By the time the wages question re-emerged later in 1982, the Area had made a concerted attempt to learn from the defeat in January. In south Wales, the main steps taken in October 1982 to support the union's official policy (calling for a weekly rate of £115 for surface workers, with appropriate differentials) were a series of high-profile rallies, the implementation of a national overtime ban and the unveiling of the new Area journal. The campaign was conducted on both wages and pit closures, with a conference on 6 October endorsing the strike call. The overtime ban, which received total support in south Wales, was an attempt to focus miners' minds on the inadequacy of their basic wage-rates and also to deplete coal stocks. Additionally, it was arranged for the Area leadership to tour the pits to argue the case for strike action. The highlight of these meetings was a mass rally at the Afan Lido in Port Talbot, addressed by the national officials. Despite these efforts, the overall ballot result was a disappointment for NUM militants, with action rejected by 125,233 votes (61 per cent) to 81,592 (39 per cent). South Wales supported the strike call, by 12,138 votes (59.25 per cent) to 8,287 (40.75 per cent). Following this, Emlyn Williams congratulated the south Wales miners on their pro-strike vote, in spite of what he described as 'a propaganda bombardment by the Coal Board and the media which surpassed any in living memory . . . [T]he Establishment were terrified of a miners' strike.'[96]

This failure prompted much deliberation in south Wales. Across the coalfield, the view was that the EC had run a very good campaign – and consequently the 59 per cent pro-strike vote was seen as quite disappointing by the Area leadership. The EC attributed the defeat to NCB and media interference, the ballot being held in the run-up to Christmas, and the belief that some men would rather take redundancy than strike. Emlyn Williams slammed the media's 'anti-working class propaganda and lies' and also had stern words for the 'greed and indifference [which] played a large part in the outcome of the vote'.[97] At the 1983 Area conference, he described the episode as 'a humiliating setback for the Union'.[98]

The ballot result may have removed the possibility of a national strike over wages but many south Wales miners still felt that decisive

---

[96] *SWM*, October, November 1982; *The Miner*, November 1982; *WM*, 12, 19 October 1982.
[97] EC, 24 November 1982; ASC, 8 December 1982.
[98] AAC, 1983.

action was necessary to prevent the run-down of their coalfield. On 8 December 1982, an Area conference demanded that the NCB increase investment in south Wales from £14 million to £500 million and allow adequate recruitment; if this was not forthcoming by 17 January 1983, the Area should instigate unilateral strike action. The pit at the centre of this campaign was Blaengwrach, which needed development work to save it from closure. Soon afterwards, lodge meetings overwhelmingly backed the strike call, by twenty-eight lodges to five. Subsequently, the South Wales leadership contacted other Areas to ask them to join the proposed strike. The intention was clearly a re-run of the strategy pursued in February 1981.

Blaengwrach and Lewis Merthyr

January 1983 looked set to repeat the events of two years earlier. However, solidarity from other Areas failed to materialise following the Scottish decision not to oppose the closure of Kinneil colliery or combine this with the south Wales campaign planned for 17 January. This lessened enthusiasm for action, causing concern within the EC that it would be compromised by making a strike call which the membership rejected – as had happened in February 1980. Moreover, in a meeting with the Area's leaders on 11 January, Weekes offered a deal: serious consideration to be given to NUM investment proposals, an end to the recruitment ban, and a guaranteed monopoly in supplying Aberthaw. As a result of these developments, the EC decided against pursuing strike action and recommended to an Area conference the following day that the planned stoppage be called off. This suggestion met with incredulity from some delegates. Charlie White (St John's) stated: 'I cannot understand what the Executive Council is doing . . . It is simply giving licence to the Board to crush us . . . [T]he men are ready to defend their jobs. We have always had promises [from the NCB] in South Wales and these new proposals are simply a waste of time.' Arfon Evans (Maerdy) was concerned that 'we have not learned the lessons and mistakes of the past'. In spite of this, the majority of delegates gave the Area leadership the benefit of the doubt and the strike was cancelled on a card vote by 379 votes to 121. Following this, Blaengwrach lodge considered picketing the most militant pits in an attempt to bring about a coalfield-wide strike. However, the Area's leaders felt that this was inadvisable and persuaded the Blaengwrach men not to go ahead – much to the annoyance of the lodge secretary and EC member Dane Hartwell. He later claimed that the situation was significant in precipitating the events that occurred soon after at Lewis Merthyr.[99] Reflecting on the episode at the 1983 annual conference, Emlyn Williams commented: 'With hindsight, I think we should have . . . struck . . . In January we could have acted in a planned, disciplined way over a general issue. It was the right issue at the right time. But instead we took the NCB at its word and allowed the heat to go out of the situation.'

While calling off the strike was inevitably unpopular with some lodges, it was justified at the time by the expectation that the NCB would deliver on its promises. In meetings with the Board in mid-January 1983, the Area pressed for investment at Blaengwrach and Lewis Merthyr and also called for reassurances regarding recruitment, exploration of coalfield reserves and the proposals for a new mine at Glyncastle. However, it soon became clear that none of this would materialise on the terms which the miners had been led to expect. In early February 1983, the South Wales NCB announced that recruitment would not increase significantly and that any which might occur would be conditional on further pit closures. George Rees expressed the Area's disgust at this news, telling the Board directors: 'You are not to be trusted and . . . have not carried out your side of the bargain which, it seems, was only used to avert a strike. We have been completely hoodwinked.' Consequently, the EC decided to convene a conference to bring the Area out on strike as from March 1983. This was overtaken by dramatic developments elsewhere in the coalfield.

The Lewis Merthyr stay-down strike of February 1983 was a significant event in its own right and the last of its kind in the history of the south Wales coalfield. It began when Weekes informed Alec Jones, MP for the Rhondda, that Lewis Merthyr would close, following which Jones tipped off the Lewis Merthyr men. In response, Des Dutfield led an immediate unofficial stay-down strike of twenty-eight miners at the colliery, which began on 21 February. Although he was South Wales vice-president, the strike began without the knowledge of the other Area officials – much to their

---

[99]   Dane Hartwell interview; EC, 25 January, 16 February 1983.

initial annoyance. Dutfield later explained that he led the strike because he felt that his ultimate loyalty was to the men with whom he worked in the pit, rather than to the EC.[100]

The stay-down strike intensified the pressure for action against closures. Lewis Merthyr struck immediately and within a few days had been joined by Trelewis Drift, St John's, Coedely, Britannia, Penrhiwceiber, Maerdy and Tower. Representatives from these lodges met the EC the day after the stay-down had begun and persuaded it to call a conference to discuss a coalfield-wide stoppage. The Area leadership decided to recommend a strike ballot to the conference on 23 February, to which the delegates agreed. However, this decision provoked anger from the lodges who were already out, since they felt that the December 1982 mandate still applied. Having secured their aim, the Lewis Merthyr strikers returned to the surface. The south Wales miners voted to strike by 9,714 votes (55.4 per cent) to 7,817 (44.6 per cent). Emlyn Williams attributed the narrowness of this margin to the difficulties in arranging for the pits that were already on strike to take part in the ballot. Although it had been a somewhat untidy process, by the end of February 1983 the south Wales miners were on strike against the run-down of their coalfield.[101]

Once the strike was underway, South Wales delegates travelled to the other coalfields to ask for their support. The possibility existed of an Area-by-Area strike; however, the emergence of dissent at several collieries in Scotland, Yorkshire and Derbyshire led the national leadership to opt instead for a ballot.[102]

The fact that the south Wales miners were already on strike offered an opportunity to influence the outcome of the ballot, with around 2,000 activists lobbying every pit in Britain to persuade them to join the struggle. Although this campaign was vital to the Area, it was by no means certain that miners elsewhere would agree, as the delegates who visited the other coalfields discovered. In coalfields such as Nottinghamshire, where the collieries were secure and the miners well-paid, the mood was one of indifference to the prospect of closures elsewhere. Ironically, given events the following year,

[100] *WM*, 22 February 1983; interviews with Des Dutfield (12 February 2004), Kevin Williams (25 February 2004), George Rees, Emlyn Jenkins (5 March 2004) and Terry Thomas.
[101] *The Guardian*, 24 February 1983; *WM*, 26 February 1983.
[102] *The Times*, 28 February, 1–4 March 1983; *The Guardian*, 4 March 1983; *WM*, 1–4 March 1983.

South Wales delegates later recalled that they fared better in Nottinghamshire than they did in Yorkshire, where they were prevented in some cases from addressing pithead meetings. As a lodge secretary later pointed out, the south Wales miners 'had a very bitter experience of going to Yorkshire in '83 – virtually feeling as if they'd been abandoned . . . It stuck in people's throats . . . that the Yorkshire Area did not support the south Wales miners in '83.'[103]

Given this mixed reception, it was perhaps not surprising that the national ballot rejected strike action, by 61 per cent (118,954 votes) to 39 per cent (76,540 votes). In south Wales – despite the absence of many activists on campaign duty – 68 per cent voted for the strike, with Garw Valley and Penrhiwceiber lodges returning majorities of 93 and 94 per cent respectively.[104] Following this defeat, the south Wales miners had no choice but to return to work. At an Area conference on 12 March, delegates voted unanimously to end the strike but at the same time attempted to draw lessons from the episode. Emlyn Williams said: 'I know there is a feeling of despondency . . . [but] we must not sit back and accept the butchery of the South Wales Coalfield'. Significantly, Mike Griffin commented that '[w]e could have won the struggle if we used the same tactics as we did in 1981', while Tyrone O'Sullivan (Tower) stated: 'In future we don't want another ballot, we must use the mandate that was achieved in the last Ballot. We should say "No more Ballots in South Wales".'

THE LESSONS OF 1983

The failure of a national ballot to support strike action against pit closures inevitably raised questions for the south Wales miners about what this meant for their policy of opposing the run-down of their coalfield. In March 1983, Oakdale lodge called for a greater effort in putting the miners' case to the public and also a strengthening of inter-Area links in preparation for a showdown with the government.[105] In May, Des Dutfield questioned the need for

---

[103] Ian Isaac interview.

[104] *SWM*, April 1983; *The Miner*, March 1983.

[105] This emphasis of the need for engagement with public opinion reflected the particular strategic perspective of Allan Baker, the Oakdale lodge secretary. See p. 42 for a fuller discussion of this.

successive ballots about closures: 'I do not believe that the continual holding of ballots on this subject is anything to do with democracy, but it is an excuse [for] . . . those who wish to avoid carrying out our policies'.[106] Speaking at the 1983 Area conference, Emlyn Williams criticised the anti-strike propaganda from the NCB, the government and the media in the run-up to the March 1983 ballot and called for a greater degree of organisation of the opposition to pit closures: 'It is a golden rule of industrial relations that if we are to be successful in a struggle against the NCB, *we* should choose the issue, the time and the place'.

In the history of the NUM, the events of February and March 1983 represent an important milestone on the road to 1984, in terms of the mobilisation of the south Wales miners and the shifting focus of tactics as to how best to effect national strike action. The ballot result convinced many NUM activists that the incentive scheme and the uneven impact of closures had made it impossible for a national ballot to support strike action against the run-down of the 'peripheral' coalfields. The Lewis Merthyr strike was in itself a turning point where history failed to turn. Regardless of the specifics of the case, retrospectively there would have been particular advantages to making a generalised stand against pit closures in 1983 as opposed to 1984. As one EC member later reflected:

[W]hen you look back, I think that *that was the time* that we should have been on strike . . . Over Lewis Merthyr . . . It was strategically the *best time*. Because . . . it was the *last* year of Thatcher's first term of office. Right? Instead of that, by . . . failing to get momentum at that time, we ended up actually coming on strike in the *first* year of Thatcher's *second* term of office . . . *Would* Thatcher have moved [against the NUM] if we had moved in the *last* year of her first term of office? *Would* she have taken those risks, y'know? . . . But, I mean, it would certainly . . . have been a *far better* position. Strategically, it would have been far better . . . I think that not enough thought went into it at that time . . . I *still* think that there were people in the Union at that time that could have shown a lot more leadership, then . . . I'm not talking about South Wales, I'm talking about *national* level . . . Arthur wasn't [as] *vocal at that time* . . . [a]s he was the year after . . . [T]he South Wales position was [that 1983] . . . was the time that it *should have* been done.[107]

---

[106] EC, 29 March 1983; ASC, 23 May 1983.
[107] Dane Hartwell interview.

THE 'MACGREGOR EFFECT' AND BRYNLLIW

The Conservatives' victory in the 1983 general election and the appointment of the 'union busting' Ian MacGregor as NCB chairman intensified the sense of crisis in south Wales. On 17 May, Emlyn Williams and W. R. Jenkins (the Area's safety officer) gave a detailed report to the EC on the situation in the coalfield, stressing that only recruitment and investment could improve collieries' viability. An Area conference six days later reaffirmed the need to oppose closures. Emlyn Williams told delegates: 'we must struggle or accept the demise of our coalfield'. In June 1983, Trelewis Drift called for an immediate national overtime ban as a prelude to an all-out strike that autumn.

In south Wales, miners soon experienced 'the MacGregor effect', with Coedely coke-works and Wyndham/Western colliery both being closed in later 1983. For the Area officials, Brynlliw was the best starting-point for a campaign against pit closures. In April 1983, Brynlliw lodge secretary and EC member Eric Davies claimed in the *South Wales Miner* that 'the Board have just had a taste during the Lewis Merthyr dispute of the kind of reaction they can expect if they try and pull the same trick at Brynlliw'. In June, however, Weekes stated that he intended to close Brynlliw as soon as possible. This news provoked local anger. Miners accused the NCB of reneging on the promise of investment and of ignoring a report which had suggested ways of extending the life of the pit by fifteen years. They were incensed that Brynlliw was being closed on a pure profit-and-loss basis, especially since it had only ended up in that position by being starved of capital for the preceding decade and used as a manpower reservoir for Betws. The NUM appealed against the decision, but at the review meeting in London in August 1983 it was clear that the NCB was determined to shut Brynlliw.[108]

With the Board intent on closing Brynlliw and the EC backing the fight to save the pit, the situation had the potential to provide the generalised offensive over pit closures for which the south Wales miners had been preparing. In June 1983, Area vice-president Terry Thomas commented: 'This is just one further attack on the mining industry. It is obvious how the miners will react to it, and I believe it will serve to unite them both in Wales and throughout Britain to

---

[108] EC, 26 August 1983; *SWM*, July 1983; *WM*, 21 July 1983.

protect their industry.'[109] The Area leadership was convinced of the need to strike but in accordance with union procedure it could only happen if the lodge called for it. However, in the time between submitting the case to review and the general meeting at the pit, the Board undermined the resolve of the workforce to fight by claiming that closure was inevitable and that the men would be better off if they transferred elsewhere – despite the campaigning efforts of the lodge committee. Consequently, Brynlliw decided to accept closure.[110]

The absence of a strike over Brynlliw later in 1983 was a setback for the South Wales leadership, but its significance was greater than was realised at the time. Brynlliw was seen as the potential 'launch-pad' for the Area to press for national action against closures, in a role similar to that of Lewis Merthyr in March 1983 – and also similar to that which Cortonwood played the following year. However, a strike over Brynlliw would have begun in October, strategically a far better month to begin a miners' strike than March. If action had begun then, it would certainly have posed a greater challenge to the Thatcher government than did the 1984–5 strike.

With their plans overturned by the Brynlliw closure, the Area officials looked for another potential catalyst for strike action. One likely contender seemed to be Penrhiwceiber. In September 1983, the lodge began an overtime ban against plans to integrate it with Deep Navigation, since this would cause redundancies and lead to the complete closure of the colliery in about two years' time. Penrhiwceiber received the support of several nearby lodges and there was the possibility that this could have developed into a broader campaign. When a Penrhiwceiber delegation met the EC, Emlyn Williams supported their efforts, stating that 'we must build up our resistance in readiness for an all out strike'.[111]

THE OVERTIME BAN

In October 1983, confrontations within the south Wales coalfield were augmented by the heightening of national-level tensions. The

[109] *WM*, 24 June 1983.
[110] Interviews with Eric Davies (30 January 2004) and Terry Thomas; *WM*, 27 August, 1 September 1983.
[111] EC, 12, 29 September 1983.

NEC decided to prepare for an impending clash by introducing an overtime ban, which would deplete coal stocks and radicalise rank-and-file opinion. The south Wales miners readily agreed to this. Addressing an Area conference about the need to reject the NCB's modest wage proposals, which were in any case tied to further cutbacks, Emlyn Williams pointed out that '[i]f we accept the wages now, we will be discussing pit closures in January, 1984. We have condemned the previous leadership nationally, but now we have a President who is not afraid to take up the cudgels on behalf of the membership.' Terry Thomas stated: 'By tying wages to closures the Board are adding insult to injury. We are now entering a struggle, not merely to protect our living standards but also our jobs and our communities.' The overtime ban began on 31 October, reducing weekly output in south Wales by up to 25,000 tonnes. As the Area's newspaper reported, '[t]he overtime ban is fouling up the Coal Board's operations. That's why Thatcher's messenger boys are suddenly bleating about "democracy". NUM members will remember the use of similar tactics in the run-up to the great strikes of 1972 and 1974.'[112]

This nationally-established initiative against pit closures enabled the Area leadership to resume its campaigning activities. Between October and December 1983, the Area leadership addressed a series of pithead meetings, in an attempt to ensure that the miners would respond positively to an imminent strike call. It was clear that events in the coal industry were building towards a decisive confrontation. By early 1984, the slightest provocation was likely to spark a major conflict.

CONCLUSION

For the south Wales miners, the years 1979 to 1983 were a period of simmering crisis punctuated by inconclusive confrontations with the NCB and the government. Their brief 'golden age' in the 1970s drew to a close under Callaghan's IMF-induced austerity measures, but it was not until the election of the Thatcher government that a major reduction in the size of the coal industry became a likely prospect. While the rate of pit closures in the early 1980s may not

[112] ASC, 14, 31 October 1983; EC, 8 November 1983; *SWM*, October, November/December 1983.

have matched that of the later 1960s, in many ways it was more of a threat to the south Wales miners. With the earlier closure programme, the underlying strategy had been to reformulate the coal industry as a smaller but more modern part of the energy sector. By contrast, by the 1980s the process was driven by the governmental aspiration to cut the industry back to its bare minimum with a view to privatising it. For the 'peripheral' coalfields, this meant their effective disappearance as mining areas. It was for this reason that the south Wales miners featured so prominently in the NUM's struggle against closures.

Throughout the early 1980s the South Wales leadership, conscious of the Area's traditional radicalism, sought to prepare the ground for the decisive struggle to defend jobs and collieries. By the 1980s most of the leaders of the south Wales miners had either participated in the struggles of the 1960s or had risen to prominence in the early 1970s, a period which seemed to prove the efficacy of militant methods. Many of the Area's senior figures in the 1980s were men who had led the unofficial movement in the 1960s, and the Area's policies reflected this. Nevertheless, resistance only developed into full-blown strikes in February 1981 and February 1983, when it was galvanised by unofficial action. The actions of the leadership in this period were defined by a dynamic that veered between its wish to strike a decisive blow against closures and its attempts to abide by official procedure. Fundamentally, both the Area's leaders and the most militant activists were in pursuit of the same goals; the only tension was over how these objectives should be attained.

While the South Wales Area may have adopted the approach of the 1960s unofficial movement, this policy was revised in the light of its experiences in the early 1980s. These episodes are also important in understanding some of the essential features of the national strike action which began in March 1984. The events of early 1980 seemed to confirm the view of NUM radicals that TUC involvement was more of a hindrance than a help. Moreover, the decision of the miners not to strike, contrary to official expectations, meant that the Area leadership became a bit more hesitant, thus reinforcing its preference for obtaining rank-and-file support before calling for industrial action. The short-lived strike of February 1981 was a very significant development for both the Area and the NUM as a whole, since it proved that it was possible to force the government to back down by means of a rapid spread of action on an Area-by-Area basis without recourse to a national ballot. This view seemed to be confirmed by the rejection of the strike call in the three ballots held in 1982 and 1983. Consequently, many NUM radicals came to believe that the NCB had made it virtually impossible for a national ballot to endorse strike action, particularly over colliery closures. Despite this, the south Wales miners were bitterly resentful about closures and were prepared to take action if given a clear lead. In this respect, their strikes in 1981 and 1983 helped them to prepare for the decisive clash in 1984.

While these events provide important insights into the NUM strategy during the 1984–5 strike, the historian should not fall into the trap of assuming that they were merely a build-up to it. Indeed, there was no intrinsic reason why any year between 1980 and 1983 should not have seen the final showdown between Thatcher and the miners – a development which, if it had happened, would have been more likely to produce a NUM victory. For the south Wales miners, this turned out to be a period of missed opportunities. As one former EC member later reflected:

> [W]e were in a situation from about 1980 up until '84 of the men didn't know if they were coming or going. One minute they thought they were coming out on strike, next minute they wasn't . . . South Wales miners wanted support from other Areas and didn't get it over Lewis Merthyr. We tried to get a national strike then and didn't get it . . . We missed *a lot* of opportunities. And I think that every opportunity we missed, the government then started to stock coal, they started to fetch in industrial laws, and all that, and then . . . we had our hands tied . . . in 1984.[113]

In the circumstances of the early 1980s, it was practically inevitable that the miners would clash with the Thatcher government. In the 'shadow boxing' between 1979 and 1983, the NUM had several chances to land a knockout blow but these either did not materialise fully or were allowed to pass in return for transitory concessions. As a result, the Conservative administration was able to survive and strengthen its position for an eventual day of reckoning with the NUM. Subsequent events would show that if the miners could not make the most of their confrontations with the NCB, the government would ensure that the decisive struggle would be fought once it was prepared for it and in circumstances of its own choosing.

---

[113] Mike Banwell interview.

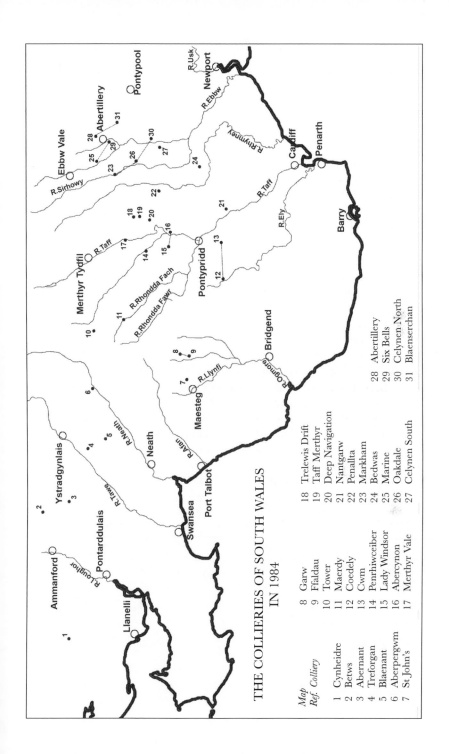

THE COLLIERIES OF SOUTH WALES
IN 1984

Map Ref.	Colliery			
1	Cynheidre	8	Garw	18 Trelewis Drift
2	Betws	9	Ffaldau	19 Taff Merthyr
3	Abernant	10	Tower	20 Deep Navigation
4	Treforgan	11	Maerdy	21 Nantgarw
5	Blaenant	12	Coedely	22 Penallta
6	Aberpergwm	13	Cwm	23 Markham
7	St. John's	14	Penrhiwceiber	24 Bedwas
		15	Lady Windsor	25 Marine
		16	Abercrynon	26 Oakdale
		17	Merthyr Vale	27 Celynen South

28 Abertillery
29 Six Bells
30 Celynen North
31 Blaenserchan

VI

THE STRIKE: 1984–1985

The miners' strike of 1984–5 was one of the most important events in twentieth-century British politics. Its scale and duration were unprecedented, with the majority of the NUM staying out for a year. Unlike the 1972 and 1974 strikes, which had been about wages, the issue for the miners in 1984 was the survival of their industry. Their eventual defeat vindicated their fears: coal-mining effectively disappeared from Britain. From an early twenty-first century perspective, the miners' strike represented the 'last stand' of an industry and a union that had been integral to British post-war economics and politics. The aftermath of the strike saw the conclusion of a major chapter in the history of south Wales.

The south Wales coalfield, which had been the paradigm example of general trends in the industry during the century, certainly fulfilled this role during the year-long dispute. After a hesitant start, South Wales was the most solid Area. As late as mid-December 1984, 21 of the 26 British pits completely free of strike-breakers were in south Wales and over 99 per cent of the Area's members were still on strike in January 1985.[1] They remained in the vanguard of the struggle throughout and were crucial to the NUM's picketing operations around Britain. The strength of the Area was a product of its traditional radicalism and the extensive support networks which grew out of the valleys' communities. No-one was more committed and loyal to the strike in 1984–5 than the south Wales miners.

How it began

The decision to strike in March 1984 was a defensive response to a direct threat. As one EC member later reflected, '[t]he miners' strike of '84–'85 was about the right to work . . . It was about trying to keep

---

[1]   Andrew J. Richards, *Miners on Strike: Class Solidarity and Division in Britain* (Oxford: 1996), p. 108.

jobs for our sons and nephews . . . to work in the industry. It was about retaining our communities – it was about retaining a way of life.'[2] In January 1985, Area president Emlyn Williams stated:

> History will record that the British miner decided on a strategy of industrial action because he could not accept that the role of families was to go to unemployment exchanges . . . This has been . . . a strike on behalf of every man, woman and child in the United Kingdom . . . [T]he miners have said, we are standing up to be counted.[3]

By early 1984, the NUM was bracing itself for a clash over the fate of the coal industry. The NCB announcement on 6 March 1984 of the closure of Cortonwood colliery in Yorkshire and Polmaise colliery in Scotland was seen by the union leadership as a signal for the long-anticipated conflict. On 8 March, NUM national president Arthur Scargill announced that the strikes underway in Yorkshire and Scotland were official under Rule 41 of the union's constitution and called on the other coalfields to support them.[4] Subsequently, at an Area conference on 9 March the EC recommended a strike, without a ballot, which was deemed unnecessary because South Wales had supported strike action in its last three ballots on the subject. Area general secretary George Rees warned that 'unless we take strike action now we can say so-long to South Wales forever . . . [E]ither we give the lead or we capitulate.' After discussion, delegates voted overwhelmingly for action as from 12 March.

This endorsement did not reflect fully the grassroots ambivalence in the coalfield. In the general meetings called to discuss the recommendation, south Wales lodges voted by 18 to 13 against a strike.[5] This outcome was an unwelcome surprise for the Area leadership, with many of these decisions seeming superficially to make little sense: 'moderate' long-life pits such as Oakdale and Betws voted for action, while many of those which rejected the strike (such as Bedwas and St John's) were themselves threatened with closure. Only a year before, however, Welsh miners had travelled to every British pit in an unsuccessful campaign to save Lewis Merthyr – and ironically

---

[2]   Interview with Ian Isaac, 2 and 8 April 2004.

[3]   *WM*, 24 January 1985.

[4]   Rule 41 empowered the NEC to give official endorsement to strike action by individual Areas.

[5]   Martin Adeney and John Lloyd, *The Miners' Strike, 1984–5: Loss Without Limit* (London: 1986), p. 96.

received a particularly hostile rejection at Cortonwood. A large proportion of the membership doubted whether Yorkshire itself would strike and were bitter about being asked to defend Cortonwood. It was not entirely surprising, therefore, that they were unenthusiastic about strike action.

Following this setback, the Area officials (Emlyn Williams, George Rees and Terry Thomas, the vice-president) met to discuss the situation. If South Wales did not join the strike there was every possibility that Yorkshire miners would try to picket it, which could have been disastrous, given grassroots bitterness over the Lewis Merthyr episode. Consequently, they decided to contact lodges that could be relied upon to move quickly and bring the coalfield out on strike. This task was left mainly to Emlyn Williams, although he used Kim Howells (the Area's research officer) as an intermediary because he could not be seen to be organising what was technically unofficial action.[6] Acting on his instructions, Howells arranged a meeting of Broad Left activists for the following day, Sunday 11 March, in Hirwaun.[7] Those present were veterans of unofficial movements dating back to 1969 and came from some of the most militant lodges: Tower, Maerdy and Trelewis Drift, to be joined later by others, notably Penrhiwceiber. Subsequently, pickets were sent to every south Wales colliery the following morning.[8]

Picketing was crucial in generating momentum in south Wales. Although generally only token pickets, these successfully focused union loyalties on support for the strike. 'At Deep Navigation colliery, a single picket turned back the coaches of miners arriving for work with the words, "Official picket, boys". In disciplined South Wales, that was enough.'[9] Once a lodge had agreed not to cross picket lines, it joined the process of spreading the strike. By the time the EC met on Monday, 12 March, Maerdy and Tower pickets were there to ask them to make the dispute official. Encouraged by the success of the stoppage, and the news that Yorkshire was out as well, the EC took the momentous decision to call the Area out on strike.

---

[6]   SWML interview with Emlyn Williams (AUD/574).

[7]   Twenty years later, Howells's opinion had changed dramatically: he described this action as 'completely unconstitutional and completely undemocratic'. BBC website, 5 March 2004, *http://news.bbc.co.uk/1/hi/wales/3532987.stm*, accessed 7 January 2012.

[8]   Hywel Francis and Gareth Rees, '"No Surrender in the Valleys": the 1984–5 Miners' Strike in south Wales', *Llafur*, 5/2 (1989), 51.

[9]   Adeney and Lloyd, *The Miners' Strike*, p. 96.

A few lodges remained reluctant: Celynen South, Bedwas, Blaenserchan and Cynheidre. Nevertheless, these were brought out over the next few days, through mass picketing and persuasion by their lodge leaderships. On 10 March a Celynen South general meeting voted overwhelmingly to reject the strike decision; five days later, a similarly comprehensive majority accepted that the colliery had stopped work.[10] Most of the pits which were reluctant to take action were in Gwent. Ray Lawrence, the Celynen South lodge secretary, later recalled a significant intervention by George Rees. In the first week of the strike, Rees told a Gwent district meeting that they would be traitors to the union if they did not fall into line – which they subsequently did. Consequently, in Lawrence's view, 'George Rees on his own saved the strike in south Wales'.[11]

Although the strike began in an untidy fashion in south Wales, the methods used to bring it about had been highly effective. Picketing was central to solidifying the strike; without it the strike might not have occurred. A key reason was the swift, unofficial way in which it began: by the time the EC met on Monday morning, it had little choice but to endorse the existing situation. Equally important was that the lodge leaderships pushed for acceptance of the conference decision and were willing to have their pits brought into the strike. As one miner later commented, 'A lot of people might disagree with the strike but . . . historically, they'll always . . . support the lodge, look. Now, if the lodge say on a Friday, "today is Tuesday", then the men will generally say "yes, it is".'[12] Once the lodges had been picketed, in most cases their leaderships convened meetings which enabled the memberships to state formally their support for the strike. In this way, a combination of unofficial militancy and union procedures had produced a total stoppage across south Wales by Wednesday, 14 March. The strike had begun. Crucially, the miners had respected the 'sanctity of the picket line' and the leadership had quickly confirmed that the strike was official, thus dispelling any lingering doubts. By the end of the week, south Wales pickets were already fanning out across the rest of Britain.

---

[10] Celynen South NUM Lodge minutes, 10, 15 March 1984.
[11] Interview with Ray Lawrence, 11 March 2004.
[12] Interview with Ron Stoate, 2 December 2003.

Strategy and timing

One of the most controversial aspects of the strike was the way in which it began. Following the lead taken by Yorkshire and Scotland, it developed on a 'domino effect' basis, with the Areas joining piecemeal without recourse to a national ballot.[13] At the time, the Labour leadership made no public comment on this matter; much later, Neil Kinnock stated that his decision not to back calls for a national ballot was the 'greatest regret of my whole life.'[14] The disadvantages of this strategy became apparent when several English coalfields failed to join the strike, which was a major blow for the NUM and a key reason for its eventual defeat. Consequently, twenty years on, some south Wales miners had come to re-evaluate this approach. George Rees reflected: 'looking in hindsight, it'd have been far better if we'd had a national ballot . . . I think had we had a national ballot, we could have won it.'[15] At the time, however, as Tyrone O'Sullivan later emphasised, once the strike was underway '*the miners of south Wales didn't want the bloody ballot*. We *agreed* with the decision we'd taken . . . The miners themselves *wanted* . . . to fight to save their jobs.'[16] Speaking at a rally in Aberdare in April 1984, for instance, Emlyn Williams demanded an all-out strike by every Area and argued against a ballot.[17]

Was March 1984 the best time for a showdown with the government? In 2004, Kim Howells stated publicly that he thought it was not.[18] However, whilst most miners were sure that the government and the NCB provoked a confrontation at the worst possible time for them, they felt there was little option but to respond as they did. Dane Hartwell, an EC member, stated:

> I was *fully aware* of the difficulties . . . that we were going into [but] . . . we were *responding* . . . to an *attack* . . . There was only two things you *could* do. You could either say, 'we'll accept what you're going to do' . . . or the only

[13] For a detailed discussion of this strategy, see Richard Hyman, 'Reflections on the mining strike', *Socialist Register*, 22 (1985), 331–5, 346–7; see also John Saville, 'An open conspiracy: Conservative politics and the miners' strike of 1984–5', *Socialist Register*, 22 (1985), 308–9.

[14] *The Guardian* website, 26 January 2004, *http://www.guardian.co.uk/politics/2004/jan/26/uk.tradeunions*, accessed 7 January 2012.

[15] Interview with George Rees, 8 December 2003.

[16] Interview with Tyrone O'Sullivan, 22 March 2004.

[17] *The Guardian*, 16 April 1984.

[18] 'Howells' miners' strike regret', BBC website, 12 March 2004, *http://news.bbc.co.uk/1/hi/wales/3506098.stm*, accessed 7 January 2012.

other alternative was to say, 'no, you're not going to do it' . . . I mean . . . it was . . . early March . . . *Strategically*, it wasn't a good time, was it? . . . [Y]ou didn't have to be a *bloody genius* to work that one out. But . . . that was all part of what had been planned . . . by the government . . . [W]e were *aware* of that. But it was a case of doing nothing or doing *something* . . . I still maintain that we *had* to do it . . . [T]he *justification* of what we did is *evident*, is *self-evident*, now.[19]

PICKETING AND THE POLICE

Once the strike was underway, the Area was soon sending bus-loads of pickets to a multitude of targets around Britain, with about 4,000–5,000 miners permanently mobilised on duty.[20] Apart from this high level of activism, also notable was the discipline and organisation of the picketing. Each colliery established its own strike committee, while overall co-ordination of activities was carried out by Kim Howells, who was accountable to the Area leadership.[21]

At the outset, the main goal of the south Wales miners was to bring every Area out on strike. By 20 March, they had picketed north Wales, with mixed results,[22] and made good progress in Staffordshire and Warwickshire. By the end of the month they had also brought out the Lancashire pits, as well as 13,000 Midlands miners.[23] Despite this, it proved increasingly difficult to persuade the more recalcitrant coalfields, particularly Nottinghamshire. The police presence there, equipped with horses and riot gear, increased the probability of confrontation. The Blaenant chairman recalled that 'we had a real rough time. By that time it has escalated into being a war situation, certainly on a hand-to-hand basis.' A Taff Merthyr miner spelt out the scale of the challenge facing the pickets: 'you couldn't get *near* the colliery gates, because there was such a heavy police presence'.[24]

[19]   Interview with Dane Hartwell, 10 December 2003.
[20]   Francis and Rees, '"No Surrender in the Valleys"', 55–6; Kim Howells, 'Stopping out: the birth of a new kind of politics', in Huw Beynon (ed.), *Digging Deeper: Issues in the Miners' Strike* (London, 1985), pp. 141–2.
[21]   In interviews conducted by the author, several miners commented on Howells's prominence and also the relatively low profile of the Area officials during the strike, with the majority being critical of various aspects of this arrangement.
[22]   For details, see Keith Gildart, *North Wales Miners: A Fragile Unity, 1945–1996* (Cardiff: 2001) pp. 173–89.
[23]   *WM*, 21, 27 March 1984.
[24]   Interviews with Phil Bowen (26 March 2004) and Colin Thomas (14 January 2004) (respectively).

The NUM inability to implement a complete national stoppage was due in no small measure to the massive police effort to impede picketing. The police made extensive use of surveillance and road-blocks: during the first six months of the strike approximately 290,000 miners were halted, sometimes hundreds of miles away from their intended destinations.[25] George Rees recalled: 'And the number of times I used to be stopped going up to Sheffield [NUM National Office]. Stopped the car on the motorway, having to pull over. And they'd say, "where are you going, Mr Rees?" And I'd say, "If you know my name, you know where I'm bloody going to!"'[26]

Mining communities were under a virtual state of siege during the strike. There were many instances of telephone-tapping, with people recounting hearing mysterious clicking noises on the phone and occasions when a third voice appeared on the line midway through a conversation.[27] Miners also found themselves being followed whenever they left the house. The Oakdale lodge chairman stated that '[i]n '72 and '74, I could get in my car and go where I wanted . . . But in '84–'85 . . . by the time I'd gone from where I'm living . . . to The Crown in Pontllanfraith, which would be about two miles, the police would be stopping me.'[28] In addition to this, local coach companies were prevented from hiring to miners. The combined effect of these activities appeared startlingly authoritarian. A craftsman from St John's colliery expressed a commonly held view: 'During the year of the miners' strike, I would say we were definitely [living in] a police state.'[29]

The main place where miners encountered police was on the picket line. The confrontational potential of these situations was exacerbated by the behaviour of some police officers, who goaded miners by boasting about their overtime earnings and also by the use of plain-clothes policemen as agents provocateurs.[30] Police picket-line attitudes varied markedly. Several miners later reflected that south Wales police were reasonably sympathetic, whereas other forces were hostile: one lodge secretary recalled that the Metropolitan

[25] *The Times*, 21 March 1984; Ben Fine, *The Coal Question: Political Economy and Industrial Change from the Nineteenth Century to the Present Day* (London: 1990), p. 162.

[26] George Rees interview.

[27] For details, see Welsh Campaign for Civil & Political Liberties and NUM (South Wales Area), *Striking Back* (Cardiff, 1985), pp. 128–44; *WM*, 7 April 1984.

[28] Quoted in Richards, *Miners on Strike*, pp. 129–30.

[29] Interview with Colin Day, 18 March 2004.

[30] *The Times*, 3 April 1984; *The Guardian*, 10 April 1984.

Police 'were like animals . . . We knew if we were encountering them, we were in for . . . a savage beating.'[31] The extensive use of police riot equipment made picket lines potentially very dangerous. Whilst some miners might not have been blameless for some of the violence, they were not the ones equipped appropriately for inflicting it. This was confirmed by the casualty figures. By December 1984, six miners had been killed on the picket lines and 3,000 badly injured; in contrast, seventy-five police had been hospitalised and 750 had been hurt. As the *Guardian* commented, 'If it was a war, you'd know which side was better armed and winning.'[32]

The war analogy was an apt one, as the government's method for tackling the strike blurred the demarcation between the police and the military.[33] During the dispute, the police adopted paramilitary tactics and a centralised chain of command, while at the same time military personnel, disguised as police, featured regularly on picket lines. On several occasions, south Wales miners had relatives in the armed forces whom they spotted wearing police uniforms, having been deployed around the English coalfields. In October 1984, a former chief constable stated publicly that a national paramilitary police force was being used to break the strike.[34] Indeed, the role of the police was sufficiently controversial to merit an Amnesty International investigation in February 1985.[35]

THE MEDIA AND THE STRIKE

Whilst the police were a direct obstacle to the miners, the national media provided a different but equally significant challenge. In some respects these institutions complemented each other, with most media reports portraying the police favourably while denigrating the strikers. Miners were dismayed by the misrepresentation. The Six Bells lodge chairman later commented: 'I used to watch the tele-vision . . . and read the newspapers [during the strike]. And I used to think to myself, "Well, that can't be the same place that I was at". It

[31] Interview with Billy Liddon, 1 April 2004.
[32] *The Guardian*, 4 December 1984.
[33] Saville, 'An open conspiracy', 309–11.
[34] WCCPL and Area, *Striking Back*, pp. 170–4; interview with Glyn Roberts, 19 March 2004; *The Guardian*, 7 May 1984; *The Times*, 17 October 1984.
[35] EC, 26 February 1985.

was *so* distorted.' Similarly, a Penallta miner recalled: 'If you picked up the newspapers – well! And I always remember one major headline in the news, in 'The Sun', at the time. It was big black bold letters . . . that the miners were "scum" . . . So, certainly not sympathetic. *At all*.'[36]

During the strike, the vast majority of media coverage centred on its most 'dramatic' aspects, primarily on picket-line clashes and national-level negotiations. This led to it being caricatured as an ideological struggle between Scargill and Thatcher. The south Wales miners were aware that this focus on Scargill was an attempt to weaken NUM unity. As one lodge secretary later pointed out:

> Arthur Scargill . . . had very little to do with *me* being on strike. And my wife, and all the families in our community staying on strike for twelve months. Most of those people had never *seen* Arthur Scargill. Half of them had never heard him on the bloody TV, even *during* the strike. They didn't need encouragement to be on strike – we knew we had *nothing* around here. *Nothing.* We had the pits in the Valleys . . . It was *all* we had here . . . and they were going to take it away. And then for [the media] . . . to believe that people working in them pits . . . had to be *encouraged* to go on strike – what a nonsense.[37]

A corollary of this media depiction was a tendency to ignore the reasons behind the miners' decision to strike. When liberal journalists and broadcasters made a more detailed investigation, it was clear that there was a genuine case against the closure programme.[38] In general, however, debate followed the terms set by the government and the NCB.

THE STRIKE AS 'A WAY OF LIFE'

After the failure of Nottinghamshire to join the strike and the decision not to hold a ballot, the south Wales miners found that by late April the situation had started to become regularised. With battle-lines drawn and routines established, the strike became almost 'a way of life' for them. There were two exceptions to this pattern in

---

[36]   Interviews with Jim Watkins (18 February 2004) and Ron Stoate, respectively.
[37]   Billy Liddon interview.
[38]   For a comprehensive rebuttal of the economic rationale for the colliery closure programme, see Saville, 'An open conspiracy', 317–21.

the coalfield during May 1984. The first of these was the occupation of the NCB's Tondu offices for several weeks in protest at the crossing of picket lines by members of APEX.[39] Additionally, the first threat to the solidarity of the strike in south Wales occurred when a few individuals attempted to return to work at Cynheidre. This was defeated by a rapid coalfield-wide response, involving a mass picket at the colliery. There was also a 1,000-strong rally at Pontyberem on 26 May, with representatives from across south Wales, striking Leicestershire miners, the Dyfed Farmers' Action Group and a wide range of political and community organisations. The exercise was successful and the return-to-work attempt was defeated.[40]

Despite the massive challenge facing them, south Wales mining communities remained convinced that they would eventually emerge triumphant. This collective optimism was reflected in support for the numerous marches and rallies: for example, a gathering of over 10,000 miners in Cardiff in April, which was addressed by Scargill and NUM vice-president Mick McGahey. In Port Talbot a week earlier, 1,200 miners and their trade union allies had marched from the town centre to a rally at the Afan Lido, cheered along by local residents. There, NUM general secretary Peter Heathfield stated that the dispute was being 'taken by the scruff of the neck' following the recent National Conference decision to declare that the strike was now considered to be national.[41] Scargill also addressed two major rallies in south Wales during the summer, comprising approximately 3,000 people at Treorchy in June and 2,000 in Abertillery in July. The biggest demonstrations of the entire strike occurred in London in early and late June, when about 1,000 south Wales miners joined with thousands of other NUM members to protest at the closure programme.

SUPPORT GROUPS AND FUNDRAISING

Faced with the prospect of a lengthy strike, the south Wales miners began to think about how to sustain themselves and their families.

---

[39] EC, 17 May, 8 June 1984; *The Guardian*, 18 May 1984.
[40] EC, 25 May, 8 June 1984; *WM*, 21–8 May 1984; Francis and Rees, '"No Surrender in the Valleys"', 57.
[41] *WM*, 21, 30 April 1984. For details of the issues surrounding the question of the national ballot, see Andrew Taylor, *The NUM and British Politics, Vol. 2: 1969–1995* (Aldershot: 2005), pp. 184–93.

Even before the EC decided in April to set up relief and fundraising facilities at its three main centres – Ammanford, Pontypridd and Crumlin – various local initiatives were already underway.[42] The reappearance of 'soup kitchens' evoked images of the heroic struggle of mining valleys' communities during the 1926 strike. By mid-May 1984, every south Wales mining village had a support group, with similar organisations emerging in Cardiff and Swansea during the summer. This community mobilisation was fundamental in enabling the miners to continue their struggle for so long.

The main business of the support groups was food-collecting and fundraising. The public gave generously: the Caerphilly Miners' Support Group, for example, raised £700 and collected £1,000 worth of food in one week.[43] This money was used to buy food for each family within the groups' 'catchment areas'. Each group had its own headquarters (typically the local miners' institute), where food supplies were collected, packaged into weekly 'ration bags' and thereafter distributed to their various 'satellite centres'. The scale of this was truly remarkable. The Gwent Food Fund (GFF), the largest support group in south Wales, distributed at least 3,500 food bags every week during the strike – and in one week prior to Christmas 1984 managed 7,000 parcels. The other groups' output was also impressive: for instance, Maerdy delivered about 700 food bags a week.[44] Support groups also assisted their communities in whatever other ways seemed necessary. Examples included advising striking miners about their social security entitlements (as the Dulais valley group did), or organising parties for local miners' children (as the Ogmore valley group did in April 1984).[45] It is not an exaggeration to see the support groups as an 'alternative welfare state' for south Wales mining families during the strike.

The support groups were also important in maintaining morale. In this respect they assumed a greater prominence as the dispute went on, with the collective response to adversity having a positive effect on community spirit. Reflecting this, one miner later commented that it 'was the best year of my life . . . It was hard work but

[42] Celynen South NUM Lodge minutes, 24 April 1984; *WM*, 19 April 1984; Francis and Rees, '"No Surrender in the Valleys"', 58.
[43] *WM*, 4 June 1984.
[44] Interviews with Hefina Headon (31 March 2004), Kay Bowen (14 April 2004), Phil Bowen and Jim Watkins; *WM*, 23 April 1984; *The Guardian*, 28 June 1984, 2 January 1985.
[45] Kay Bowen and Phil Bowen interviews; *WM*, 24 April 1984.

it was tremendous just to see people coming together . . . It was worth being alive for, to be quite honest, because people were absolutely tremendous.'[46] Furthermore, the year-long confrontation with a government determined to defeat the miners almost inevitably had a politicising effect on the support groups. This could be seen, for instance, in the rally organised by the Gwent and Rhymney groups in Cardiff in November 1984, and the series of public meetings run by the Bridgend group in January 1985. Looking back on the strike, one miner reflected that 'with a lot of the women it . . . made them politically aware. And a lot of them became active in politics.'[47]

Women played a vital role in the support groups.[48] Widespread female involvement was itself a potent propaganda force, showing that the strike was about the defence of entire communities. Many south Wales women were involved in public demonstrations, such as the march by 500 miners' wives through Aberdare in August 1984. Some even went to picket: at Port Talbot and Llanwern steelworks and also at Point of Ayr colliery in north Wales. After this, the Area leadership stated that it would encourage female participation in strike activities.[49] The South Wales Women's Support Group was formed in June 1984. This attended several high-profile events, such as an all-women lobby of a Conservative Party conference in Porthcawl in June and a national demonstration by women's support groups in London in August. Many women came to play an important role as organisers, fund-raisers and propagandists. For many female activists, the strike had a profound impact on their lives. Reflecting on her role in organising a support group, attending picket lines and speaking to mass meetings, one woman from Seven Sisters later commented: 'I didn't know that I could do what I did . . . But I did it . . . without thinking about it.' Another Dulais valley woman pointed out: 'I think the majority of us thought then that we [didn't want] . . . just to be housewives anymore. There was *far more*

---

[46] Colin Day interview.
[47] Interview with Eric Davies, 30 January 2004; EC, 30 October 1984, 21 January 1985.
[48] Much has been written elsewhere on this important topic. See, for example, Jill Miller, *You Can't Kill The Spirit: Women in a Welsh Mining Valley* (London: 1986), Vicky Seddon (ed.), *The Cutting Edge: Women And The Pit Strike* (London: 1986), and Meg Allen, '"Weapons of the Weak": Humour and consciousness in the narratives of Women Against Pit Closures', *Socialist History*, 25 (2004), 1–19.
[49] *WM*, 14–17, 24, 25 May, 6 August 1984.

that we were capable of doing out there . . . It altered me as a person totally – it gave me confidence and made me . . . question things, not . . . take [them] . . . on face value.'[50]

Once it became apparent that it would be a lengthy strike, fund-raising assumed a central role in NUM activities. Fortunately, the support around Britain for the miners meant that this was not an insurmountable task. As they discovered, goodwill towards them was not confined to the labour movement but was widespread amongst the Afro-Caribbean, Pakistani, Turkish, Indian and Sikh communities, in addition to London's gay and lesbian groups. In order to tap into this, the south Wales miners realised that support groups would have to be set up outside their coalfield. This process was underway by May 1984 and soon developed into a network of large centres in London, Reading, Oxford, Liverpool, Bristol, Birmingham, Swindon and Southampton, as well as many smaller bases elsewhere, from Plymouth to Aberystwyth and Cambridge. The lodges which established these retained a semi-permanent presence there: at Oxford, for instance, the support group – in which car-workers and students were especially active – was developed by Maerdy and Merthyr Vale miners, some of whom stayed for the rest of the strike. In Wales, an array of left-wing groups combined with local pickets at the Trawsfynydd and Wylfa nuclear plants to twin Anglesey, Bangor and Blaenau Ffestiniog with west Wales mining communities. These kinds of arrangements enabled the various support groups to be virtually self-sufficient in funding their food distribution activities in the valleys.[51]

In addition to this fund-raising work, the Area received significant financial support from the trade union movement, which provided about £2 million during the strike. One of the most generous unions was SOGAT, raising £9,000 in donations at its annual conference in May 1984 and also buying and delivering thousands of pounds' worth of food for south Wales mining families.[52] Most grassroots assistance came from the various left-of-centre political parties. The Labour Party was by far the biggest of these and local Labour activists worked hard to help to keep the strike going. This was

---

[50]   Hefina Headon and Kay Bowen interviews, respectively.
[51]   Various interviews with south Wales miners; EC, 17, 25 May 1984; *The Guardian*, 11 June 1984; Francis and Rees, '"No Surrender in the Valleys"', 58.
[52]   EC, 17 May 1984; *WM*, 15 June 1984; Emlyn Jenkins (5 March 2004) and Tyrone O'Sullivan interviews.

appreciated by the miners, who generally remained loyal to Labour after 1985. The Communist Party played a fairly peripheral role, although its membership continued to aid the south Wales miners. Another significant left-wing force in 1984 was Militant. The Cwm lodge secretary, for instance, later commented that some of the most committed Labour supporters of the strike were also Militant activists.[53] Ian Isaac, the Area's leading Militant figure in that period, also pointed to the constructive role which it played in assisting the miners and organising support rallies during the strike.[54]

In south Wales, local councils assisted NUM members considerably during the strike – not least because they recognised the miners' historical role in shaping valleys' communities. The first support arrived in April 1984, when Blaenau Gwent council gave food vouchers to every miner residing within its boundaries, while Torfaen waived miners' rents for the duration of the dispute. Subsequently, other councils gave aid, donating to the food funds, lending the use of premises or providing free school meals to children. All of this helped to maintain the impressive solidarity of the south Wales miners.

Aid for the miners was truly international in scope, with donations received from as far afield as the USSR, New Zealand, Australia, Canada and Japan. The Area's overseas fundraising efforts focused on Europe, with delegations receiving generous donations as a result of tours there. Meetings of over 10,000 were addressed by Welsh miners in Italy. Ireland was also a key source of funds, with over IR£1 million being raised.[55]

INDUSTRIAL SUPPORT

Although the financial assistance the NUM received was consider-able, much less forthcoming in 1984–5 was active trade union solidarity.[56] Most miners recognised that the victories of 1972 and 1974 owed much to the help of other unions. In 1984, consequently, the NUM was quick to enlist the aid of the TGWU, NUR and NUS. The TUC was divided by Thatcher's anti-union drive: some unions

[53]   Billy Liddon interview.
[54]   Ian Isaac interview.
[55]   EC, June 1984–January 1985 passim; interviews with numerous south Wales miners; Jonathan Saunders, *Across Frontiers: International Support for the Miners' Strike, 1984/85* (London, 1989), pp. 80–9.
[56]   Saville, 'An open conspiracy', 312–13.

embraced the 'new realism',[57] while others argued for defiance of the 1984 Trade Union Act. A Penallta miner later commented:

> [A] lot of legislation was brought in to stop . . . secondary picketing . . . But then again, . . . if you follow the law all the time, we'd still be working seven days a week and women wouldn't have the vote, would they? Sometimes you got to buck the system to get a result . . . I think what the unions are for . . . [is] to support each other . . . And if they thought our cause was just . . . perhaps they should've worked harder to take a bit more action. But, there we are. We didn't get the support, did we?[58]

Crucially, industrial support was much lower than in 1972 and 1974. As George Rees later pointed out, '[w]e had an awful lot of verbal support – but we wanted more than verbal support, we wanted action. On the picket lines, for a start. We wanted people *inside* the power stations [and] . . . inside the steelworks to say, "we're not prepared to handle this coal".' Furthermore, several unions refused to help the NUM. The EETPU and the EPEA leaderships called for their members to cross NUM picket lines at power stations, and in September 1984 they rejected the TUC's endorsement of the NUM appeal for sympathetic industrial action.[59]

Nevertheless, several unions *were* willing to take industrial action in support of the miners. In March 1984, a one-day strike by bus drivers paralysed public transport in the Rhondda, forcing the management to reverse its ban on hiring coaches to NUM pickets. NUPE members joined the picket lines outside Port Talbot steelworks in late March and staged half-day stoppages at hospitals and council offices throughout south Wales. At the outset of the strike, the rail unions, TGWU, NUS and ISTC, all agreed to prevent the transport of coal and oil across NUM picket lines. Even by the end of the year, several unions remained prepared to keep to this: for instance, NUR general secretary Jimmy Knapp told a miners' rally in Swansea in October 1984 that his union would continue supporting the NUM 'physically, financially and industrially'.[60]

---

[57] 'New realism' was a term used by left-wingers as a critique of those who were critical of the use of the strike weapon in the 'new' political and economic environment of the 1980s.

[58] Ron Stoate interview.

[59] George Rees interview; *The Times*, 2 September 1984.

[60] *The Guardian*, 29 March 1984; *WM*, 22, 23 March, 29 October 1984; *The Miner*, 2 April 1984. For details of the TGWU docks strikes of July and August 1984, see Taylor, *The NUM and British Politics, Vol. 2*, pp. 238–9.

Once it had become clear that Nottinghamshire would not join the strike, the South Wales NUM began to focus on alternative methods of attaining victory. A key concern was coal imports; consequently, many south Wales miners spent much of the strike picketing docks around Britain. As they discovered, however, the main problem was not the large shipping ports but rather the multitude of small unregistered ports. Given the difficulties this presented, the Area leadership attempted to solve the problem from the other direction. In May 1984 George Rees led a delegation to Holland, the main source of coal imports, to attempt to persuade Rotterdam dockers and the Federatie Nederlandse Vakverbond (the Dutch TUC) to implement an embargo. With the failure to reach an agreement however, imports remained a problem which could not be resolved completely, regardless of the picketing efforts of the south Wales miners.[61]

THE POWER STRUGGLE

The main measure of success for a strike by coal miners in a modern society is its impact on electricity generation. The 1984–5 strike was no exception to this, although continued working by the Nottinghamshire Area hindered this task considerably. The south Wales miners were in the vanguard of this campaign, picketing twenty-two power stations across Wales and England by late March 1984. They also picketed oil-fired and nuclear facilities: for example, by April Blaenant men were turning away CO_2 tankers at Trawsfynydd, near Blaenau Ffestiniog. In May, Welsh pickets persuaded EEPTU members at Fawley to 'black' plant maintenance work. Similarly, at Didcot (one of Britain's largest power stations), round-the-clock picketing by Merthyr Vale miners prompted workers to vote in June to refuse to accept coal delivered by road. Additionally, by September 1984 it was reported that all electricity production from coal in Wales had ceased.[62]

With the onset of autumn, the Area stepped up its efforts to generate more support from power station workers. On one day in

---

[61] *The Guardian*, 15 May 1984; interview with Arfon Evans, 1 April 2004; Saunders, *Across Frontiers*, pp. 52–5.

[62] *WM*, 29 March, 30 May, 1, 30 June, 24 September 1984; *The Guardian*, 3 April 1984; interview with Bill King, 4 March 2004.

October 1984, for example, over 300 south Wales pickets descended on Oldbury nuclear plant, near Bristol, while 100 went to the oil-fired Pembroke station and a further fifty visited Berkeley power station in Gloucestershire. Later that month, south Wales also provided many of the 500-strong mass picket at Didcot, in protest at the oil deliveries occurring there. Furthermore, following a meeting with activists in other unions in November 1984, the Area leadership decided to invite power station shop stewards to discuss future joint action with them, to take up the EEPTU offer to publish their case in its newspaper, and also to print leaflets for distribution to power station workers. One of the clearest examples of the determination of the south Wales miners was provided by the ten Merthyr Vale miners who spent Christmas week manning the Didcot picket line. As late as January 1985, Welsh miners could still be found among a picket of Tilbury power station organised by London-based support groups. No-one in the NUM did more to halt the power stations than the south Wales miners.[63]

THE STEEL BLOCKADE

In addition to shutting down the power stations, a key NUM strategic objective was to hit steel production. For South Wales, the first task was to persuade the Port Talbot and Llanwern unions not to handle imported coal. The failure of these negotiations led to hundreds of south Wales miners picketing the steelworks. By April, it was reported that supplies were on the verge of exhaustion.[64] However, the EC realised that starving the steelworks completely would be counter-productive, since without a minimum usage of coking coal their blast furnaces and ovens would collapse. This would jeopardise the jobs of the steelworkers and also of the miners whose collieries depended on supplying BSC. Consequently, after meeting steel union representatives in April and May 1984, the Area leadership agreed to allow Llanwern the minimum amount of coal necessary for safety purposes (which would cut steel output by around 40 per cent), to be transported there in carefully-monitored quantities by the NUR and ASLEF. In return, the ISTC promised to

---

[63]   *WM*, 6, 25 October, 22 December 1984; EC, 12 November 1984, 21 January 1985.
[64]   *WM*, 20, 29 March, 4, 6 April 1984; *The Guardian*, 5 April 1984; *The Miner*, 2 April 1984.

use only rail-delivered coal, thereby allowing the NUM to retain control of the situation. In early June, the EC confirmed that Area policy was to ensure that this commitment should continue to be met.[65]

The output-limiting agreement did not last. The first signs of a harder stance emerged at the NUM rally in Cardiff in late April 1984, when Scargill said: 'The time has come to begin to tighten the knot . . . The quicker other industries are affected the quicker the Government will change their attitude.'[66] Moreover, by late May there was evidence that the deal was not quite as 'watertight' as had been supposed. It had been reported that the ISTC was not keeping to the agreed quota; for example, Llanwern had also been receiving coal from Dowd's Wharf in Newport.[67] On the other hand, Terry Thomas later argued that the complete blockade was a strategic mistake because it alienated steelworkers, who saw it as an attempt to close them down.[68]

The total blockade of the steelworks began in June 1984. Established by the NEC to oversee all strike-related decision-making, the first act of the union's National Co-ordinating Committee was to ask ASLEF to stop all fuel deliveries to the steelworks from midnight on 19 June if the ISTC did not agree to reduce steel output – which it subsequently did not. This came as an unwelcome surprise to the Area leadership, which had not been informed beforehand and had previously spelt out to the NEC that the Gwent pits were completely dependent on Llanwern. Nevertheless, once the decision had been made the Area adhered to it. Within two days, Llanwern's output was down by around 33 per cent (below the financial break-even point), with reports of serious fuel shortages. Llanwern delegates told the Area's leaders on 20 June that furnace linings there were already damaged and that their plant was vulnerable precisely because it used Welsh coal, whereas other steelworks relied on imports. The EC, however, remained resolute in enforcing the national decision.[69]

The attitude of the steelworkers was a fundamental factor in this situation. The NUM had called for reciprocity for its support for the steelworkers during their strike in 1980 – in other words, no

[65] EC, 27 April, 17, 25 May, 1 June 1984; *WM*, 11 April, 5, 16 May 1984.
[66] *WM*, 30 April 1984.
[67] EC, 25 May 1984.
[68] Interview with Terry Thomas, 16 February 2004.
[69] EC, 15, 20 June 1984; *WM*, 15–22 June 1984 passim; *The Guardian*, 16, 20, 21 June 1984.

production of finished steel. In early July 1984 however, the ISTC pledged to maintain maximum output at all plants. It was this complete failure of solidarity that was the ultimate reason for the failure of the blockade of the south Wales steelworks.

The NUM plan was for the total blockade of Llanwern to be implemented by means of the NUR and ASLEF ensuring that the coal trains which supplied the steelworks would not cross picket lines. Within a week, however, lorry convoys had been established and were travelling daily between Port Talbot (where the coal docked) and Llanwern on the M4, an operation which continued for the remainder of the strike. In retaliation, the NUM instructed the rail unions also to blockade iron ore, since it was believed to be impossible for BSC to supply Llanwern by road because of the vast quantities required (around 50,000 tonnes a week). This expedient seemed initially to work – but by the end of June the convoy had begun to move iron ore as well, with a hundred lorries (each carrying twenty-five tonnes of ore) arriving every day, in addition to the sixty-five coke-carrying lorries. Eventually, massive convoys of up to 200 giant haulage lorries – which were covered with additional metal grilles and panels especially for the purpose of blockade-running and many of which were neither roadworthy nor safe for other motorists – were making the journey between the steelworks twice a day. Although the rail blockade was maintained, this was insufficient to halt Llanwern.[70]

Enforcing the road blockade was a formidable task. At Llanwern, the management told employees not to use the plant's eastern entrance, so as to enable the convoy to drive at high speed through picket lines. Hundreds of miners and their supporters tried their best but despite an array of tactics and picketing of both steelworks month after month, the convoy was never halted for more than a few days.[71] The inherent dangers of trying to stop a high-speed lorry convoy were illustrated tragically in September 1984, when two Penallta miners were killed while on picket duty outside Llanwern.[72]

[70]   EC, 15, 20 June 1984; *The Guardian*, 21–8 June 1984; *WM*, 21 June–3 July 1984.

[71]   EC, 6, 17 July 1984; *The Guardian*, 22 June, 5 July 1984; *The Times*, July–November 1984 passim; *WM*, July–September 1984 passim; John Mason (24 February 2004), Tyrone O'Sullivan, Ian Isaac, Kevin Williams (25 March 2004), and Lyn Harper (29 March 2004) interviews.

[72]   In addition to these two men, another Penallta miner was killed during the strike, in an accident at the pit in April while carrying out safety work. Interviews with Don Jones (23 February 2004) and Ron Stoate; EC, 27 April, 11 September 1984.

Retrospectively, even committed activists acknowledged the practical impossibility of physically stopping the convoy: 'It became in the end a futile exercise to be picketing because . . . if you stood on the road they'd knock you down – *knowing* that they'd get away with it.' Similarly, another miner commented that '[y]ou can't really stop a convoy that's in full flow unless you've got rocket launchers [– but] . . . we're not Osama bin Ladens, we're south Wales coal miners'.[73]

Whatever the merits of the NUM national plan to blockade the steelworks, it did not work in practice. By October 1984, 600 lorry movements a day meant that Llanwern was receiving its entire materials requirements – and significantly more than the amount allowed before the 'total blockade' had been declared. Instead of limiting output, the abandonment of the local agreement meant that steel production in south Wales reached a three-year highpoint. The failure of the blockade was a significant blow to the NUM's ability to achieve outright victory.[74]

<h3 style="text-align:center">ORGREAVE</h3>

The most notorious incident of the strike was the 'battle of Orgreave', a mass picketing action that came to a climax on 18 June 1984. Picketing coke-works and the use of mass pickets had been central to the strategy and tactics of the national NUM leadership since the outset of the strike, partly at least because of the symbolic significance of the closure of the Saltley coke depot during the 1972 strike.[75] In contrast, the EC was unenthusiastic about picketing Orgreave because reconnaissance had indicated that it was an open and remote site, whereas Saltley had been an enclosed depot in the Birmingham suburbs, from where it was easier to obtain physical support from other trade unionists. The NUM's failure to prevent the movement of coking coal from Orgreave coke-works was a key turning point. As Emlyn Williams later commented, 'Saltley made Arthur – and Orgreave destroyed him.'[76]

---

[73] Quotes taken from (respectively) Billy Liddon and Colin Day interviews.
[74] *WM*, 13 October 1984; EC, 16 October 1984.
[75] For a discussion of mass picketing as a tactic during the strike, see Hyman, 'Reflections on the mining strike', 335–7, 347–50.
[76] Emlyn Williams SWML interview; EC, 8 June 1984.

At Orgreave approximately 6,500 miners, including approximately 1,000 south Wales pickets, converged on the site.[77] Unlike elsewhere, the police did not hinder their arrival – and even supervised the parking of the miners' coaches. Consequently, many miners later claimed that the government had engineered the confrontation to strike a decisive blow against the NUM. Once in position, the pickets were met by upwards of 4,000 police, equipped with riot gear, dogs and horses: '[t]he result was the greatest violence seen in a British industrial dispute since before the First World War'.[78] In the view of one lodge secretary, '"The battle of Orgreave" should have been described as "the massacre of Orgreave". Because if ever anything was constructed to brutalise and savagely beat working-class people, it was Orgreave . . . [I]t will live in bloody infamy for what the British government did to working-class people.'[79]

Even working in a dangerous environment, and their picket-line experiences earlier in the strike, did not prepare miners for what they faced at Orgreave. Dressed typically in jeans, T-shirts and trainers, the miners were unprepared for a clash with police fully equipped with truncheons, body armour and riot shields. During the struggle, police staged mounted charges of unprecedented ferocity and used Alsatians to maul the pickets. Mounted police chased pickets down nearby streets and through gardens, lashing out indiscriminately at them. Welsh miners who were there that day later recalled their experiences of police brutality; as one commented, 'They done everything bar turn guns on us.'[80] A Maerdy man stated: 'If you was in the front, up against the shields, you'd had it . . . And you seen a lot of heads getting cracked open . . . You had to be there to believe what happened. It was carnage . . . The police were going nuts.'

---

[77] *WM*, 19 June 1984; EC, 15 June 1984. This is not undisputed: both Taylor and Beckett and Hencke state that there were 10,000 pickets, although neither provides a source for this figure. Taylor, *The NUM and British Politics, Vol. 2*, p. 225; Francis Beckett and David Hencke, *Marching to the Fault Line: The Miners' Strike and the Battle for Industrial Britain* (London: 2009), p. 100.

[78] Alex Callinicos and Mike Simons, *The Great Strike: The Miners' Strike of 1984–5 and its lessons* (London: 1985), p. 101. Estimates as to the number of police officers present vary: Beckett and Hencke say there were about 4,000, Taylor says 4,163, and Milne says 8,000. Beckett and Hencke, *Marching to the Fault Line*, p. 100; Taylor, *The NUM and British Politics, Vol. 2*, p. 225; Seumas Milne, *The Enemy Within: The Secret War Against The Miners* (London: 1995), p. 24.

[79] Billy Liddon interview.

[80] Quoted in Richards, *Miners on Strike*, p. 128; WCCPL and Area, *Striking Back*, pp. 99–100.

Similarly, the Tower lodge secretary said that 'I've never seen so much blood in my life . . . Everybody seemed to be marked with blood.'[81] The miners' shock was expressed vividly by a Penallta collier:

> Orgreave was a *major* experience in my life. I'll never forget that at all . . . It was like something . . . that happened in Chile or Uruguay, or one of these South American countries . . . How the police behaved was abominable, to say the least . . . *Even now*, I'm bitter about it . . . It was absolutely *terrible* what they done . . . [O]nce they got us all in one place, then they cut loose . . . Dogs. Horses. Policemen with short, round shields. Policemen with long, tall shields. Padded up . . . And done with military precision . . . It was horrendous.[82]

The media's depiction of Orgreave added insult to injury, portraying the miners as the instigators of the violence. This image augmented government depictions of the miners as 'the enemy within' and was a potent propaganda weapon against them. Pickets who attended Orgreave stated that this was a complete misrepresentation of events – a view confirmed by later revelations and some history programmes broadcast to mark the twentieth anniversary of the strike. One EC member stated: 'the media . . . showed the miners charging the police, when in fact it was the other way around . . . And there's *no doubt* about that . . . [T]he police were *lying*, the media was lying – but that was a *concerted effort* . . . to try and alienate the public against the miners.'[83]

If Saltley was a symbol of NUM victory in 1972, then Orgreave was a harbinger of the miners' eventual defeat in 1985. The fundamental reason for this difference lay not in the specifics of the coke-works' location or in the systematic police violence in 1984 (though these factors were important) but in the glaring absence of physical assistance from other trade unionists. As an EC member later asserted:

> Saltley Gates was *symbolic* . . . in 1972 . . . [However,] the tactic Arthur was using was *wrong* [in 1984] . . . Saltley Gates wasn't closed by the miners [but] . . . by the *car-workers*. It was that *solidarity* of the trade union movement which you had in '72 – which you *didn't* have in '84 . . . Now, Arthur was

[81]   Kevin Williams and Tyrone O'Sullivan interviews, respectively.
[82]   Ron Stoate interview.
[83]   Eric Davies interview; Milne, *The Enemy Within*, p. 24.

trying to repeat that in Orgreave. The problem was [that] . . . the
Establishment wanted Orgreave to take place. It was the battleground which
was, again, of their choosing . . . [a]nd it was a *trap*. And it was a trap that
could have been *foreseen*.[84]

Following Orgreave, the pressing need within the NUM became
the attainment of some successes, however symbolic, as a way of
sustaining morale and momentum. After the dispute was over,
Emlyn Williams conceded that there had been a failure to come to
terms with this defeat and also a confusion between rallies attended
by committed activists and genuine mass support: 'we were failing to
communicate [with the membership] – only through mass rallies.
And those mass rallies were made up mainly of men . . . who adored
Arthur Scargill. And the men in the house, of course, we were not
getting at.'[85]

This perspective was not solely the product of hindsight. An
important exception to the lack of strategic planning was the
internal discussion document by Kim Howells entitled *Some
Observations on the Strike in the 3ʳᵈ Month*, circulated in mid-May to all
south Wales lodges. This criticised 'much confusion and lack of
direction amongst certain area and national leaderships', focusing on
the failure to stop coal movements, ineffective picketing, the inability
to create national machinery to feed NUM members and the
absence of any 'short, simple demands or targets'. The document
concluded on the question of financing the exorbitant costs being
incurred by Areas such as South Wales. These tensions between the
national leadership and the Area officials, implicit even at this stage,
did not emerge publicly until January 1985.

THE STATE AND THE STRIKE

Orgreave and the steelworks blockade highlighted with brutal clarity
the lengths to which the state was prepared to go to defeat the NUM.
This was also evident in the courts' treatment of miners who had
been arrested. Here, the typical sentence was that of being bound
over to keep the peace and a prohibition of attending other picket
lines. Although nominally a judicial measure, the blanket imposition

[84] Dane Hartwell interview.
[85] Emlyn Williams SWML interview; EC, 20 June 1984.

of this judgment emphasised its underlying political purpose, namely, to weaken the NUM's ability to win the strike.[86] The social security system was another arm of the state used to exert pressure on miners and their families. From the strike's outset, single miners were denied benefits, despite being without any income. Additionally, the government imposed a cut of £15 per week for miners' families, together with a further £1 a week reduction in November. This occurred because the miners were deemed to be receiving strike pay, even though it was apparent that the NUM could not afford this. The cut remained in force even after the sequestration of union funds, demonstrating that it was essentially about attempting to force the NUM into submission. It was with some justification that the Cwm lodge secretary could later comment: 'It was a *war* by Margaret Thatcher on what she saw as the enemy . . . I hope that sometime in the future . . . people will recognise that this government declared war on a part of society, because of their political trade union beliefs. That's what happened.'[87]

Although the government claimed that it was defending Britain from NUM 'lawlessness', miners were acutely aware that the Thatcher administration's definitions of illegality were tailored precisely to its overall objective of defeating the strike. As one lodge activist commented, '[y]ou didn't have to be guilty of a crime if you were a miner – you'd be arrested and removed from the picket line . . . And yet here was this government deliberately and calculatingly breaking the law', through ignoring the Mines and Quarries Act, encouraging the operation of unsafe lorry convoys and sequestrating NUM assets.[88] There was also evidence of the government using more clandestine methods: for example, the Press Council reported that two 'moles' inside the NEC had been leaking material to the *Daily Mail* and *Yorkshire Post*. Similarly, in February 1985, the *Guardian* reported that former MI5 intelligence officers had made allegations of widespread spying on the NUM and that political information about the strike had been passed to the government, in direct

---

[86] Saville, 'An open conspiracy', 311, 326–7.

[87] Billy Liddon interview.

[88] Billy Liddon interview. For a more detailed discussion of this subject, see Huw Beynon, 'Decisive power: the new Tory state against the miners', in Beynon, *Digging Deeper*, pp. 29–45, and John McIlroy, 'Police and pickets: the law against the miners', in Beynon, *Digging Deeper*, pp. 101–22.

contravention of MI5's charter.[89] This authoritarian application of 'law and order' methods by the government to its opponents, as well as a readiness to ignore any legislation that impeded its overarching political goals, led several south Wales miners to express the view that Thatcher in 1984 appeared to be on the verge of establishing a fascist state.

SEQUESTRATION AND RETALIATION

Late summer and early autumn 1984 saw several developments that impeded the union's ability to win an outright victory. For the Area, one of the most significant of these was the sequestration of its assets because of its refusal to comply with a High Court order banning picketing at Port Talbot steelworks. South Wales was the first victim of the new 'Tebbit laws', whose political intent was clear: it was singled out because of its importance to national NUM picketing operations.

On 1 August 1984, the South Wales NUM's bank accounts, including its food funds and those of some support groups, were frozen. Anticipating this development, the EC had taken steps to disperse the Area's funds and transfer its assets to offshore accounts. On the day that sequestration occurred, around 2,000 south Wales miners converged on their Area headquarters in the AUEW building in Pontypridd to prevent any prospective attempts by High Court commissioners to gain access. Additionally, a contingent of over a hundred miners (including the entire Area leadership) barricaded themselves inside the Area office on the third floor, where they remained for several days. Speaking via a megaphone from the office window, Emlyn Williams told the crowd below: 'We are here as a result of the insidious legislation created by a neo-fascist government . . . The South Wales miners will stand . . . There is no going back. There is no surrender. We fight, we win, or we die in the attempt.'[90] Within days, however, the sequestrators had seized several of the Area's accounts – including the main account, which had been transferred to Jersey. Fortunately for those who depended on them,

---

[89] EC, 27 July 1984; *The Guardian*, 21 February 1985. See also WCCPL and Area, *Striking Back*, pp. 128–44.
[90] *The Guardian*, 2 August 1984.

many lodges and support groups had been able to withdraw their funds from their bank accounts and they operated for the remainder of the strike on a purely cash-based system. All the actions taken by the EC regarding this episode were subsequently endorsed by an Area conference on 29 August.[91] Even after sequestration, the south Wales miners were still able to maintain their food centres and picketing operations. Nevertheless, the Area's picketing ability was inevitably curtailed: travel and sustenance expenses effectively ceased, while large-scale picketing actions became less common.[92]

These developments did surprisingly little to demoralise the strikers and their communities. The survival of the Area for another seven months of struggle without the use of its own bank accounts was due largely to strong local support and the organisational discipline which permeated the struggle. Sequestration inadvertently reinforced social relationships in the valleys and created conditions for a wider mobilisation across Wales in support of the miners. Major rallies were held in Aberdare, Treorchy, Newport and Ferndale during August; mass demonstrations were still being held in October 1984, when hundreds of people attended gatherings in Cardiff and Cwmbrân. An entirely different manifestation of this defiance occurred in August 1984, when fifteen Maerdy miners staged an eight-hour occupation of the Birmingham offices of sequestrators Price Waterhouse in protest at their seizure of community hardship funds.[93]

The Price Waterhouse occupation was the forerunner of two even more audacious initiatives by south Wales miners. The first hint of these occurred at an Area conference on 29 August, when Emlyn Williams announced 'a number of special actions' at 'crucial picketing targets during the 48 hours following this conference'. As predicted, miners conducted two daring and meticulously-planned occupations in this period, under cover of darkness and within an hour of each other. Over one hundred strikers infiltrated the huge Port Talbot steelworks and occupied the three massive wharf cranes to prevent the unloading of coking coal. Additionally, a group of miners took over the Newport Transporter Bridge, suspending the bridge's gondola midstream and blocking shipping access to

---

[91] *The Times*, 4, 7 August 1984; *WM*, 6, 7 August 1984; EC, 20 August 1984.

[92] EC, 13, 15 August, 11 September, 9 October 1984.

[93] *WM*, 6, 7, 16, 20, 28 August, 22 October 1984; *The Guardian*, 16 August 1984.

Llanwern's coal wharves. At Port Talbot, British Transport Police staked out the cranes over several days, until the miners could be persuaded to give themselves up; in contrast, Gwent Police forced a more violent conclusion to the Transporter Bridge occupation.[94]

How did these occupations fit into the South Wales strategy? At the time, Kim Howells stated that the pickets had been given a week's food and instructed to stay in position for as long as possible, since it was believed that Llanwern and Port Talbot had less than a week's supply of coking coal left. To maximise their effect, the raids were also timed to coincide with the ongoing dockers' strike. Retrospectively, miners seem to have been more ambivalent about the occupations. For one EC member, they were a morale-boosting exercise, 'highlighting the determination of the miners [and] . . . showing that basically the miners aren't prepared to go down without a fight'. In contrast, another EC representative recalled that his private opinion at the time was that it was 'absolutely crazy' to place over a hundred of the Area's best pickets in a situation practically guaranteed to end with them being arrested and barred from any further picketing. Looking back, George Rees said that the whole exercise 'was *bound* to fail, but at least it showed that the Union wasn't sitting back doing nothing . . . It had gone to a stage where we'd try *anything*.'[95]

PREVENTING STRIKE-BREAKING IN SOUTH WALES

August 1984 also saw the first significant attempts at a co-ordinated 'return to work' movement. Unlike most other coalfields, which saw real breaches in their solidarity, in south Wales there were only a few solitary strike-breaking attempts. These prompted a massive spontaneous reaction, with which neither the police nor NCB could cope. At Garw, Cwm, Bedwas and the Aberaman Phurnacite plant, individual strike-breakers admitted defeat in the face of over-whelming community opposition, with NCB bus drivers refusing to cross picket lines and in one case a milkman boycotting a strike-breaker's house. After five months of struggle the south Wales miners remained literally 100 per cent solid.

[94]   *WM*, 31 August, 1, 3 September 1984; *The Guardian*, 1 September 1984; interviews with miners involved in these occupations.
[95]   *WM*, 31 August 1984; Eric Davies, Dane Hartwell and George Rees interviews, respectively.

This unity was very impressive but did not mean that the situation was problem-free. By August 1984, for instance, there were rumours of discontent in Gwent, where a few pits had not been overly enthusiastic about the strike from the outset. Celynen South was where this was most apparent; Emlyn Williams and George Rees tackled this problem by addressing a lodge general meeting and persuading them to remain loyal to the strike. Nevertheless, the EC remained concerned about any potential NCB attempt to organise a 'return to work'. An Area conference on 29 August resolved to take decisive action if any strike-breaking occurred, including mass picketing and the coalfield-wide withdrawal of safety cover for at least twenty-four hours. On 3 September, the Area also responded positively to Scargill's call for miners to picket their own workplaces.[96]

THE TURN OF THE TIDE

Although the strike remained solid in south Wales, the trend of events during early autumn 1984 was troubling for the union. There had been the sequestration of the Area's assets, the return of the first strike-breakers in other important coalfields, the cancellation of planned strike action by NACODS and the failure of the TUC to offer effective assistance.[97] NUM-NCB talks broke down again in October; '[i]t is now generally agreed that the failure of these talks was the last occasion when some sort of settlement which did not involve the defeat of the NUM was practicable.'[98] Neil Kinnock began having regular Saturday morning breakfast meetings with Kim Howells, a former militant who now believed that Scargill was leading the union to disaster. Kinnock later recalled that Howells 'was telling me what was going on on the inside; we wanted to try to save something.'[99] Both Emlyn Williams and George Rees came to believe that Thatcher's overriding objective was to smash the NUM,

[96]   Celynen South NUM Lodge minutes, 21 August 1984; *WM*, 11 August, 4 September 1984; EC, 22 August 1984.
[97]   For details on the 'NACODS crisis', see Ned Smith, *The 1984 Miners' Strike: The Actual Account* (Whitstable: 1997), pp. 163–83. For details on the TUC's role, see Geoffrey Goodman, *The Miners' Strike* (London: 1985), pp. 93–116.
[98]   Saville, 'An open conspiracy', 314. For a detailed personal account of the national-level NUM-NCB talks, see Smith, *The 1984 Miners' Strike*, pp. 113–31.
[99]   Beckett and Hencke, *Marching to the Fault Line*, p. 108.

not merely to win the dispute.[100] Their concerns were reinforced by
no less a figure than Will Paynter, the former NUM national general
secretary and Area president. George Rees recalled:

> Paynter . . . [called] in on us . . . I can remember him saying, 'start looking
> for a way, George, to end this strike. If you don't, the Union will be
> destroyed . . . [Y]ou can't win it. It's gone on too long' . . . And from
> September on . . . we used to have discussions amongst ourselves in the office
> . . . And whilst we were in full support [of the strike], there were appre-
> hensions starting to build in our minds. Especially when you had people like
> Paynter telling us, 'Start to look for a way out, boy.' I mean, you're talking
> about a man whose experience had been through it all.[101]

As the autumn drew on, doubts began to grow amongst the Area
leadership about the likelihood of *any* kind of eventual NUM victory.
One EC member later commented:

> [I]t was a very worrying time . . . [T]owards the latter part of that year . . .
> I'd be going down to Pontypridd. Emlyn [Williams] would say, 'come on in,
> come in the office'. And then he'd say, 'what do you think . . . about the
> strike? . . . What do you *really* think?' . . . [And] towards, say, November, I
> remember saying to Emlyn Williams, 'To be honest with you,' I said, 'I think
> we're in *terrible* trouble'. And Emlyn said, 'I know' . . . Emlyn was of the
> same opinion.[102]

As 1984 drew to a close, the Area's miners and their supporters
found that the struggle was becoming increasingly a defensive one.
Changing circumstances shifted their activities from picketing and
campaigning around Britain to shoring up the south Wales coalfield.
For the first time since the strike began, the miners found themselves
picketing their own collieries. Although the Area remained
significantly more solid than any other, the long and painful retreat
had finally reached south Wales.

CYNHEIDRE AND THE FIRST CRACKS IN SOUTH WALES SOLIDARITY

In early November 1984, the NCB orchestrated another 'back to
work' campaign. Up until that point south Wales had been the only
coalfield to remain absolutely solid, but even here, as the strike began

[100] EC, 18 September 1984; Emlyn Williams SWML interview.
[101] George Rees interview.
[102] Dane Hartwell interview.

to crumble elsewhere, a small strike-breaking movement emerged, centred on Cynheidre colliery. Remarkably, however, despite considerable resources and NCB and police collaboration, the predicted surge failed to materialise: only nineteen men broke the strike in south Wales on 5 November, sixteen of them at Cynheidre. The other lodge committee which faced difficulties was Celynen South, although to a much lesser extent. Of the tiny number of south Wales miners who had become strike-breakers by late 1984, most were at Cynheidre and Celynen South. On 20 November, for instance, 73 of the 85 strike-breakers came from these collieries (with 53 at Cynheidre and 20 at Celynen South). This trend persisted for the rest of the strike: in early January 1985, for example, 87 out of the coalfield's 136 strike-breakers were from Cynheidre.[103]

Cynheidre was the weak link for the south Wales miners because of a combination of factors. Ever since mining began there in the early 1960s, the lodge had a reputation for moderation somewhat out of step with the traditional radicalism of the Area, whose leadership had generally come from the more militant central valleys. This tendency had been reinforced by the colliery's 'receiver pit' role. Located at the western extremity of the coalfield, Cynheidre faced several geographical problems, principally that its workforce was drawn from a wide catchment area including Llanelli, Cross Hands and all the small villages across rural southern Carmarthenshire. Consequently, the NUM lodge was not as integral to the local communities as it was elsewhere in south Wales. This had obvious implications for maintaining solidarity and operating an effective support network. The glaring contrast was with places like Tower and Maerdy, whose workforces were mainly from the tight-knit Cynon and Rhondda valleys respectively – and where there were *no* strike-breakers throughout the dispute. These factors were exacerbated prior to the strike by specific intra-lodge developments: the retirement of veteran lodge secretary Howard Jones in December 1983 and the ballot which replaced Tony Hollman as lodge chairman by the younger and more dynamic Tony Ciano. In this situation, the embittered ex-chairman chose to become a strike-breaker in order to advance his own standing. It is significant that the only pit where a prominent ex-lodge leader was a dedicated opponent of the strike was the least solid colliery in south Wales.

[103] *WM*, 6–20 November 1984 passim, 5 January 1985; Celynen South NUM Lodge minutes, 7, 12, 14 November 1984.

Unfortunately for the south Wales miners, the activities of individuals such as Hollman had an impact far beyond their own localities. George Rees later commented that 'people like Tony Hollman . . . the press made him out to be a hero. He was going to take on the South Wales Area, going to smash the South Wales Area.'[104] This handful of prospective strike-breakers was in contact with the wider movement aimed at undermining the NUM: as early as July 1984, secret meetings had been held in London and south Wales, with rumours that 'Silver Birch', a leading strike-breaker, had travelled to the coalfield to assist them. By October, Hollman and his associates were writing letters to the local media on behalf of an organisation known as the National Working Miners' Committee and soliciting companies for financial support for their schemes. Their efforts culminated in a legal action against the Area for alleged 'misuse' of NUM rules.[105]

PHILIP WEEKES

Throughout the strike, the relative absence of confrontation in south Wales was at least partly due to the unwillingness of South Wales NCB director Philip Weekes to take aggressive steps to force the miners into conceding defeat, remaining unenthusiastic about the attempts by a few individuals to return to work and also the harsh methods used by MacGregor.[106] The clearest example of this was the series of secret meetings between Weekes and the Area officials, which enabled the Area to obtain a more sympathetic local treatment than would otherwise have been the case.[107]

Weekes may have been relatively empathetic towards the miners but it was still his job to be an NCB director. Des Dutfield, an EC member at the time, later commented that 'Philip Weekes was no different from all the other Coal Board officials . . . [H]e was just a nicer man, a gentleman . . . but he carried out the policies of the Coal Board, of MacGregor.'[108] As from November 1984, the

---

[104] George Rees interview.
[105] *The Times*, 25 July 1984; EC, 9, 16, 30 October 1984; *WM*, 25 July, 27 October 1984.
[106] The Diary of Philip Weekes (Philip Weekes Papers, NLW, 1/10).
[107] Philip Weekes Diary; Terry Thomas interview; Emlyn Williams SWML interview; BBC website, 5 March 2004, *http://news.bbc.co.uk/1/hi/wales/3532987.stm*, accessed 7 January 2012; Beckett and Hencke, *Marching to the Fault Line*, p. 179.
[108] Interview with Des Dutfield, 12 February 2004.

combined pressure from the handful of dedicated strike-breakers and the national NCB finally forced the Board to take a more combative stance in south Wales – hence the first emergence of strike-breakers there. Weekes later told Emlyn Williams that MacGregor had given him an ultimatum: either conform to NCB policy or be sacked.[109] This new approach was apparent in his public calls for a return to work and also the attempt to use a Christmas bonus to coax men into abandoning the strike. Although Weekes denied it publicly, it was rumoured that colliery managers had received training on how to break the strike, systematically targeting vulnerable individual miners and placing them under immense pressure to return to work.[110]

THE SOLIDARITY OF SOUTH WALES MINING COMMUNITIES

Despite the NCB's efforts, the strike proved extraordinarily solid in the valleys. By 19 November, 99.6 per cent of the south Wales miners were still out (the highest percentage of any Area), compared with the national average of 73.7 per cent. Even though a mass return to work did not materialise, the threat brought out several thousand men on picket duty across south Wales. By mid-December 1984, the total number of strike-breakers in the coalfield had stabilised at around 120 – out of a total workforce of about 21,000. At that time, twenty-one of the twenty-six British pits still completely free of strike-breakers were to be found amongst the twenty-eight south Wales collieries. Speaking at a memorial meeting for Will Paynter (who had died in early December) shortly before Christmas, Emlyn Williams restated the miners' defiance: 'We are still amongst the most militant section of the working class movement . . . We will not be destroyed . . . [T]he South Wales miners will show their loyalty. We don't intend to live in a society of unemployment. We don't intend to see our children in the dole queues.'[111]

By late 1984, a key task for the miners and their supporters was to maintain morale. The Area leadership did this by encouraging lodges to hold general meetings, to disseminate information and to

[109] Emlyn Williams SWML interview.

[110] *WM*, 3, 24 November 1984; *The Guardian*, 24, 27 November 1984. In his diary, Weekes noted that the South Wales Board contacted over 700 selected 'possible dissidents' to try to persuade them to return to work. Philip Weekes Diary, 19 November 1984.

[111] *WM*, 13 November–24 December 1984 passim; Richards, *Miners on Strike*, pp. 108–9.

dispel any return-to-work talk. The lodge committees found that the best solution was to involve as many people as possible in the struggle, whether through picketing or fundraising. As one Penallta collier recalled:

> [T]he morale of the people I was involved with was *always* high, because they were always active. I think if you wasn't active . . . you become isolated then, don't you? . . . Whereas when you're active, you realise you're not the only one who is in that situation . . . And also, by being active, you made yourself available to information as to what to do in certain situations. If you *did* have . . . heavy letters coming through about debts, then the advice was there on how to deal with it . . . So, morale was high amongst those that was active and focused on the strike, and *believed* in it . . . Those that weren't involved, then their problems became their own.[112]

The most remarkable aspect of the strike in south Wales was the immense solidarity of the miners and their supporters. Undoubtedly, the radicalism that had shaped their history was an important factor. One lodge secretary later reflected that '[i]n many places, if you took Arthur [Scargill] out of the game, it would fall apart. In south Wales, you could take Arthur out – or anybody else – and the lodges was just as strong . . . So that's why we didn't break.' Emlyn Williams underlined this point: '[t]he South Wales coalfield has always been possibly the most militant coalfield . . . In the 1926 strike they were the last to go back . . . The bastion of the trade union movement . . . is the South Wales miners.'[113]

This traditional radicalism shaped the politics of Area activists and also created a culture of solidarity amongst the wider member-ship, in which the vast majority of south Wales miners would never contemplate crossing a NUM picket line. Towards the latter part of the strike, it was this instinctive loyalty that kept the strike solid in the valleys. As one Maerdy miner expressed it: '*Miners in south Wales have always been loyal to the Union.* Once they're out, they're out . . . [M]en *wanted* to go back to work. There's no argument about that – the hardship was *there*. But you was in the struggle – until the Union told us to go back.'[114]

This unshakeable loyalty of the south Wales miners cannot be explained without understanding the importance of the Area to its

---

[112] Ron Stoate interview.
[113] Tyrone O'Sullivan interview; *WM*, 24 January 1985.
[114] Interview with Mike Richards, 27 January 2004.

members. The primary original economic rationale of many valleys towns and villages was mining and the union had been a key part of the social fabric there from the outset. As one Tower miner expressed it, 'the Union was *everything*. The tradition . . . of the NUM, the Fed in south Wales – we all grew up with it . . . If you was living in the Valleys, yes, you can go and be a bus driver or anything else, but to be a *miner* . . . was a tradition, part of the culture.' The lodges were involved in community life, whether through the miners' institutes, local brass bands and rugby teams, or whatever. Although the historian must be careful not to over-romanticise the point, it was this cultural importance, together with the continued significance of mining within the coalfield, which prompted the Maerdy lodge chairman to comment that '[t]he heart of the community *was* the Union. It influenced all of your life. And not just on the pit life – it was in the traditions of communities. And I think miners respected that. And they respected when the Union said, "let's go" – they went.'[115] The union had a tangible local presence: lodge leaders were not remote figures but instead worked at the same coalfaces and attended the same social clubs as everyone else. This combination of factors meant that the lodge leadership's role was overwhelmingly about helping people with their problems, and it was precisely this that generated the immense rank-and-file loyalty during the strike. As a Maerdy miner pointed out, 'the NUM in South Wales is much more than an industrial union, it represents the community more closely than any other organisation'.[116]

The affinities between NUM lodge and community in south Wales meant that the former took seriously its responsibilities towards the latter. One example of this was the decision by Celynen South lodge to organise teams of volunteers to distribute firewood to local pensioners who required it.[117] It was this type of altruism, together with the lodges' positive social role and the widespread local understanding that the miners were fighting to defend the economic basis of many south Wales communities, which explains the solidarity shown by the coalfield's population towards the strike; for example, some retired mineworkers paid their pension into strike funds every week during the dispute. Miners were able to survive through assistance from their lodge and support group and also from their

---

[115] Quotations from Glyn Roberts and Arfon Evans interviews respectively.
[116] *The Guardian*, 2 January 1985.
[117] Celynen South NUM Lodge minutes, 17 March 1984.

friends and extended families. This collective response to adversity demonstrated precisely what the strike was all about for the mining communities of south Wales.

STRIKE-BREAKING IN SOUTH WALES

By November 1984, the south Wales miners were faced with the unpleasant reality that there were strike-breakers in their coalfield. Although they were only a tiny minority, the EC decided on a tough policy towards them, including disciplinary action, a significant increase in picketing and the withdrawal of safety cover at any pit where there was strike-breaking. The Area also circumvented NCB return-to-work plans by getting its TGWU and GMBATU allies to prevent colliery buses from leaving their depots. In January 1985, Emlyn Williams underlined this uncompromising stance towards strike-breakers: 'We shall never forgive them. To us, they are scabs. And no different from 1926 and 1911. They will be treated as scabs when the strike is over.'[118]

Where established methods failed, more unorthodox approaches were sometimes adopted to deter strike-breakers. Women's groups were now increasingly prominent, strengthening picket-line resistance and undertaking some of the more imaginative protests, for example, occupying the pithead baths and the manager's office at Cynheidre. On another occasion, over a hundred pickets gathered in Ystradgynlais outside the house of a strike-breaker and sang hymns in an attempt to persuade him to change his mind.[119] The most incongruous episode occurred just before Christmas at Celynen South, the scene of some of the worst clashes in south Wales. Here, lodge officials appeared on the picket line dressed as Father Christmas and sang carols to the strike-breakers, while the police were offered – though they declined – presents of plastic toy pigs. Lodge chairman Carl Browning explained: 'We wanted to enter the festive spirit and show the scabs coming in that we are human beings'.[120]

The general valleys reaction to strike-breaking during the strike was one of bitter, visceral opposition. The unremitting enmity of entire communities was a powerful deterrent to any prospective

[118] EC, 6 November 1984; *WM*, 10, 13 November 1984, 24 January 1985.
[119] *The Times*, 10 November 1984; *WM*, 10, 20 November 1984, 10, 18 January 1985.
[120] *The Guardian*, 22 December 1984.

return-to-work attempt. Valleys people have long memories when it comes to strike-breaking: for example, a Six Bells miner recalled that, during the dispute, his mother drew comparisons between those who had returned to work and the various local strike-breakers of 1926 whose names had been etched in her memory. Similarly, one strike-breaker was 'named and shamed' by graffiti painted on the old Llanhilleth pithead baths; elsewhere, hundreds of people staged peaceful demonstrations outside a strike-breaker's home in Merthyr Tydfil.[121]

Significantly, some of the leading strike-breakers were socially marginal elements or newcomers to south Wales mining communities.[122] One support group leader alleged that '[s]ometimes they are miners whom the union has repeatedly had to save from dismissal. Sometimes they are religious fanatics. Sometimes they are disturbed, come from unhappy homes, or live isolated from the community.' This assertion was reiterated by a Swansea district EC member, who stated his belief that the Cynheidre strike-breakers were 'led by wife-beaters, reprobates, and other people . . . [M]ost of the ones that went back in Cynheidre were the bad attenders, the poor performers, men which the lodge had *defended*.'[123] Several others came from military backgrounds and were alien to the trade union ethos. A prominent example was Gordon Fjaellberg, one of the few strike-breakers at Cwm colliery, a former RAF member who spoke with a Home Counties accent and who had only worked at the pit for about a year before the strike began. In the view of the Cwm lodge secretary, Fjaellberg's actions proved that he 'could *never* have become a miner as long as he lived'.[124]

At this time, the Area leadership's main fear was a violent backlash from communities hitherto self-disciplined but which were confronted increasingly by police and poverty and who regarded the strike-breakers as traitors. This was encapsulated by events at a 5,000-strong rally in Port Talbot on 13 November, at which TUC general secretary Norman Willis was one of the main speakers. This rally was always a potential flashpoint situation, as Willis had hitherto

[121] Jim Watkins interview; EC, 20 November 1984; *The Guardian*, 21 November 1984.

[122] Tony Hollman at Cynheidre represents a noteworthy exception to this general observation.

[123] Quotations from *MS*, 15 December 1984, and Eric Davies interview, respectively. Obviously, it is very difficult for the historian to assess the accuracy of such statements.

[124] Billy Liddon interview; *WM*, 2 January 1985.

been unwilling to offer unconditional support for the miners' strike. At the rally, Scargill received a rapturous reception. In contrast, when Willis appeared to distance himself from their struggle, he provoked uproar. In a grim symbolic gesture which had presumably been planned in advance, furious strikers lowered a noose from the ceiling above him, while a spokesman likened the speech to the TUC's 'great betrayal' in 1926. Although the EC subsequently felt that the 'noose incident' had detracted from the rally and that the media's distortion of events had been unhelpful, the episode demonstrated graphically the intensity of feeling in the coalfield.[125]

The return of the first strike-breakers in November 1984 brought to south Wales the picket-line scenes that had become commonplace in every other coalfield. The scale of the confrontations dwarfed the actual number of those returning to work; on 12 November, for example, the fifty-four strike-breakers caused stand-offs between about 2,000 strikers and a similar number of police. During the last weeks of 1984, picketing occurred mainly at Cynheidre, Marine, Celynen South, Merthyr Vale, Abernant, Nantgarw, Cwm and the Aberaman Phurnacite plant, with the numbers of strikers in each case ranging from about 100 up to 800. Allan Rogers MP condemned the use of hundreds of police to force a few strike-breakers into otherwise solid pits: 'Is it right for these vast sums of money to be spent on this particular exercise? Why doesn't the Coal Board . . . stop tearing the communities apart?' Similarly, Kim Howells warned that NCB tactics were leading to escalating levels of confrontation.[126]

One of the most tragic events in south Wales during the dispute occurred on the last day of November. David Wilkie, a taxi-driver, was killed by a concrete block dropped from a bridge as he drove a strike-breaker to Merthyr Vale. As soon as he heard the news of this, Kim Howells, one of the main organisers of the south Wales pickets, rushed to the union offices and destroyed documents and maps relating to the Area's picketing activities because, as he later recalled, he feared that the union might be implicated.[127] A few days before the tragedy, Ted Rowlands, MP for Merthyr Tydfil, had telephoned Weekes to ask him to stop the two strike-breakers, whose activities

---

[125] EC, 20, 26 November 1984.

[126] *WM*, 26 November 1984; *The Guardian*, 27 November 1984.

[127] 'Minister's secret role in miners' strike death inquiry', *The Guardian* website, 26 January 2004, *http://www.guardian.co.uk/politics/2004/jan/26/uk.tradeunions*, accessed 7 January 2012.

were causing intense resentment and increasingly unpleasant picket-line scenes, but Weekes refused, in line with NCB policy. Merthyr Vale was a flashpoint because of its proximity to Aberfan and its location in the most solidly pro-strike district in Britain. Wilkie's death and the arrest of three young miners, two of whom later stood trial for murder, did little to weaken the strike in south Wales because it was such an aberration. It did, however, have a calming effect on the coalfield, epitomised by Bill King, the veteran Merthyr Vale lodge secretary. The following morning, at the picket line, a miner recalled: 'we stood in the pouring rain, Bill King asked . . . for two minutes' silence for everyone who had died as a result of the strike that was forced upon us. And we stood there, rain dripping off our noses, stunned . . . But still [the strike-breaker] came back to work . . . in the convoy.'[128]

CHRISTMAS QUESTIONS

By December 1984, the immediate concern in south Wales mining communities was to get the best Christmas possible in the circum-stances. The Area leadership and the support groups worked to ensure that every miner's family received a turkey, in addition to their usual provisions. Special efforts were made for the children, with a generous supply of donated toys (including several lorry-loads of gifts from French, Dutch and Belgian trade unionists) and parties organised for them across the coalfield. The solidarity that had sustained the miners throughout the year enabled their families to have a decent Christmas.[129]

This focus on getting the miners and their families through Christmas meant that – as the EC was aware – questions about the progress of the strike would soon return in an even more acute form. Christmas 1984 represented a psychological turning-point for the NUM membership. Across south Wales, leaders at both Area and lodge level noticed a changed atmosphere among the membership, and a belief that it was not now possible to win the strike. This was most pronounced in Gwent and the west of the coalfield but was

---

[128] Quoted in Francis and Rees, '"No Surrender in the Valleys"', 63; *The Guardian*, 23, 27 November, 1 December 1984; *WM*, 22, 23, 24, 30 November, 1, 4 December 1984; Bill King interview.

[129] *WM*, 18 December 1984; *The Guardian*, 22 December 1984.

even discernible in places where the strike was still completely solid. As the dispute carried on into 1985, it was becoming apparent that the only thing keeping many miners going was their loyalty to the NUM.[130]

LOYALTY AND DESPERATION

Sustaining the strike was placing a major strain on the south Wales miners by early 1985. Union officials recalled occasions when tough and determined men came to them in distress or cried publicly in lodge meetings. At a Cynheidre general meeting, George Rees was faced with a cry of anguish: 'I've lost my wife, my family, my house. Don't turn me into a scab.'[131] As the Oakdale lodge secretary commented: '[t]he writing was on the wall . . . Men were exhausted. They were losing their homes, their marriages were breaking up . . . [T]hey were despondent and demoralised – and it was crazy, it was all bloody crazy.' One stark indicator of this was the increased number of calls to the Samaritans from south Wales men and also the tragic suicide of a young Trelewis Drift miner in January 1985.[132]

By January 1985, union loyalty was the main bond between committed activists and the majority of strikers, whose participation consisted of hanging on in the struggle. Where appeals for loyalty failed, lodge officials became 'social workers' and visited strike-breakers' homes, some of which were in truly desperate straits. One EC member stated: 'If you saw . . . some of the things that *I* saw, in terms of repossessions, houses [with] no coal, no heating, burning shoes [in the fireplace] . . . [T]here was no money. People had gone into debt . . . You attended meetings of miners and you could see this – it was building up.' In the view of a Taff Merthyr miner, 'these boys that tried to break the strike, they must have been *desperate* . . . Because once you go back, that will live with them *forever* . . . I think they must have gone back in *desperation*.'[133] Francis and Rees observe that 'In such circumstances, "loyalty" took a perverse new meaning.

---

[130] EC, 18 December 1984; Emlyn Williams SWML interview; Phil Bowen, Ray Lawrence and Terry Thomas interviews.

[131] Quotation from Francis and Rees, '"No Surrender in the Valleys"', 64; interviews with Graham Bartlett (20 February 2004) and Terry Thomas.

[132] Allan Baker interview; *WM*, 18 December 1984, 19 January 1985.

[133] Eric Davies and Colin Thomas interviews, respectively.

As the lodge chairman of Blaenant . . . began to say publicly, "Does the last striker have the right to call the last but one a 'scab'?".[134]

The hardships endured by the south Wales miners make the resilience of the vast majority who stayed on strike even more remarkable. In early January there were still only 117 strike-breakers in the coalfield. Although this figure increased gradually over the following weeks, the percentage involved was tiny. On 9 January, only 0.8 per cent of South Wales was back in work (the next most solid Area was Yorkshire, with 7.0 per cent). By late January, seventeen of the thirty south Wales lodges were still completely free of strike-breakers. As late as 20 February, 97.5 per cent of the Area's members remained on strike. Maerdy, Tower, Garw, Penrhiwceiber, Taff Merthyr and Trelewis Drift all stayed 100 per cent solid to the end (the only pits in Britain to do so), while strike-breaking numbers in eleven other collieries did not exceed single figures. Of those back at work, over half were concentrated at just four collieries: Cynheidre, Abertillery, Bedwas and Celynen South.[135]

January 1985 saw the NCB intensify its efforts to undermine the strike in south Wales, with MacGregor and Weekes appealing publicly for miners to return to work. A formidable array of strike-breaking measures were used, including sending letters to miners encouraging them to organise return-to-work groups; promising that anyone returning to work would receive up to £325 for doing so; and even allegedly taking prospective strike-breakers out to dinner. Kim Howells commented caustically that '[the NCB] must be spending more on getting a few scabs in than they've invested in some pits in the last ten years'.[136]

The main response of the south Wales miners was through mass picketing at pits where there had been a dent in unity: on one day in late January, for instance, over 900 pickets were deployed across the coalfield, including 300 at Bedwas. A serious blow to the Area's ability to maintain the strike occurred in February, when twenty south Wales strike-breakers acquired a High Court order restricting the number of pickets at each pit to six. This judgment was highly controversial, creating legal precedent by giving a statutory limitation to picketing numbers. An Area conference on 13 February

[134] Francis and Rees, ' "No Surrender in the Valleys" ', 64.

[135] The Times, 3, 10 January, 26 February 1985; WM, January–February 1985 passim; EC, 21 January 1985.

[136] The Guardian, 2, 12 January, 22 February 1985; WM, 7, 12, 25 January 1985.

decided that there was no alternative but to accept it: however, this proved difficult to do in practice, since the news had caused large spontaneous picket-line gatherings to demonstrate the community's support for the NUM.[137]

Following this legal ruling, several south Wales lodges decided that their sole remaining option was to withdraw safety cover at their pits. This was done at St John's in late January after seventeen men returned to work; similarly, Oakdale lodge temporarily withdrew cover in protest at the emergence of a few strike-breakers there. The NCB claimed that, as a result of the strike, ten south Wales coalfaces had been ruined. In response, Terry Thomas said that the Board had exaggerated this damage, commenting sardonically that 'I only wish the coal board had been as concerned before the strike about the condition of pits and coal faces as they appear to be now.'[138]

A key issue at this time was the reinstatement of thousands of miners who had been sacked during the dispute. Unlike in many other Areas, only forty-two south Wales miners had been dismissed and most of these had been for minor offences, though there were a few exceptions, such as the three Nantgarw men who had occupied the winding-gear of a Staffordshire colliery. An Area conference on 14 December agreed that the strike should continue until there was an amnesty for every sacked miner, a demand which the EC reaffirmed in mid-February 1985. There was no progress on this issue until after the strike, when it soon became apparent that almost all of the dismissed south Wales miners would be reinstated.[139]

For the South Wales NUM, possibly the most ominous dismissal case was that of the 'St John's Four'. Here, four lodge officials were sacked in what appeared to be a 'set-up'.[140] The intent was clear: to discourage the Area from preventing miners from abandoning the strike. The EC was concerned that the Board would use this precedent to 'decapitate' the lodge leaderships right across the coalfield. At the same time as this victimisation was occurring, the NCB was encouraging leading strike-breakers to establish alternative lodge committees. The prospect of a 'scab union' had a

[137] *WM*, 7, 30 January, 12, 14 February 1985; *The Times*, 12, 13 February 1985.

[138] *WM*, 24 January, 4, 13–15 February 1985; *The Times*, 4 February 1985.

[139] EC, 13, 19 February 1985; *WM*, 28 February 1985; *The Times*, 28 February, 5 March 1985.

[140] Ian Isaac, the lodge secretary, was one of the men who were sacked. For his perspective on this episode, see Ian Isaac, *When We Were Miners* (n.p., 2010), pp. 99–100. *WM*, 12 February 1985; Ian Isaac interview.

particularly haunting resonance for miners who remembered the 1930s and for whom industrial unity was paramount.[141]

ENDGAMES

By early 1985, NUM policy was to stand firm in the hope that unexpected developments would enable the union to obtain a favourable settlement.[142] Despite the accelerating break-up of the strike elsewhere, the fact that less than 2 per cent of the south Wales miners were back in work meant that an Area conference on 25 January could endorse the continuation of the struggle. By mid-February, however, growing discontent prompted the leadership to convene a further conference to head off return-to-work calls from several pits. This repeated the Area's clear support for the official NUM line, but also requested a National Conference to discuss the strike. Although the representatives of the lodges that were still completely solid reiterated their defiance, delegates from lodges where men were returning to work stated that resistance was on the verge of crumbling. Other concerns were expressed about what would happen to those who remained on strike once the national percentage of men back in work exceeded 50 per cent and that the NUM was 'running the risk of being crushed in'. As late as 22 February, however, an Area conference accepted the EC's request to stand firm, despite growing fears of an impending collapse.[143]

The preferred South Wales conclusion to the dispute was a negotiated settlement, with the leadership endorsing the solution promoted by the Welsh Council of Churches which it had helped to draft. This plan proposed to establish an independent review body to examine the coal industry in the context of a long-term energy policy. Although (or possibly *because*) these proposals received the formal backing of the Area and of thirty-six Opposition MPs, they were never taken seriously by the government.[144]

[141] EC, 12 February 1985; ASC, 13 February 1985.

[142] Goodman, *The Miners' Strike*, pp. 101–3, 171–94.

[143] EC, 19 February 1985; ASC, 13 February 1985; *The Guardian*, 28 January, 20 February 1985; *WM*, February 1985 passim; Celynen South NUM Lodge minutes, 12, 23 February 1985.

[144] Emlyn Williams SWML interview; EC, 8, 21 January, 2 February 1985; *WM*, 8, 9, 16 January 1985.

A prominent feature of the final weeks of the dispute was the point-blank refusal of the government to negotiate. By late January 1985, Thatcher was demanding that the NUM state in writing its acceptance of the closure of 'uneconomic' collieries as a pre-condition of any discussion. It was becoming obvious that the only outcome acceptable to Thatcher and MacGregor was total NUM surrender.[145] In the last weeks of the strike, the absence of any significant TUC aid inevitably provoked NUM recriminations. The TUC was negotiating with ACAS and the NCB, but its solution was completely unacceptable because it offered no safeguards against further closures. By mid-February, the EC was informed that there was a distinct threat of the NUM being destroyed if the TUC did not quickly produce a more positive proposal. At an Area conference several days later, Emlyn Williams attributed TUC unwillingness to intervene effectively to its determination to ruin Scargill's reputation as a union leader.[146]

Throughout the strike, the south Wales miners had been its most solid supporters. The Area leadership had adhered faithfully to national NUM policy, even when it disagreed with particular decisions. By 1985, however, it had begun to speak out. For many of the coalfield's leaders, the primary concern by this stage had become the struggle to ensure the survival of the NUM. In January, Emlyn Williams stated: '[Thatcher] is out to grind the miners into the dust . . . This is no longer an issue of strike – [for her,] it is an issue to destroy the NUM.' Although the South Wales leadership reiterated that it would stand firm, evidence of tension was apparent in the Area officials' frustration at a statement by Scargill that he would rather see the return-to-work continue than 'prostitute his principles' by bringing the strike to an end.[147]

A controversial figure in these intra-union tensions was Kim Howells. Although never an elected representative, by early 1985 he was being used by Emlyn Williams as a channel to express viewpoints about the strike which did not conform to NUM policy, and that displeased Scargill intensely.[148] As Howells later put it:

[145] Smith, *The 1984 Miners' Strike*, pp. 150–61; Taylor, *The NUM and British Politics, Vol. 2*, pp. 235–43; Goodman, *The Miners' Strike*, pp. 171–94; WM, 25, 29 January 1985; EC, 2, 19 February 1985; *The Guardian*, 8 February 1985.

[146] EC, 12, 19 February 1985; ASC, 22 February 1985; *The Times*, 27 February 1985.

[147] EC, 21 January, 12, 19 February 1985; WM, 3, 26 January 1985.

[148] Emlyn Williams SWML interview; Beckett and Hencke, *Marching to the Fault Line*, p. 197.

Things had become inconceivably desperate, and many of us in the coal-fields had recognized that there seemed to be a serious credibility gap between what Arthur [Scargill] and Peter [Heathfield] were saying on public platforms at these huge rallies and what was happening on the ground. There seemed to be no recognition of the appalling problems which miners' families were suffering . . . [C]ompromise didn't seem to be on [Scargill's] agenda. He was going for total victory and the corollary of that is total defeat. Many of us began to think how it might be possible to save the union.[149]

During January 1985, Howells claimed publicly that south Wales miners were becoming disillusioned with the lack of initiative from the national leadership and criticised the union's mass picketing tactics. The following month, he suggested that South Wales might possibly return to work without a settlement and made veiled criticisms of Scargill's conduct of the strike. These statements met with incredulous opposition within the Area; in response, Howells was suspended as Area spokesman, though he was reinstated a few days later. The episode highlighted clearly the pressures and tensions within the NUM hierarchy as the miners were forced to confront the unpleasant reality of the probability of impending defeat.

Throughout the Area early in 1985, the dominant miners' viewpoint was unstinting opposition to any 'sell out' agreement. This led to a further difference of opinion between Scargill and the majority of the Area leadership. The national president insisted on a negotiated conclusion to the strike on terms that suited the union, even though the prospect of this seemed remote. In contrast, by late January some south Wales miners were inclining towards a general return-to-work without a settlement, since this would avoid agreeing to a closure programme and would allow the struggle to continue locally on a 'guerrilla' basis. A few weeks later, the Area's representatives were arguing unsuccessfully on the NEC for a national return-to-work without an agreement. Matters were not helped by Scargill's statements at that time that the strike was not 'national' and that Areas could do as they pleased, a suggestion that the EC felt was extremely dangerous. In response, Emlyn Williams reaffirmed that there would never be a unilateral return-to-work by the South Wales NUM.[150]

[149] Quoted in Beckett and Hencke, *Marching to the Fault Line*, p. 198.
[150] EC, 25, 29 January, 5 February 1985; *The Times*, 19, 29 January, 7 February 1985; *The Guardian*, 6 February 1985; *WM*, 11 February 1985.

THE WRITING ON THE WALL

Despite the solidity of the south Wales miners, the accelerating abandonment of the strike elsewhere increased the prospect of a return-to-work. By the end of February, as the number back in work across Britain approached 50 per cent, it became possible to foresee the Area having to withstand the entire weight of the NCB onslaught alone. As the Aberpergwm lodge secretary later reflected, '[w]e could see the end coming . . . [S]tories of them drifting back in other Areas *was* beginning to dishearten our men . . . I would say the last three weeks before we did go back to work, the feeling was getting strong that we had to go back.' The Area leadership was aware of this: later in February, Terry Thomas stated that 'We will do our utmost to get a national settlement . . . But . . . we would not see South Wales miners kept out in isolation. I can only assure all South Wales miners of that.'[151]

Even the incredible resilience of the south Wales miners had its limits. The last fortnight of February 1985 indicated that there were several places where there was a possibility of the strike collapsing, as it had done already in many other coalfields. An early indication of this was when a large section of the audience failed to join in the customary standing ovation for Scargill when he addressed a Cynheidre lodge meeting in early January. Throughout February there was also sustained grassroots pressure at Celynen South for a mass return-to-work. If Celynen South had abandoned the strike, many other Gwent collieries would probably have followed suit; as it transpired, their union loyalty just about kept them from breaking ranks.[152] These tensions were even being felt to a lesser degree in the central valleys. Although the EC was aware that several lodges were threatened by a mass return-to-work, as late as mid-February it agreed to support the NEC's 'stand firm' line, on the understanding that the national leadership was working to obtain a negotiated settlement.[153]

The numbers of miners abandoning the strike accelerated in late February. In south Wales, this trebled between 19 and 28 February,

---

[151] Interview with Harry Samuel, 20 January 2004; *WM*, 20 February 1985.

[152] *The Guardian*, 8 January, February 1985 passim; *WM*, February 1985 passim; ASC, 13 February 1985; Celynen South NUM Lodge minutes, 12 February 1985; Ray Lawrence interview.

[153] EC, 12, 19 February 1985.

from 478 (approximately 2.5 per cent of the workforce) to 1,471 (7.5 per cent). Most of these were at the six pits which had seen the greatest difficulties in maintaining solidarity: Cynheidre, Abertillery, Six Bells, Marine, Celynen South and Bedwas. By this stage, the numbers back in work at these pits ranged from over 40 per cent to about 15 per cent. This decline was much more serious elsewhere: after South Wales, the next most solid Area (Yorkshire) had 21 per cent back in work, while nationally the number on strike barely exceeded 50 per cent. This process continued until the last day of the strike, when there were 1,739 men at work in south Wales – and many more across Britain as a whole.[154]

The deteriorating situation facing the NUM was reflected in the changing attitude of the EC towards continuing the strike. By early 1985, some members had concluded that the miners faced imminent defeat and that a national return-to-work was the best form of damage limitation. A Swansea district EC representative later recounted:

> [A] few of us on the Executive, by early '85 . . . felt that we wouldn't win . . . It was obvious. We had lost. And it was . . . about the survival of the Union. Because if you didn't have the Union, whatever came after would be ten times worse. And many of us took that view – I certainly took that view. The onslaught is going to come – but the Union has got to be there, to do the best they can out of a bad job.[155]

Within the EC at this time, the contrasting viewpoints were the maintaining of the status quo and a call for a nationally-organised end to the strike. On 13 February, the EC agreed to support the view of the national leadership, though it also called for a National Conference. Six days later, fears were expressed on the EC about the imminent possibility of the collapse of the strike, although the majority opinion was to stand firm and await further national developments. The EC meeting on 22 February reaffirmed the need to keep the strike going but also revealed the reservations felt by a growing minority of its members. The main 'stand firm' exponents were the Aberdare, Merthyr and Rhondda district representatives, backed by the Maesteg district members and the Area officials; by

---

[154] Although the numbers quoted are NCB figures, the trend which they illustrate is undeniable. *WM*, 20–8 February, 1, 5 March 1985; *The Times*, 27 February 1985; *The Guardian*, 26 February 1985.

[155] Eric Davies interview.

contrast, the Swansea representatives called for a National Conference to organise a return to work without a settlement, while the Rhymney and Gwent members doubted the ability of the NUM to survive in any meaningful form if the drift back to work continued. The balance of opinion was tipped further towards ending the strike by events in the last days of February: the decision by the Nottinghamshire Area to end its overtime ban, the beginnings of a collapse in parts of south Wales, together with a formal appeal from Cynheidre, Betws and Cwmgwili lodges for an immediate Area conference.[156] It was this small but decisive shift which changed the EC majority viewpoint from one of maintaining the status quo to one of contemplating finishing the strike.[157]

By the end of February 1985, the Area leadership had become convinced of the necessity for an official national return to work without a settlement. Although most south Wales miners initially were in favour of continuing the struggle, the failure of the various peace initiatives meant that support increased for an organised return rather than to watch the strike crumble. On 27 February, Terry Thomas stated: 'I don't see . . . us getting the kind of victory now that we thought of in March 1984 . . . [W]e must . . . not abuse the loyalty that has been given to us by many thousands of miners . . . and if we don't give them leadership then I fear for the unity of the NUM.' On 26 February, the EC decided – given the increasing drift back to work and the prospect of the establishment of rival lodge committees as a first possible step towards the formation of a 'scab union' – to convene an Area conference and call for a National Conference to have a 'realistic appraisal' of the situation.[158]

THE BITTER END

In response to these developments, on 1 March a South Wales conference decided by 374 votes to 90 to accept the EC recommendation and call for a national return to work without a settlement. Speaking at the conference, Emlyn Williams stressed the need to save

[156] EC, 13–26 February 1985 passim.

[157] This seems the best explanation for the Area leadership's actions in late February 1985. The alternative view, articulated by a minority of lodge activists, was that the Area officials capitulated under pressure from Kinnock and Weekes.

[158] The Times, 28 February 1985; The Guardian, 27 February 1985; EC, 1 March 1985.

the NUM, emphasising 'the vital necessity not merely to come out on strike under leadership, but also to go back under leadership' and that leaders should not 'hide in the shadows'. This decision was not about saving Welsh collieries; many delegates who voted for a return knew that their own pits would not survive the year.

The decision to call for an end to the strike was arguably the most contentious step ever taken by the South Wales NUM. Consequently, it is not surprising that it provoked bitter opposition from a minority of the membership: at Trelewis Drift, for instance, miners accused Emlyn Williams of 'treachery'. Even twenty years later, some lodge activists still condemned the Area officials for leading the return to work, arguing that continuing the strike for a few more weeks might have forced power-cuts or a rebellion against Thatcher by Conservative MPs.[159] In contrast, other south Wales miners felt that there was no choice but to end the strike. The Six Bells lodge chairman, for example, stated that 'I believe what he [Emlyn Williams] did was right because we'd lost by then and all we were doing was prolonging the agony and throwing money away'. Similarly, an EC member commented: 'some people . . . said, "oh damn, if we'd stopped out . . . another fortnight, we'd have won". Well, *we bloody well wouldn't have won* . . . [W]hen we had gone as far as the March . . . [of 1985], *they knew* we'd lost it . . . [L]et's not pretend anything different, it was lost.'[160]

Fundamentally, the NUM had no realistic option in March 1985 other than to end the strike. There were several reasons for this: the government had ensured that other key unions received above-inflation pay rises, thereby preventing the opening of a 'second front'; there was no further prospect of TUC support; the intransigence of MacGregor and Thatcher meant that negotiations were futile; coal was being moved around Britain; and the police were ensuring that power stations kept working. Furthermore, the situation within the union was dire: the strike was collapsing (or had already collapsed) in most Areas and even in south Wales many miners were close to breaking point. As one EC member recalled, 'it was *evident* from the feedback we were getting from the lodge officers . . . that the lines couldn't be held indefinitely . . . [T]he men had had enough, then.' Another EC representative concurred: '[T]he

---

[159] *The Guardian*, 5 March 1985; interviews with Dai 'Dosco' Davies (19 March 2004), Glyn Roberts, Tyrone O'Sullivan, and Billy Liddon.

[160] Jim Watkins and Dane Hartwell interviews, respectively.

floodgates *were* going to burst . . . I don't think that strike would have gone on beyond another fortnight.' Emlyn Williams also later pointed to the reports of total chaos in coalfields such as Yorkshire and Scotland, where the leaderships were phoning South Wales every day to beg its officials, in the most solid Area, to call a National Conference. Consequently, the Area led the return to save the NUM from destruction. As George Rees put it, 'we could see no conclusion . . . [o]ther than defeat. *Utter, complete defeat.* The *smashing* of the Union. That's why we decided to [end the strike] . . . [W]e could see the destruction of the Union facing us. And it was more important to get the Union to survive at the end of this twelve months than anything else.'[161]

This decision by South Wales did little to endear it to Scargill and the NUM national headquarters, which instead argued that the drift-back be allowed to continue until there remained a hard core of activists whose refusal to work would force the NCB to concede terms. This proposal was seen overwhelmingly in south Wales, and ultimately by the National Conference, as a retrograde step that would enable the NCB to sack the most committed activists and ultimately disfranchise the majority of Britain's miners from membership of what would remain of the NUM – in other words, the destruction of the union. For many of the Area's miners, Scargill's biggest failing was not in the decision to strike in March 1984 or in how he conducted the dispute, but in his inability to accept that it had to come to an end in March 1985.

The circumstances of the decision to end the strike were soon eclipsed by the drama of the return on Tuesday, 5 March 1985. There was disruption at several south Wales pits: Trelewis Drift men refused to cross token picket lines of Kent miners; at Merthyr Vale, the miners would not work until a prominent strike-breaker had been transferred out of the coalfield; at Penrhiwceiber and Six Bells, NUM members were sent home for the day after NACODS claimed that they were unmanageable. One Penrhiwceiber miner later recalled that the mood of the men was 'absolute despondency': '[i]f ever you saw the face of defeat, it was that morning in Penrhiwceiber'. Elsewhere, the return was subdued. As Garw lodge chairman John Jones put it, '[w]e went back with our heads down . . . there was nothing to celebrate'. At several collieries, however, the men

---

[161] Quotations from Dane Hartwell, Eric Davies and George Rees interviews, respectively; Emlyn Williams SWML interview.

marched back behind the lodge banner, in a show of solidarity: pits where this occurred included Penallta, Cwm and – significantly – Cynheidre and Celynen South. One of the most enduring images of the entire strike occurred that morning at Maerdy. There, a thousand-strong crowd of miners, their families and supporters marched behind the union banner and colliery band to the pit, where they were addressed by Arfon Evans, the lodge chairman – emotional scenes that were subsequently broadcast world-wide. United, defiant and unrepentant, the Maerdy miners epitomised the strengths which had enabled the NUM to remain on strike for a whole year.[162]

Across the south Wales coalfield, the reaction to the end of the strike was summarised by a Penallta collier, who later commented that 'relief was the first feeling. Bitter disappointment as well . . . [I]t would rip my guts out to think of Margaret Thatcher and MacGregor in Chequers that weekend we went back to work, sipping champagne and saying, "we won".'[163] There was an understandable enmity shown towards strike-breakers, though at places like Cynheidre a distinction was drawn between the 'super scabs' and those who had returned to work in the last month of the dispute. Another commonly held view was that some other Areas (particularly Nottinghamshire) and sections of the labour movement (particularly the TUC) had not done enough to help the miners. The wife of a Blaenant miner reflected:

> You'd . . . struggled for *so long*. And all your struggling . . . wasn't for extra pay or better conditions – you just wanted your husband to have a job to bring the money in. And all of a sudden you're thinking, a whole year – for nothing. To struggle *for nothing* . . . [A]ll the way through the strike . . . you'd got doubts . . . but you keep on thinking that maybe at the end . . . you'll still have a job to hang onto. And then you know your colliery's going to close . . . And what are you going to have, because there's no other industry in the area? *Nothing.*[164]

A Penrhiwceiber miner later called the strike 'a story of heartbreak. Absolute heartbreak. No glory in it . . . [I]t was the greatest defeat

---

[162] Quotation from Dai 'Dosco' Davies interview; *WM*, 6 March 1985; *The Times*, 6 March 1985; *The Guardian*, 6 March 1985; Ron Stoate, Eddie Thomas (17 March 2004), Arfon Evans, Ivor England (27 February 2004) and Mike Richards interviews.

[163] Ron Stoate interview.

[164] Kay Bowen interview.

ever inflicted on any trade union movement . . . And the rest of the British trade union movement fell with us . . . You was in a war – you either win it or lose it . . . But we lost it.'[165]

CONCLUSION

Although the 1984–5 strike could not have been begun or sustained for as long as it was in south Wales without the support of the rank-and-file membership, the Area leadership nevertheless played a crucial role in shaping the strategy and conduct of the dispute. Throughout the year-long stoppage, the essential policy of the South Wales Area leadership had been one of loyalty to the NUM and its members. Conscious of the traditional radicalism of the south Wales miners and also the likely impact of the Thatcher government's colliery closure programme, throughout the period 1979–84 the Area officials worked to galvanise the NUM into strike action against pit closures – not surprisingly, as Emlyn Williams and George Rees had championed this approach during the 1960s. Whatever reservations they may have had about the strategic wisdom of beginning a strike in March 1984, both Emlyn Williams and George Rees played an important, albeit not particularly high-profile, role in mobilising support among the South Wales membership for the national leadership's call for strike action. Although never an elected leader of the south Wales miners, once the strike was underway, Kim Howells came to assume a prominent role within the Area, both as its official spokesman and as the main co-ordinator of its picketing activities. The Area officials loyally abided by the national leadership's decisions – including those with which they personally disagreed, such as the total blockade of the steelworks. Even so, they still maintained their own ideas as to how best the strike should be conducted, both within south Wales and further afield. By autumn 1984, the turn of events meant that both Emlyn Williams and George Rees had privately reached the conclusion that it was unlikely that the strike could be won outright. Thereafter, they began to think in terms of limiting the potential damage to the NUM, so as to enable it to survive after the strike was over. It was this differing appraisal of the strike situation and the prospects of victory that led

---

[165] Dai 'Dosco' Davies interview.

to a divergence of views between the Area officials and Scargill in the last two or three months of the strike. Kim Howells was the main target of Scargill's ire in this respect; his criticisms of Scargill's strategy, his closeness to the Area officials and his growing political affinity with Kinnock made Howells a prominent advocate of moderation within the South Wales NUM. Nevertheless, despite the tensions, NUM loyalty remained a strong factor: as late as 22 February 1985 the Area officials were arguing dutifully in EC meetings in support of the national leadership's 'stand firm' line. Ultimately, though, having considered both the situation at national level and also in their own coalfield, by March 1985 the south Wales miners as a whole had reached the same conclusion as that of the Area officials: namely, that it was now impossible to win the strike and that it should be brought to an end.

For south Wales, the defeat of the miners in 1985 signified the end of an era. The ensuing closure programme all but eliminated mining from a region once synonymous with it. It was fitting, then, that events there during the dispute exemplified the core NUM strengths and yet posed in their sharpest form the main problems facing the miners. In March 1984, unofficial picketing was the key factor in bringing the Area out on strike. Despite a hesitant start, south Wales was the most solid coalfield, a reflection of the strength of the historical bond between union and community in the valleys. South Wales miners were central to picketing strategic targets across Britain; however, the failure of the steelworks blockade reflected a key internal NUM controversy about methods which was heightened by events at Orgreave. Finally, the role played by the Area leadership in ending the strike emphasised the importance of South Wales in the NUM. In keeping with the trend throughout the twentieth century, the Area encapsulated many aspects of the broader coal-mining picture during the 1984–5 strike. The solidarity and traditional radicalism of the south Wales miners in the face of adversity remained a defining feature of their history to the end.

CONCLUSION

Following the miners' defeat in 1985, the coal industry shrank at a staggering rate. When Labour left office in 1979, there were 235,000 miners in Britain; by early 1992 there were 32,000. South Wales felt this impact as fully as anywhere else. Before the strike, 20,000 miners had worked at twenty-eight pits; by 1994, the government was attempting to shut Tower, the last deep-mine in the coalfield.[1] These closures were followed rapidly by the collieries' demolition, resulting in coal-mining literally being wiped off the map.

In the NUM, appraisals of the outcome of the strike varied. Scargill did not see it as a shattering defeat and remained positive about the union's potential strength. While this view was based on a realistic assessment of the role of coal in British electricity generation, it clashed with the majority of opinion in the union. The Six Bells chairman, for instance, argued: 'How can it be a victory when we lost all our money, people was in debt . . . and we *still* lost the pits? . . . I'd like to say, "yes, it was a victory." But it wasn't. It was a defeat.' George Rees was even blunter: 'Arthur still thinks he *won* [the strike] . . . As I said to him, "if this is a victory, God help us we didn't have a *bloody hammering!*"'[2]

INDUSTRIAL COLLAPSE

In the aftermath of the strike, the closure programme began in earnest. South Wales was devastated by closures in 1985: Celynen South on 6 June, Bedwas on 31 August, Markham on 20 September, Treforgan on 30 September, Aberpergwm on 7 October, Penrhiwceiber on 8 October, Abertillery on 9 October, St John's on 22 November, and Garw on 13 December. Despite widespread bitterness and anger, only at St John's was there a concerted

---

[1]   Mike Parker, *The Politics of Coal's Decline: The Industry in Western Europe* (London: 1994), p. 49.
[2]   Jim Watkins (18 February 2004) and George Rees (8 December 2003) interviews, respectively.

campaign of opposition.[3] In 1986, Blaenserchan, Coedely and Abercynon were finished as separate units, followed that autumn by Cwm and Nantgarw. In October 1983 there had been 21,500 mineworkers in the coalfield but three years later there were only 11,943. South Wales had long suffered closures, but those of 1985–6 removed mining completely from large swathes of the valleys.[4]

These closures were the first wave of a programme designed to remove Britain's dependence on coal. Inevitably, they were not the end of the story: Six Bells shut in 1987, Abernant and Lady Windsor in 1988, Marine, Cynheidre, Oakdale, Trelewis Drift and Merthyr Vale in 1989, Blaenant and Maerdy in 1990, Penallta and Deep Navigation in 1991, and Taff Merthyr in 1992. The consequences were all too predictable. The closure of Oakdale, for example, led the local council to speak of the 'social and economic devastation' caused by the overnight jump in the unemployment rate from 15 to 25 per cent. Research published in 2005 revealed that south Wales remained the coalfield worst hit by the collapse, with the overwhelming majority of the jobs lost never having been replaced.[5]

The dramatic collapse of the industry was accompanied by profound changes in its labour relations. Just as coal was formerly the 'paradigm case' of nationalised industrial consensus, so it became a byword for managerial authoritarianism and job insecurity in the later 1980s. Colliery managements disregarded established practices and introduced contracts that undercut previous agreements with the lodges. Nationally, British Coal increased the level of piecework in the wage system, undermining payment structures that had been in place for thirty years. A Tower miner commented that 'there was a big difference with management . . . [I]t was, "we are the bosses now, you do as you're told" . . . It went back to how it was in the Thirties.' Similarly, a Betws worker stated: 'I never enjoyed the work after the '84–5 strike – in fact it was a nightmare up until . . . I finished [in 1989]. We were squeezed . . . and squeezed by the managers. It was a totally different atmosphere. We had to give up

[3]   For details of this campaign, see Ian Isaac, *When We Were Miners* (n.p., 2010), pp. 105–17, 125–8.

[4]   EC, 26 February–17 December 1985 passim; *SWM*, September 1985, September, October/November 1986; *WM*, March–December 1985 passim; Hywel Francis, and Gareth Rees, '"No Surrender in the Valleys": the 1984–5 Miners' Strike in south Wales', *Llafur*, 5/2 (1989), 67.

[5]   Andrew J. Richards, *Miners on Strike: Class Solidarity and Division in Britain* (Oxford: 1996), p. 211; *WM*, 4 March 2005.

concessions which we'd fought for, and maintained, for many, many years.'[6] The increased power of the management after 1985 enabled it to coerce miners into accepting an accelerated closure programme. In August 1989, for instance, when the closure of Merthyr Vale was announced, British Coal threatened to withdraw redundancy payments within forty-eight hours if the workforce did not agree to closure.[7]

LIFE AFTER THE STRIKE

South Wales communities remained understandably bitter at the outcome of the dispute. The main targets for this acrimony were the strike-breakers and the haulage companies blacklisted for their role in the NUM defeat. In the collieries, anger was controlled by lodge discipline and the fear of victimisation; this was not always the case elsewhere, however. An attack on the wife of a 'super scab' while she was driving her car out of Aberaman Phurnacite plant led indirectly to the sacking of five activists. None of these was apparently involved in the incident and this action prompted sympathy strikes at neighbouring pits. On 17 May 1985, two miners – Dean Hancock and Russell Shankland – were found guilty of the murder of David Wilkie. The large demonstrations in their support at Rhymney and Cardiff showed a continued commitment to the struggle.[8]

Within the Area, the key concern was to consolidate the NUM's position following its grave setback. In order to save the union as a viable organisation, the Area purged its contempt of court, thereby freeing its sequestrated assets. The leadership also negotiated on behalf of its sacked members and by the end of March 1985 all bar five of them had been reinstated.[9] Crucially, the south Wales miners never turned against the NUM: only a handful of individuals joined the breakaway UDM and these were soon won back. The disappearance of the 'super scabs', through early redundancy or transfers to other coalfields, reaffirmed the NUM's hegemony.

    [6]   Interview with Dennis Davies, 19 March 2004; Betws miner as quoted in Richards, *Miners on Strike*, p. 208.
    [7]   Hywel Francis, 'Denial of Dignity', *New Statesman*, 1 September 1989, 10–11.
    [8]   *WM*, March passim, 20, 27 May 1985; EC, 12 March, 21 May, 24 September, 8 October 1985; Francis and Rees, '"No Surrender in the Valleys"', 66.
    [9]   ASC, 9, 30 March 1985; EC, 9, 12, 26 March, 9, 19, 23 April, 4, 18 June, 16 July, 8 October 1985; *WM*, March 1985 passim; Francis and Rees, '"No Surrender in the Valleys"', 66–7.

South Wales was the only Area where the UDM made no impact whatsoever.

Significantly, rank-and-file activism was not completely extinguished in the post-strike period. In November 1985, militant lodges were demanding strike action against the closure programme. Localised disputes remained commonplace. In 1986, only fifteen out of Britain's 125 mines were free of industrial action, while there were widespread strikes during 1987–8. In April and May 1987, British Coal lost £2 million because of unofficial stoppages at eight south Wales pits. In this respect, the south Wales miners' long-standing culture of resistance remained, despite the difficulties they faced.[10]

NUM DIVISIONS

At national level, defeat intensified NUM inter-Area divisions while also de-aligning traditional left-right factionalism. Encouraged by the NCB and right-wing businessmen, in July 1985 the Nottinghamshire Area seceded from the NUM, thereby weakening the position of the old-style 'moderates'. The UDM was established in October 1985. The Left caucus also disintegrated, with South Wales and Scotland becoming critical of Scargill's policies. An important underlying factor here was the historical identification of the leaderships of these Areas with the CP. In contrast, particularly in the post-strike period, Scargill's activist support base came mainly from the extra-CP Left – from Militant, the SWP and so on – as well as from non-aligned young miners who had been politicised by Scargill and the events of the strike. In this way, internal NUM disputes became bitter political dogfights.

The post-strike adoption of 'realism' by the South Wales leadership was a crucial development. The Area officials had disagreed with some of Scargill's policies during the strike and between January and March 1985 developed their own strategies for resolving the dispute. In the aftermath of the defeat, the main differences between them focused on the potential for renewing the struggle through industrial action, the necessity of a public campaign to reinstate sacked miners, and the centralisation of decision-making within the NUM at the possible expense of local democracy. Given

[10] ASC, 16 November 1985; EC, 19 November 1985; *WM*, 23 April 1985, 21 November 1987; *SWM*, July 1987; *SWE*, 24 August 1987; Richards, *Miners on Strike*, p. 216.

the extent of the crisis, the Area's leaders decided that the only way to avoid the elimination of mining in south Wales was to be prepared to negotiate with British Coal. Flexible working patterns were a key topic where they led the 'moderate' dissenters, an issue that came to a head when British Coal announced that development of the proposed Margam 'super pit' was conditional on the acceptance of flexible working. South Wales decided to break with national policy and in March 1987 Area president Des Dutfield agreed to discuss flexible working.[11] This willingness to be accommodating, however, could do nothing to change the government's total opposition to any expansion of coal production.

The new outlook of the South Wales leadership was not without its critics, one of the most persistent of whom was Tyrone O'Sullivan, the Tower lodge secretary. There were also a few attempts to establish this opposition on a formal basis. In late March 1985, there was an unsuccessful campaign by EC member Des Dutfield and Cwm lodge secretary Billy Liddon to unseat Emlyn Williams and George Rees as the Area's representatives on the NEC, in protest at their role in ending the strike.[12] A more significant opportunity was the election for Area president in November 1985, following the retirement of Emlyn Williams. Terry Thomas – as vice-president – was the 'continuity candidate' but he was beaten by Dutfield, who was then regarded as being a more pro-Scargill figure. The election also demonstrated the increased activity of Militant in the Area, with Ian Isaac (the St John's lodge secretary) standing for president and running a controversial campaign that had the support of the Militant Tendency and also the tacit approval of Scargill. Isaac met with disapproval from the Area hierarchy but nevertheless received 22 per cent of the first-round vote, a reasonably successful result considering he had a far lower union profile than did the other candidates. As he later explained, 'I stood in that election because I felt the industry was collapsing . . . [and] there was a *strong feeling* amongst the rank and file that we should continue to fight the NCB, to keep our jobs and to . . . protect our industry as best we could'.[13]

[11] *SWM*, March, June, July, December 1987.
[12] *WM*, 14 March 1985; ASC, 30 March 1985; interview with Billy Liddon (1 April 2004).
[13] Interview with Ian Isaac (2 and 8 April 2004); EC, 5, 12, 19 November, 3, 17 December 1985; ASC, 18 October, 16 November 1985; *WM*, 12 June 1985. For Isaac's perspective on this campaign, see Isaac, *When We Were Miners*, pp. 118–23.

TOWER

The story of Tower colliery, the last deep-mine in south Wales, provided the only relief in the unrelenting gloom of coal's decline in the 1990s. Despite the pit making £28 million profit between 1991 and 1994, in October 1993 British Coal reduced its output targets and called for 200 'voluntary' redundancies. In response, 2,000 people marched through Aberdare in protest.[14] Despite this, by the end of the year British Coal had halved Tower's workforce. When the closure was announced in April 1994, the miners decided to put the pit through the review procedure rather than accept an extra £9,000 each in redundancy payments, thereby forcing British Coal to keep Tower open. However, the management insisted that continued mining was conditional on massive wage cuts and reduced conditions, seemingly leaving the miners with no alternative but to accept closure. Despite this, the imminent privatisation of the industry provided an unlikely salvation. Tower was bought by its employees in January 1995 and this courageous decision enabled the mine to prosper under workers' ownership, despite fierce energy market competition.[15] The success of Tower, although never one of the coalfield's 'star performers', showed that the post-strike decimation of the industry was fundamentally the product of political policies rather than of straightforward economic considerations.

THE ROAD FROM 1985

The 1984–5 dispute was a defining event in twentieth-century British politics. For the Thatcher government, defeating the miners fulfilled a key aim of its Ridley plan to subdue the unions and enable it to proceed with its monetarist agenda. The ensuing pit closure programme was more severe than even the worst predictions, effectively finishing mining as an industry of any significance. Although coal continued to produce 33 per cent of Britain's electricity, over two-thirds of the supplies were imported.[16] The peripheral coalfields were the worst affected by this decline. Whole communities were stripped of the focus that had shaped their political consciousness and social and cultural affiliations, often becoming

[14] Richards, *Miners on Strike*, pp. 225–6.
[15] Tower colliery eventually closed in 2008, as it was unable to raise the necessary capital investment to permit further mining operations.
[16] *Professional Engineering*, 8 February 2006.

unemployment black-spots. By March 2005, only 19 per cent of the south Wales jobs lost following the closure programme had been replaced by employment in other sectors.[17] The valleys and west Wales continued to count officially as among the poorest regions in the EU, which is why they received Objective One and Convergence funding. In this respect, the outcome of the strike continued to cast a shadow over south Wales at the beginning of the twenty-first century.

*   *   *

The years between 1964 and 1985 represent the final phase in the history of coal-mining in south Wales as a major source of employment. This period saw the effective demise of an industry which had shaped and epitomised south Wales and also the end of the distinctive contribution to the labour movement made by the South Wales NUM as a sizeable organisation. Retrospectively, this decline might seem to have been inevitable, though this was not the viewpoint of men who had spent their working lives in the industry. It is true that there had been protracted crises and recurrent threats of colliery closures, but there was also an unbroken theme of struggle, with miners fighting to make coal-mining an industry worth working in and to provide a secure future for their families and communities. There was nothing inevitable about their eventual defeat and we should heed E. P. Thompson's warning about 'the enormous condescension of posterity' when studying their actions.[18]

This book is an attempt to write a mining union history within a historical materialist framework which avoids simplistic structural reductionism and acknowledges the semi-autonomous role of cultural and ideological factors in miners' decision-making, while maintaining that ultimately these factors arose from the miners' interaction with material conditions. Despite this awareness of the complexities involved, the history of the south Wales miners demonstrates that it *was* possible for them to retain their long-standing tradition of militancy. Following the approach outlined by Harrison in *Independent Collier*, of stressing the centrality of the realities of historical experience in shaping coalfield cultures, this

---

[17]   Christina Beatty, Stephen Fothergill and Ryan Powell, 'Twenty years on: has the economy of the coalfields recovered?', p. 19, *www.shu.ac.uk/cresr/news/index.html*, accessed March 2005.

[18]   E. P. Thompson, *The Making of the English Working Class* (London: 1991), p. 12.

book rests on the understanding that this vanguard role was not at all an inevitability but was the outcome of a myriad of specific factors. The south Wales miners made their own history, though not in circumstances of their own choosing.

The south Wales coal miners were consistently one of the most militant groups of workers in Britain in the later twentieth century, both in terms of industrial combativeness and political radicalism. Broadly speaking, their distinctive industrial politics can be explained as the combined effect of particular geological-economic, social and ideological factors: the difficult geology of the coalfield, which produced a tendency towards antagonistic industrial relations and therefore provided a greater impetus for militancy than existed in many other coalfields; the social centrality of the miners and their union in valley communities, in which the identities and interests of the two overlapped to a significant degree; and the traditional radicalism of the south Wales miners, which was a response to their socio-economic environment and also an ideology produced by activists in the South Wales NUM and spawned by the workforce's collective memory of earlier struggles.

This radicalism was articulated by the south Wales miners via their union, its official Area structures and its lodge-level activists. The analysis of the period 1964–85 presents a complex picture of the interactions between the respective layers of the South Wales NUM and the tension between militancy and moderation, which overlapped and contradicted each other at different times and in different places. Far from being either an irrelevance or a 'Red menace', left-wing activists played a key role in developing and implementing Area policy, a role which was at its greatest when it reflected the basic values of the broader union membership and the mining communities of the valleys. In the South Wales NUM, the overall trend was for the containment of rank-and-file activism within official structures. The leaders of the 1960s 'unofficial move-ment' had become the senior figures in the Area by the 1980s, thereby helping to steel the miners against the challenges threatening their industry. This development was part of a long-term tendency for the south Wales miners to work through their union in order to effect political change, together with the participatory structure of the Area which enabled them to do so. South Wales miners' 'rank and filism' was always located squarely in the colliery lodges, the bedrock on which the Area was built.

A central theme of this book is the class/community synthesis produced by the links between South Wales NUM lodges and their respective mining communities. As a result of the centrality of coal-mining in the valleys, the union, its traditions and culture, had been integral to the social fabric from the outset. The Area had a tangible local presence: lodge leaders were very much a part of the same work-force and community as were all the other miners. This combination meant that their role was overwhelmingly about helping people with their problems, and it was precisely this solid day-to-day work that generated the immense rank-and-file loyalty to their lodge and their union. In this way, the South Wales NUM represented the community more closely than did any other organisation. It is only by a union-orientated study such as this that the historian is able to produce an overarching social history of the south Wales miners.

This picture over a twenty-year period is naturally not a static one. There were undeniably long-term trends at work in the later twentieth century which were reducing the hegemonic role of coal-mining in the regional economy, and consequently the social centrality of the NUM. Nevertheless, the pattern that emerges is a clear one: the mobilisation of entire communities behind the banner of the NUM, and the impressive solidarity shown by the south Wales miners during the 1984–5 strike demonstrate that they remained a central force in the valleys.

In its most general and non-determinative aspects, the 'archetypal proletarian' image resonates with the historical experience of the south Wales miners, located within a class/culture synthesis of valley communities as outlined in both *The Fed* and this book. Community solidarity was a material factor in the history of these communities, as demonstrated during the strikes of 1972, 1974 and 1984–5. Ironically, in a historiographical context, this correspondence in several key respects to the ideal type of a coalfield society makes the south Wales mineworkers something of an exceptional case.

The coal miners of south Wales have an exceptional vanguard place in British labour history. They succeeded in maintaining this role in the later twentieth century in a struggle to defend their livelihoods and their communities. Even in defeat, and with their industry all but eliminated, the south Wales miners remained 'the conscience of the labour movement'.[19]

[19] Seumas Milne, *The Enemy Within: The Secret War Against The Miners* (London: 1995), p. 425.

BIBLIOGRAPHY

A. ORAL HISTORY EVIDENCE AND DIARIES

I. *Interviews*

Allan Baker (Pentwynmawr), 13 February 2004
Mike Banwell (Williamstown), 9 March 2004
Graham Bartlett (Abertillery), 20 February 2004
Gordon Bartley (Cefn Fforest), 22 January 2004
Tommy Bowden (NUM Offices, Pontypridd), 19 January 2004
Kay Bowen (Dyffryn Cellwen), 14 April 2004
Phil Bowen (Dyffryn Cellwen), 26 March 2004
Dan Canniff (Hengoed), 17 February 2004
Dai 'Dosco' Davies (Tower Colliery, Hirwaun), 19 March 2004
Dennis Davies (Tower Colliery, Hirwaun), 19 March 2004
Eric Davies (Transport House, Cardiff), 30 January 2004
Howard Davies (Neath), 26 February 2004
Colin Day (Blaengwynfi), 18 March 2004
Des Dutfield (NUM Offices, Pontypridd), 12 February 2004
Ivor England (Llwyncelyn), 27 February 2004
Arfon Evans (Penderyn), 1 April 2004
Lyn Harper (Port Talbot), 29 March 2004
Dane Hartwell (Hirwaun), 10 December 2003
Hefina Headon (Seven Sisters), 31 March 2004

Ian Isaac (Port Talbot), 2 April 2004 and 8 April 2004
Emlyn Jenkins (Tonteg), 5 March 2004
Browell Jones (NUM Offices, Pontypridd), 19 January 2004
Don Jones (Cefn Fforest), 23 February 2004
Howard Jones (Pontyates), 10 February 2004
Bill King (Merthyr Tydfil), 4 March 2004
Ray Lawrence (Oakdale), 11 March 2004
Billy Liddon (Pontypridd), 1 April 2004
John Mason (Nantyglo), 24 February 2004
Tyrone O'Sullivan (Tower Colliery, Hirwaun), 22 March 2004
Verdun Price (Maesteg), 15 March 2004
George Rees (NUM Offices, Pontypridd), 8 December 2003
Mike Richards (Maerdy), 27 January 2004
Glyn Roberts (Tower Colliery, Hirwaun), 19 March 2004
Harry Samuel (Glynneath), 20 January 2004
Ron Stoate (NUM Offices, Pontypridd), 2 December 2003
Colin Thomas (Cefn Fforest), 14 January 2004
Eddie Thomas (Llantrisant), 17 March 2004
Terry Thomas (Gowerton), 16 February 2004
Jim Watkins (Six Bells), 18 February 2004
Kevin Williams (Tower Colliery, Hirwaun), 25 March 2004
Viv Williams (NUM Offices, Pontypridd), 25 February 2004

II. *Interviews undertaken by the South Wales Coalfield History Project*
Dai Coity Davies, 19 June 1976 (AUD/382)
Brian Elliott, 7 May 1981 (AUD/123)
Dai Francis, 1979-82 (AUD/131)
Mike Griffin, 27 January 1981 (AUD/31)
Don Hayward and Emlyn Jenkins, 19 June 1976 (AUD/381)
Berwyn Howells, 3 March 1980 (AUD/21)
Haydn Matthews, 22 October 1980 (AUD/134)
Ben Morris, 1979–82 (AUD/22)
Will Paynter, 1979–81 (AUD/105)
George Rees, 22 October 1980 (AUD/140)
Emlyn Williams, 19 June 1976 (AUD/161)
Emlyn Williams, 22 October 1980 (AUD/33)
Emlyn Williams, 1 June 1986 (AUD/574)
Glyn Williams, 20 March 1973 (AUD/258)
Glyn Williams, 1979–82 (AUD/113)
Ron Williams, 28 January 1981 (AUD/115)

III. *Diaries*
The Diary of Philip Weekes (Philip Weekes Papers, National Library of Wales,
    1/10)

B. Official Records

Premier's papers PREM13 / 1610
Premier's papers PREM13 / 2769
Premier's papers PREM13 / 3311
Report of the Tribunal appointed to inquire into the Disaster at Aberfan on
21 October, 1966

C. Trade Union Records and Publications

I. *Trade Union Records*
NUM Report of Annual Conference 1989
NUM Report of Reconvened Special Conference 19 April 1984
NUM (South Wales Area) colliery files 1984–5 strike period
NUM (South Wales Area) Conference minutes
NUM (South Wales Area) Executive Council Annual Reports
NUM (South Wales Area) Executive Council minutes
Celynen South NUM Lodge minutes

II. *Miscellaneous Trade Union Publications*
Howells, Kim, *Some Observations on the Strike in the Third Month* (mimeo, May 1984)
 – together with a response by A. Baker, Oakdale
Howells, Kim (on behalf of NUM South Wales Area), *South Wales Coal & The
 Common Market Energy Strategy* (South Wales Miners' Library, 1982)
NUM Rules, Model Rules & Standing Orders (1985 edition)
St John's NUM & Communities Action Campaign Committee, *Keep Mining In
 Maesteg* (Maesteg: 1985)

D. Political Party Records and Publications

I. *Political Party Records*
CPGB Executive Committee minutes and papers
CPGB Industrial Department papers
CPGB Political Committee minutes and papers
CPGB Welsh Committee District files
Labour Party Annual Conference Reports
Labour Party Wales Annual Conference Reports
Labour Party Wales Executive Committee Annual Conference Reports

II. *Miscellaneous Political Party Publications*
CPGB pamphlet, *A Plan For The Miners*, by Will Whitehead and Bert Wynn (1964)
CPGB pamphlet, *What Is The Socialist Way Forward?*, by John Gollan (1970)

Labour Party National Executive Committee, *The Socialist Alternative: A Statement By The National Executive Committee Of The 1981 Conference* (1981)

E. NEWSPAPERS AND PERIODICALS

Coal News
Daily Mirror
Daily Worker
The Economist
The Guardian
Labour Monthly
Labour Weekly: The Newspaper of the Labour Party
Marxism Today
Militant
The Miner: The Magazine of the South Wales Area of the National Union of Mineworkers (ceased publication 1968)
The Miner: Voice of the National Union of Mineworkers (began publication 1969)
Morning Star
The Observer
Professional Engineering
Socialist Worker
South Wales Echo
South Wales Miner (began publication 1982; ceased publication 1988)
The Sunday Times
The Times
Western Mail

F. THESES AND DISSERTATIONS

Curtis, Ben, 'The South Wales Miners, 1964–1985' (Ph.D., University of Glamorgan: 2006)
Howells, Kim, 'A View From Below: Tradition, Experience and Nationalisation in the South Wales Coalfield, 1937–1957' (Ph.D., University of Warwick: 1979)
Zweiniger-Bargielowska, Ina-Maria, 'Industrial Relationships and Nationalization in the South Wales Coalmining Industry' (Ph.D., University of Cambridge: 1989)

G. PUBLISHED WORKS

Ackers, Peter, and Payne, Jonathan, 'Before the storm: the experience of nationalization and the prospects for industrial relations partnership in the British coal industry, 1947–1972 – rethinking the militant narrative', *Social History*, 27/2 (2002), 184–209

Adeney, Martin, and Lloyd, John, *The Miners' Strike, 1984–5: Loss Without Limit* (London: 1986)

Allen, Meg, '"Weapons of the Weak": Humour and consciousness in the narratives of Women Against Pit Closures', *Socialist History*, 25 (2004), 1–19

Allen, V. L., *The Militancy of British Miners* (Shipley: 1981)

Arnot, Robin Page, *South Wales Miners, Vol. 1: 1898–1914* (London: 1967)

Arnot, Robin Page, *South Wales Miners, Vol. 2: 1914–1926* (Cardiff: 1975)

Ashworth, William, *The History of the British Coal Industry, Vol. 5: 1946–1982, The Nationalised Industry* (Oxford: 1986)

Bain, George Sayers (ed.), *Industrial Relations in Britain* (Oxford: 1983)

Ball, Stuart, and Seldon, Anthony (eds), *The Heath Government 1970–74: A Reappraisal* (London: 1996)

Barron, Hester, *The 1926 Miners' Lockout: Meanings of Community in the Durham Coalfield* (Oxford: 2009)

Beckett, Francis, and Hencke, David, *Marching to the Fault Line: The Miners' Strike and the Battle for Industrial Britain* (London: 2009)

Berger, Stefan, Croll, Andy, and LaPorte, Norman (eds), *Towards a Comparative History of Coalfield Societies* (Aldershot: 2005)

Beynon, Huw (ed.), *Digging Deeper: Issues in the Miners' Strike* (London: 1985)

Burge, Alun, and Davies, Keith, '"Enlightenment of the Highest Order": The Education Programme of the South Wales Miners, 1956–1971', *Llafur*, 7/1 (1996), 111–21

Callaghan, John, 'Industrial Militancy, 1945–79: The Failure of the British Road to Socialism?', *Twentieth Century British History*, 15/4 (2004), 388–409

Callinicos, Alex, and Simons, Mike, *The Great Strike: The Miners' Strike of 1984–5 and its lessons* (London: 1985)

Campbell, Alan, 'Exploring Miners' Militancy, 1889–1966: I', *Historical Studies in Industrial Relations*, 7 (1999), 147–63

Campbell, Alan, Fishman, Nina, and Howell, David (eds), *Miners, Unions and Politics, 1910–1947* (Aldershot: 1996)

Campbell, Alan, Fishman, Nina, and McIlroy, John (eds), *British Trade Unions and Industrial Politics, Vol. 1: The Post-War Compromise, 1945–64* (Aldershot: 1999)

Carter, Pete, 'Striking the Right Note', *Marxism Today* (March 1985), 28–31

Church, Roy, Outram, Quentin, and Smith, David N., 'The "isolated mass" revisited: strikes in British coal mining', *Sociological Review*, 39/1 (1991), 55–87

Cronin, James E., 'Neither exceptional nor particular: towards the comparative study of labor in advanced societies', *International Review of Social History*, 38/1 (1993), 59–75

Curtis, Ben, 'A Tradition of Radicalism: The Politics of the South Wales Miners, 1964–1985', *Labour History Review*, 76/1 (April 2011), 34–50

Curtis, Ben, 'The Calm Before the Storm? The South Wales Miners versus the Thatcher Government, 1979–1983', *Llafur*, 10/2 (2009), 117–40

Curtis, Ben, 'The Wilson Government and Pit Closures in South Wales, 1964–1970', *Llafur*, 9/1 (2004), 59–70

Darlington, Ralph, and Lyddon, Dave, *Glorious Summer: Class Struggle in Britain 1972* (London: 2001)

Edwards, Ness, *The History Of The South Wales Miners* (London: 1926)

Edwards, Ness, *History of the South Wales Miners' Federation, Vol. 1* (London: 1938)

England, Joe, *The Wales TUC, 1974–2004: Devolution and Industrial Politics* (Cardiff: 2004)

Feldman, Gerald D., and Tenfelde, Klaus (eds), *Workers, Owners and Politics in Coal Mining* (Oxford: 1990)

Fine, Ben, *The Coal Question: Political Economy and Industrial Change from the Nineteenth Century to the Present Day* (London: 1990)

Fishman, Nina, *Arthur Horner: A Political Biography, Vol. 1, 1894–1944* (London: 2010)

Fishman, Nina, *Arthur Horner: A Political Biography, Vol. 2, 1944–1968* (London: 2010)

Fishman, Nina, 'Coal: Owned and Managed on Behalf of the People', in Fyrth, Jim, (ed.), *Labour's High Noon: The Government and the Economy, 1945–51* (London: 1993), pp. 61–77

Francis, Hywel, 'Denial of Dignity', *New Statesman*, 1 September 1989

Francis, Hywel, 'Emlyn Williams (1921–1995)', *Llafur*, 7/1 (1996), 5–7

Francis, Hywel, *History on Our Side: Wales and the 1984–85 Miners' Strike* (Ferryside: 2009)

Francis, Hywel, *Miners Against Fascism: Wales and the Spanish Civil War* (London: 1984; 3rd edn, 2012)

Francis, Hywel, 'Mining the Popular Front', *Marxism Today* (February 1985), 12–15

Hywel Francis, 'The Anthracite Strike and Disturbances of 1925', *Llafur*, 1/2 (1973), 58-62 (1972–5 compendium edition), 53–66

Francis, Hywel, and Rees, Gareth, '"No Surrender in the Valleys": the 1984–5 Miners' Strike in south Wales', *Llafur*, 5/2 (1989), 41–71

Francis, Hywel, and Smith, David, *The Fed: A History of the South Wales Miners in the Twentieth Century* (London: 1980)

Gidwell, David Ingli, 'Philosophy and Geology in Conflict: The Evolution of a Wages Structure in the South Wales Coalfield, 1926–1974', *Llafur*, 1/4 (1975), 194–207

Gildart, Keith, 'Coal strikes on the Home Front: miners' militancy and socialist politics in the Second World War', *Twentieth Century British History*, 20/2 (2009), 121–51

Gildart, Keith, 'Cooperation and Conflict: Episodes from the North Wales Coalfield, 1925–35', *Historical Studies in Industrial Relations*, 12 (2001), 27–56

Gildart, Keith, 'Mining memories: reading coalfield autobiographies', *Labor History*, 50/2 (2009), 139–61

Gildart, Keith, *North Wales Miners: A Fragile Unity, 1945–1996* (Cardiff: 2001)

Golden, Miriam A., *Heroic Defeats: The Politics of Job Loss* (Cambridge: 1997)

Goodman, Geoffrey, *The Miners' Strike* (London: 1985)

Gormley, Joe, *Battered Cherub: The Autobiography of Joe Gormley* (London: 1982)

Gramsci, Antonio, *Selections from Political Writings, 1910–1920*, ed. Quintin Hoare, (London: 1977)

Harrison, Royden (ed.), *Independent Collier: The Coal Miner as Archetypal Proletarian Reconsidered* (Hassocks: 1978)

Hobsbawm, E. J., *On History* (London: 1997)

Howell, David, *The Politics of the NUM: A Lancashire View* (Manchester: 1989)

Howell, David W., and Morgan, Kenneth O. (eds), *Crime, Protest and Police in Modern British Society* (Cardiff: 1999)

Howells, Kim, and Jones, Merfyn, 'Oral history and contemporary history', *Oral History*, 11/2 (1983), 15–20

Hyman, Richard, 'Reflections on the mining strike', *Socialist Register*, 22 (1985), 330–54

Hyman, Richard, 'The sound of one hand clapping: A comment on the "Rank and Filism" debate', *International Review of Social History*, 34/2 (1989), 309–26

Isaac, Ian, *When We Were Miners* (n.p., 2010)

Jackson, Michael P., *The Price of Coal* (London: 1974)

James, Peter, *The Future of Coal* (London: 1982)

Jenkins, Islwyn (ed.), *The Collected Poems of Idris Davies* (Llandysul: 2003)

John, Angela V., 'A Miner Struggle? Women's Protests in Welsh Mining History', *Llafur*, 4/1 (1984), 72–90

Jones, Bill, Roberts, Brian, and Williams, Chris, '"Going from Darkness to the Light": South Wales Miners' attitudes towards Nationalisation', *Llafur*, 7/1 (1996), 96–110

Kerr, Clark, and Siegel, Abraham, 'The interindustry propensity to strike – an international comparison', in Kornhauser, Arthur, Dubin, Robert, and Ross, Arthur M. (eds), *Industrial Conflict* (New York: 1954), pp. 189–212

Lawrence, Ray, *Celynen South, 1873–1985: A Short History to Commemorate the Closure of the Colliery* (n.p., 1985)

Lieven, Mike, 'A "New History" of the South Wales Coalfield?', *Llafur*, 8/3 (2002), 89–106

Manners, Gerald, *Coal in Britain: An Uncertain Future* (London: 1981)

Manners, Gerald (ed.), *South Wales in the Sixties: Studies in Industrial Geography* (Oxford: 1964)

McCormick, B. J., *Industrial Relations in the Coal Industry* (London: 1979)

McHugh, John, and Ripley, B. J., 'The Neath By-Election, 1945: Trotskyists in West Wales', *Llafur*, 3/2 (1981), 68–78

McIlroy, John, *Trade Unions in Britain Today* (Manchester: 1988; second edition, 1995)

McIlroy, John, and Campbell, Alan, 'Still setting the pace? Labour history, industrial relations and the history of post-war trade unionism', *Labour History Review*, 64/2 (1999), 179–99

McIlroy, John, Fishman, Nina, and Campbell, Alan (eds), *British Trade Unions and Industrial Politics, Vol. 2: The High Tide of Trade Unionism, 1964–79* (Aldershot: 1999)

McLean, Iain, and Johnes, Martin, *Aberfan: Government and Disasters* (Cardiff: 2000)

Miller, Jill, *You Can't Kill The Spirit: Women in a Welsh Mining Valley* (London: 1986)

Milne, Seumas, *The Enemy Within: The Secret War Against The Miners* (Pan edition, London: 1995)

Morgan, Kevin, 'Harry Pollitt, Rhondda East and the Cold War collapse of the British Communist electorate', *Llafur*, 10/4 (2011), 16–31

Morgan, Kenneth O., *Rebirth of a Nation: Wales, 1880–1980* (Oxford: 1981)

Mòr O'Brien, Anthony, 'Patriotism on trial: the strike of the South Wales miners, July 1915', *Welsh History Review*, 12/1 (1984), 76–104

O'Sullivan, Tyrone, with Eve, John, and Edworthy, Ann, *Tower Of Strength: The Story of Tyrone O'Sullivan and Tower Colliery* (Edinburgh: 2001)

Parker, Mike, *The Politics of Coal's Decline: The Industry in Western Europe* (London: 1994)

Parker, M. J., *Thatcherism and the Fall of Coal* (Oxford: 2000)

Richards, Andrew J., *Miners on Strike: Class Solidarity and Division in Britain* (Oxford: 1996)

Robens, Lord, *Ten Year Stint* (London: 1972)

Salway, Gareth, *Penallta: A Pit and its People* (Abertillery: 2008)

Samuel, Raphael, Bloomfield, Barbara, and Boanas, Guy (eds), *The Enemy Within: Pit Villages and the Miners' Strike of 1984–5* (London: 1986)

Saunders, Jonathan, *Across Frontiers: International Support for the Miners' Strike, 1984/85* (London: 1989)

Saville, John, 'An open conspiracy: Conservative politics and the miners' strike of 1984–5', *Socialist Register*, 22 (1985), 295–329

Scargill, Arthur, 'The New Unionism', *New Left Review*, 92 (July–August 1975), 3–33

Scargill, Arthur, and Kahn, Peggy, *The Myth of Workers' Control* (Nottingham: 1980)

Seddon, Vicky (ed.), *The Cutting Edge: Women And The Pit Strike* (London: 1986)

Smith, Dai, *Aneurin Bevan and The World of South Wales* (Cardiff: 1993)

Smith, Ned, *The 1984 Miners' Strike: The Actual Account* (Whitstable: 1997)

Supple, Barry, *The History of the British Coal Industry, Vol. 4: 1913–1946, The Political Economy of Decline* (Oxford: 1987)

Sutcliffe, Lesley, and Hill, Brian, *Let Them Eat Coal: The Political Use of Social Security During the Miners' Strike* (London: 1985)

Swain, Fay, and Williams, Cory (eds), *Penallta: A Brief History of Penallta Colliery in the Rhymney Valley* (Ystrad Mynach: 1994)

Tanner, Duncan, Williams, Chris, and Hopkin, Deian (eds), *The Labour Party in Wales, 1900–2000* (Cardiff: 2000)

Taylor, Andrew, *The NUM and British Politics, Vol. 1: 1944–1968* (Aldershot: 2003)

Taylor, Andrew, *The NUM and British Politics, Vol. 2: 1969–1995* (Aldershot: 2005)

Thompson, E. P., *The Making of the English Working Class* (London: 1991)

Town, Stephen W., *After the Mines: Changing Employment Opportunities in a South Wales Valley* (Cardiff: 1978)

Unofficial Reform Committee, *The Miners' Next Step* (Tonypandy: 1912; new edition, n.p., 1991)

Welsh Campaign for Civil and Political Liberties and NUM (South Wales Area), *Striking Back* (Cardiff: 1985)

Wigham, Eric, *Strikes and the Government, 1893–1974* (London: 1976)

Williams, Chris, *Capitalism, Community and Conflict: The South Wales Coalfield, 1898–1947* (Cardiff: 1998)

Williams, Gwyn A., *When Was Wales?* (London: 1985)

Williams, John, *Digest of Welsh Historical Statistics, Vol. 1* (Cardiff: 1985)

Williams, John, *Was Wales Industrialised? Essays in Modern Welsh History* (Llandysul: 1995)

Winterton, Jonathan, and Winterton, Ruth, *Coal, Crisis and Conflict: The 1984–85 Miners' Strike in Yorkshire* (Manchester: 1989)

Zweiniger-Bargielowska, Ina-Maria, 'Miners' militancy: a study of four south Wales collieries during the middle of the twentieth century', *Welsh History Review*, 16/3 (1993), 356–89

H. Internet-based Material

Beatty, Christina, Fothergill, Stephen, and Powell, Ryan, 'Twenty years on: has the economy of the coalfields recovered?', *www.shu.ac.uk/cresr/news/index.html*, accessed March 2005

'Howells' miners' strike regret', BBC website, 12 March 2004, *http://news.bbc.co.uk/1/hi/wales/3506098.stm*, accessed 7 January 2012

'Hurt and pain of the Coal War', BBC website, 5 March 2004, *http://news.bbc.co.uk/1/hi/wales/3532987.stm*, accessed 7 January 2012

'Minister's secret role in miners' strike death inquiry', *The Guardian website*, 26 January 2004, *http://www.guardian.co.uk/politics/2004/jan/26/uk.tradeunions*, accessed 7 January 2012

INDEX